# An iceberg as big as Manhattan

## REPORTING FROM SCIENCE'S NEW FRONTLINES

## DAVID SHUKMAN

Environment and Science Correspondent, BBC News

PROFILE BOOKS

First published in Great Britain in 2011 by
PROFILE BOOKS LTD
3A Exmouth House
Pine Street
London EC1R 0JH
www.profilebooks.com

10 9 8 7 6 5 4 3 2 1

Printed and bound in Great Britain by
CPI Bookmarque Ltd, Croydon, Surrey

A CIP catalogue record for this book is available from the
British Library.

ISBN 978 1 84668 888 1
eISBN 978 1 84765 787 9

# An iceberg as big as Manhattan

## REPORTING FROM SCIENCE'S NEW FRONTLINES

**David Shukman** has been a BBC television reporter for nearly three decades. He reported from East Berlin during the fall of the Wall and from conflicts in Bosnia, the Caucasus and Africa. He has broadcast from more than ninety countries and became Environment and Science Correspondent in 2003.

# Contents

*To Jess, Jack, Harry and Kitty*

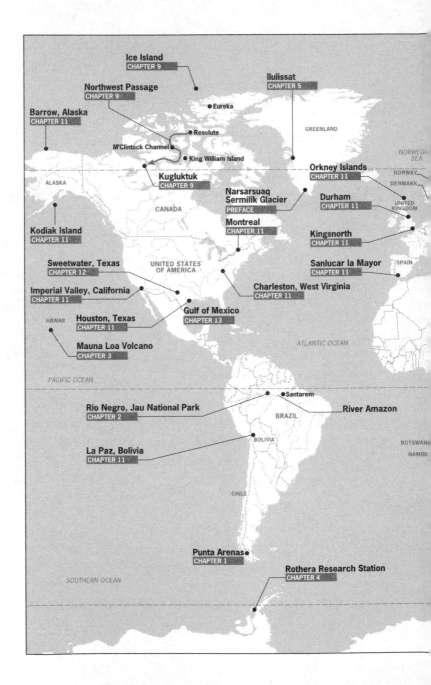

Ice Island
CHAPTER 9

Northwest Passage
CHAPTER 9

Barrow, Alaska
CHAPTER 11

Ilulissat
CHAPTER 5

• Eureka

GREENLAND

• Resolute

M'Clintock Channel •

• King William Island

ALASKA

Kugluktuk
CHAPTER 9

Orkney Islands
CHAPTER 11

NORWEGI
SEA

NORWAY

DENMARK

Narsarsuaq
Sermilik Glacier
PREFACE

CANADA

Durham
CHAPTER 11

UNITED
KINGDOM

Kodiak Island
CHAPTER 11

Montreal
CHAPTER 11

Kingsnorth
CHAPTER 11

Sweetwater, Texas
CHAPTER 12

UNITED STATES
OF AMERICA

Sanlucar la Mayor
CHAPTER 11

SPAIN

Imperial Valley, California
CHAPTER 11

Charleston, West Virginia
CHAPTER 11

HAWAII

Houston, Texas
CHAPTER 11

Gulf of Mexico
CHAPTER 13

ATLANTIC OCEAN

Mauna Loa Volcano
CHAPTER 3

PACIFIC OCEAN

• Santarem

Rio Negro, Jau National Park
CHAPTER 2

BRAZIL

River Amazon

La Paz, Bolivia
CHAPTER 11

• BOLIVIA

BOTSWAN

NAMIBI

CHILE

Punta Arenas •
CHAPTER 1

Rothera Research Station
CHAPTER 4

SOUTHERN OCEAN

ARCTIC OCEAN

**Whaling route**
CHAPTER 1

nsø
North Cape
Gamvik

SIBERIA

**Cherskii**
CHAPTER 5

Arctic Circle

**Copenhagen**
CHAPTER 12

Kolyma

RUSSIA

Yakutsk

**Belchatow**
CHAPTER 11

**Moscow**
CHAPTER 5

POLAND
ROMANIA

**Aral Sea**
CHAPTER 1

UZBEKISTAN

CHINA

**Copsa Mica
Transylvania**
CHAPTER 8

**Midway Atoll**
CHAPTER 7

INDIA

PACIFIC OCEAN

u Forest
LOGUE

BANGLADESH

**Nairobi**
CHAPTER 6

**Gabura Island**
CHAPTER 10

Equator

KENYA

**Kajaro**
CHAPTER 6

INDONESIA

**Tuvalu**
CHAPTER 10

INDIAN OCEAN

**Bali**
CHAPTER 11

AUSTRALIA

SOUTH
AFRICA

**Kalahari Desert**
CHAPTER 6

SOUTHERN OCEAN

Antarctic Circle

ANTARCTICA

# An iceberg as big
# as Manhattan

# PREFACE

# An innocent in the Arctic

A sharp wind flicks my legs as I climb out of a helicopter and stumble into my first discovery about reporting on global warming: that the Arctic can still feel miserably cold. For some reason I'd convinced myself that chinos would be robust enough; they aren't. I'm in Greenland in July and, although the forecast was mild, something known as a katabatic wind descends from the heights inland, gathering chill over a thousand miles of ice, and successfully targets a poorly protected spot just above my ankles. I wrestle with the idea of tucking my trousers into my socks but know how that kind of thing can look ruinous on television. Vanity wins.

I then discover that those crystal-clean, chocolate-box pictures you often find in coffee-table books of the Arctic don't exactly tell the whole truth. In fact the scene I've entered is startlingly ugly, a mess of ice and rock, a giant's dump for oversized rubble. From the air, glancing at Greenland out of the window on flights between Europe and America, there isn't much to see except a beautiful, rather restful white. Close-up, this bit couldn't seem more disturbed.

I didn't arrive wholly ignorant; I knew that Greenland was covered by an ice sheet, it's just that I now realise how

I never understood what that meant. Standing here, I learn that the so-called ice sheet isn't a sheet at all, and that the phrase is misleadingly genteel. Sheets are thin and delicate, soft enough to lie between. This gargantuan mass of ice is incredibly thick – sometimes nearly two miles thick – and rock-hard. Ludicrous that anyone would call it a sheet. It's more like a monstrous mountain of ice that's lying sideways on the land. Its edges are some of the biggest cliffs I've ever seen, numbingly sharp, skyscraper-tall. There are lurid blue fissures the size of urban canyons, chunks of ice as big as office buildings, a jumbled frozen version of a ruined Manhattan.

Until now my closest encounters with snow and mountains have been in the benign surroundings of the European Alps and in fact, in the rush to get ready for this trip, the chinos aren't my only failing because I have managed to bring nothing more robust than my usual anorak, a bright red thing better suited to a hike in the hills. Not quite the gear for this raw, unforgiving spot. I also can't help thinking that if you get into trouble in the Alps you're rescued in minutes while, if we get stuck here, there's only one other helicopter within a day's flying of us.

I look down and get another shock. The ice I'm scrunching over is not pristine. Instead this jagged, shattered surface, a blasted wilderness stretching towards the North Pole, is actually grey or even black in patches. A bit like a building site littered with dirt. A landscape that ought to be unsullied is menacingly dark.

I shuffle about, testing the ground because all around me the ice is scarred with deep crevasses. My mind keeps churning over the thought that the Arctic ought to be white, that something's not quite right up here. I bend down to look at the surface more closely. I can actually see thousands of little black flecks in the ice. It looks like it must be possible to scoop them up so I take off a glove and reach out but my fingertips meet solid ice, clear, incredibly smooth and unyielding. The dark particles are locked inside. I picture one of those tourist ornaments where plastic snowflakes tumble around a landmark except that in this case the snowflakes would be a sinister black and frozen in place.

As the giant white island at the top of the Atlantic, Greenland should be one of the purest corners of the planet. I'm on what's called the Sermilik glacier at its southern tip and the nearest settlement is the little town of Narsarsuaq, not a place many have heard of. In fact it's so out of sight that this corner of the country has an eerie history: the Americans chose it as the site for a vast, discreet hospital to treat their wounded from the Korean War. Of the secret wards that housed hundreds of injured soldiers beyond the gaze of the US public, only the foundations remain.

Now, from where I'm standing on the ice, there are only pockets of people for thousands of miles around. So where did the dark dust come from? There's no industry here, hardly a power station.

I call out to the scientist who has brought us along, a Danish polar expert called Carl Boggild. He doesn't reply at first. He's a short distance away, with his anorak pulled over his head to keep the sunshine off the screen of his laptop. He's focused on his work.

Carl does not look like the stereotypical scientist. In fact he'd pass for someone big in mountain rescue, his hair cropped short and his face burnished. A hands-on, outdoors type, he's trying to get hard facts about Greenland and its fate, which is why we've joined him, to bypass what campaigners are saying about the Arctic and see what frontline field researchers are actually measuring.

With a series of automatic monitoring devices, spindly tripods like stick insects, his instruments record the weather and the height of the ice. Usually the evidence from these fragile robots is transmitted by satellite back to Copenhagen but, whenever he can, Carl visits them and downloads the data directly into his laptop. Not the sort of person to trust technology, he's also very cautious about jumping to conclusions: he wants his own figures to help form his own judgement about what's happening in the Arctic, which is just the kind of approach I'm after.

Job done, Carl stands up, data downloaded, and pulls his anorak back on. It's not just me that's feeling the cold.

It's probably from China, he calls back.

China? Soot from China?

Or maybe Europe, the big industries.

It's a startling idea, that soot could travel so far. It turns out that whatever belches out of the chimneys of the world's biggest industrial heartlands – the north-east United States, China or northern Europe – is whisked into the weather systems and carried around the world within about 10 days. Carl explains that much of the soot is scattered but a lot gets caught in the air circulating northwards, the wind acting as a spiralling conveyor belt carrying the plumes of black smoke to the Arctic. And the darker the surface, the warmer it'll get, and the faster the ice will melt.

I look down again at the much-travelled particles, and it strikes me that for all the talk of a global village I'd never thought to ask what happens to the village's exhaust, where it goes, where it ends up. I can tell that Carl is being deliberately patient with me, watching the reactions of a slow student in a new class. And the cold isn't helping.

I've been here only a few minutes and I'm confused, a supposedly seasoned correspondent surprised to be so out of his depth. The trouble is, I'd always seen pollution as something that afflicted the industrial corners of the old Soviet Union or the choked streets of Asia, not the distant white Eden of the polar bear, not the ice beneath my boots. I need time to think all this through. But the helicopter pilot keeps glancing at his watch and checking the sky for an approaching

weather front. We have to get on with our filming. And my
ankles are starting to feel numb.

**Dressed to chill:** as an ice-sheet novice, I underestimate the cold of Greenland in July.
The soot covering Sermilik glacier near Narsarsuaq is also a surprise: note the darker
patches in what should be a pristine polar Eden.                                    *BBC*

I'd never imagined being on assignment to a place like this, let
alone becoming an Environment & Science correspondent covering an issue like climate change. The idea had never occurred
to me and, when it came, the proposal was a real shock. The
sunshine in an editor's office suddenly seemed brighter, the
objects starker, and I had that slow-motion feeling that can
kick in when faced with something momentous. It was the
summer of 2002: the Iraq invasion was on the horizon. Four
small televisions were tuned to the rolling news channels – our
two, CNN and Sky – and all were carrying a Bush speech live.
The sound was down. My first reaction: could I contemplate
switching jobs and then miss being involved in such a huge
international event as a war in the Gulf?

Taking the Environment & Science job would mean
leaving Foreign News where I'd spent most of my career

and joining Home News. This might sound like an administrative detail but the two departments are almost tribally distinct. Foreign reporting, I felt, had been my natural home for fifteen years and it was on foreign assignments that I'd had some of my most searing and formative experiences.

I was in East Berlin to witness the fall of the Wall, seeing the tears of a family who in the 1960s had watched the brutal grey barrier being assembled outside their apartment and who were now overcome as it was breached. In Armenia, during the conflict following the collapse of the Soviet Union, my crew and I were given dinner by a group of rebels and realised that everyone else around the table was armed. In the war in Angola I'd interviewed three brave, polite sisters who'd each gone to fetch water and had then each lost a leg to landmine. In the golden light of a Bosnian summer evening, I'd winced at the sight of two children, familiar faces from a house close to the BBC's, lying in our lane bleeding from a sniper's bullets; they survived but I'll always recall how the impact had blasted the girl's new shoes from her feet.

Part of me worried that the environment brief would feel comparatively tame, even dull. But another part realised that I'd had my fill of horror, that I was becoming too uncomfortable, too nervous about the hazards of reporting conflicts. The precise tipping point came when I was in the dust of Central Asia. Tajikistan, once part of a superpower, was gripped by a famine after several years without rain and, by macabre coincidence, we checked in to our Soviet-era hotel just as the South Tower of the World Trade Centre collapsed. It was 9/11. The assumed perpetrators were from Al-Qaeda. And Al-Qaeda's base was Afghanistan, the country just next door. Tajikistan, fly-blown and forgotten, was suddenly on the map and we were there.

An opportunity quickly came up to cross into Afghanistan with the Northern Alliance, the group opposed to the then

Taliban government, and, though it was a potentially clever move, I was worried. We were to be ferried by helicopter, battered machines which I'd seen, forlorn and unserviced, at the airport. Our route was to be over Taliban-held territory at an altitude well within range of their surface-to-air missiles – I'd been a defence correspondent and knew about the risks of these things. But these were mere details: fundamentally I'd come to see that I just wasn't prepared for that level of danger anymore. When I rang London I explained that my decision not to go was not a safety issue or an editorial one. It was about me, and it was hard to talk about. The editor at the other end fell silent as the implications of what I was saying sank in: that this chapter in my career was closing.

Fast forward to that bright office and Bush on the box with the sound down. It was one thing to stop heading off to conflicts, quite another to become Environment & Science correspondent. Was I really that interested in agricultural policy and fish quotas? While covering the European Union in Brussels I'd had a heavy dose of protests by muck-spreading farmers and all-night talks over cod stocks. And did I really want to spend time in labs filming test tubes or be on the receiving end of press releases about yet another threat to the whales? I'd always seen myself as someone involved in stories that were part of the major currents of history – presenting a profile of Mikhail Gorbachev on the night the Soviet Union ended; reporting on the launch of a major global currency, the euro; developing contacts in Washington, London and Moscow that yielded scoops on nuclear weapons and Iraq and terrorism.

And, most significantly, if I thought about it all, I'd have described myself as cynical about green causes and quite distrustful of the sincerity of some environmentalists. Not that I ever articulated it but, if pressed, I'd have declared myself sympathetic to the view that economic development in a capitalist system is broadly a good thing, that industry and cars and jets have improved our lives, and that returning to some eco-friendly rural idyll simply isn't realistic. I'd seen how the old Communist regimes not only failed to deliver the basic things people wanted but also crushed their aspirations. And trips to developing countries had shown me how it's human nature to want to be more secure and comfortable, not just to have basics like running water and electricity, but also to enjoy the comfort that comes from controlling our immediate surroundings. Standing in front of a vent of chilled air in the summer heat of Disneyland in California was a real pleasure and I understood why a family in China or Mozambique would save up to buy, above all else, a fan or an air-conditioning unit. In hot countries, a potent form of apartheid between haves and have-nots is whether you can afford to keep cool.

It was a colleague who first identified my dilemma. With long experience covering environmental issues, he made a very personal and perceptive point: that he'd never seen me as someone who'd be instinctively comfortable with things ecological, or even interested in them, joking that he didn't see me as 'one of us bunny huggers'. He was right. I definitely did not see myself as in any way green or even particularly interested in a green agenda. In fact I never even liked the word 'environment'.

One reason is that I've always disliked being branded. In Northern Ireland, as a middle-class reporter from London with a posh voice, colleagues semi-jokingly accused me of being a spy. Working as defence correspondent, learning about weapons and spending time with the military, led to the easy assumption that I was virtually clad in khaki myself. And being based in Brussels for four years, reporting on the European Union, convinced many that I'd gone native, morphing into a Euro-acolyte. So the thought of having an 'eco' label attached to me as well was a step too far.

And I've always been mildly allergic to the more strident campaigners, turning off anything that smacks of a lecture about lifestyles. So when a friend joked that if I took the job I'd have to build my own bike and make my children walk to school, I bridled.

But then came a line from my editor so persuasive that I'd have been a fool to even hesitate over it: that the job would be global, that it was about reporting the planet and its changes, that it was a role to generate strong visual stories on major themes. Put more simply, I was to cover anything I might see featured on the front of National Geographic magazine – or even imagine seeing there. Amazing wildlife, polar bears, rainforests, pollution, that kind of thing ...

So that's how I come to be in our helicopter, a frail little craft, hovering above Greenland's cliffs of ice. We've been hopping around different locations to get the best footage. I ask the pilot to set us down again. It's so loud in the cabin we're talking over headsets. Where, he asks. Anywhere safe, I reply. Towards its margin, the ice is scarred by vast cracks and those closest to the coast are more like chasms. This regular pattern of deadly crevasses will eventually delineate the contours of the icebergs which will crash into the sea. It was an iceberg from Greenland that reputedly sank the Titanic. We head a bit further inland and, where the scars in the ice aren't so deep, we make a gentle touchdown.

We're about to start filming when there's another surprise. Carl has three of his monitoring devices at this spot but can't see one of them. It's not the sort of place where things get stolen; a polar bear might have wrecked it but surely not carried it off. We all hunt around and find the device lying on its side in a shallow crevasse.

The ice has moved so far and so fast in the past few months that it's tipped the tripod over.

I can't believe it, says Carl. The ice is vanishing so quickly.

Until now, the most recent estimate had come from the American space agency NASA which said that parts of the margins of the ice sheet were falling by up to one metre every year. That's what I'd read in a scientific journal and had come to see for myself. But what Carl says his tripped-up tripod has revealed is that the ice, in this area, at the height of summer, is dropping at a far greater speed – it's vanishing at a rate of one whole metre every month. It takes us a few moments to digest this. A metre a month – that means the ice is in effect collapsing.

We rescue the tripod and manoeuvre it back into position. Cameraman Steve Adrain reminds me that we've a lot to do, that different programmes require separate recordings, and we're aware that it's cost a lot to get us here. People often ask if I've ever been scared on assignment. The truth is that nothing sharpens the mind like the fear of failing to gather the right material.

While we're working, we keep hearing booms and cracks. Down at the distant seafront, where the glacier is breaking into the sea, huge blocks must be crashing into the waters. It's the iconic image of global warming but from where we are, we can't see it. So I suggest to Steve that we wrap up at this location and get the pilot to fly us to a position on a rocky hill overlooking the edge of the ice. Maybe we'll get lucky and catch an iconic shot ourselves.

It isn't as easy as it looks. We set up the camera and Steve starts filming. Of course, nothing happens. He keeps running tape and still no ice breaks away. One of the batteries packs up and needs changing. Then a tape runs out so we install a new one. Minutes pass, and we're still waiting, desperately scanning the now silent, motionless ice. It's always said that nothing's less predictable than filming children or wildlife but a camera-shy ice sheet should be added to the list.

Now and again, there's a burst of thunder and we frantically search the ice front to seek the telltale puff of snow and a big lump tumbling. But the sound echoes around the fjord and we can't tell where it's come from. The ice front is nearly a mile wide so, even if we do spot a decent break, the chances are that Steve will be pointing in another direction. It's incredibly frustrating.

And then the temperature rises. Not much, but enough to cross some invisible but biologically critical threshold. From nowhere, clouds of mosquitoes emerge. These are more like daddy-long-legs in scale – large, floppy, clumsy fliers that swarm onto our necks and faces, and into our ears and nostrils. I wave my hands almost continuously around my head. Steve just keeps his face pressed tight to the eyepiece but he occasionally twists in annoyance.

We need the shots but can't take too much of this. Our patience with the insect life of warming Greenland is running out. In the course of a tortured hour Steve manages to capture a few icefalls, he's done well in the circumstances, so we can return with enough shots of collapsing ice to compile an effective report, our heads reasonably high.

We climb back into the helicopter, always a fiddly process because it's so cramped. Steve clambers to the back, gets strapped in and I hand him the camera. He then realises he needs to switch from his regular lens, the best for the ice shots, to the wide angle lens which is better for working inside the helicopter. Because I'm still not strapped in, it falls to me to help him. No problem. I move towards the luggage locker at the back of the helicopter, open its little door, reach for a small metal flight case and pull out the lens.

And it's at that moment that I hear a terrible series of explosions. It's like an artillery barrage. I get a flashback to a night in Bosnia when the heavy guns of the Croats roared into action not far from our house, the booms so resound-ingly deep and ferociously loud as the shells flew overhead that you could actually feel your guts quiver. I feel the same shaking now but there's no gunpowder here, no warheads erupting. Instead, it's the ice.

A monumentally large wall of it, a series of tower-block cliffs, is slowly tearing away from the ice sheet and start-ing a mesmerising, inching, deafening collapse towards the sea. It's the biggest break-up of the day. By far. It's our money shot, what we've waited for. But Steve is strapped in and has a camera without a lens. And I'm holding a lens without a camera. It's a television journalist's nightmare. I grab a smaller video camera that we have as backup and run towards the action. But it's not a camera I've ever used before and, as I fumble over the controls, I can hear and see what was meant to be our dream shot bursting into the ocean, thousands of tons of ice splashing and rising and splitting.

I've had tricky moments, potentially brilliant television robbed by bad luck, but this is one of the worst. I feel a bit sick. Steve's face is white. I'm sure mine is pale green. Sud-denly, we feel the strain of working in this weird, treacher-ous land. We lift off, tired and itchy.

The ice passes below us, no longer interesting. We're slumped, exhausted. But the pilot, a steady sort, casts us the kind of look you might shoot at spoiled children, as if urging us to get over it, and comes up with a suggestion. Maybe he is sympathetic to our dented morale.

A little off our route, he says, on the edge of a small settlement down by the coast, there's a farm.

A farm, so what? I'm not thinking clearly, I'm hungry and irritable.

A farm where they grow potatoes.

Potatoes? In the Arctic? It turns out that it's been so warm the past few summers that the ground is now soft enough and the growing season long enough for an intrepid fisherman to lay down his nets and take up a shovel to dig spuds instead.

Of course we stop, it's a great idea. We're now out of the wind and it's like entering yet another new world, one in which I'm far too hot. We walk with the farmer, Ferdinand Egede, and his sons over to their plot; these Inuit men with lined, impassive faces are apparently unmoved by the unexpected arrival of a helicopter bearing a sweating BBC news team.

We're deep in mud. The fjord beside us is festooned with icebergs, brilliant against the green of the hills which could be the Alps in high summer. The farmer shows us his rows of vibrant plants and, when he pulls one up, rich soil spills from a clutch of bright white potatoes, a scene from Ireland, not Greenland. For Ferdinand, cultivating the land is a novelty, an activity outside his family's memory – his father never had the chance, nor his grandfather. There's simply nothing in the culture here about having a summer season warm enough to yield any useful growth.

I turn to Carl, the robust, no-nonsense scientist, to discuss what this means.

He's clearly surprised at what Ferdinand and his sons are doing. But he's also cautious. It's likely, he says, that this isn't the first time that vegetables have been grown in Greenland. There's evidence that this has happened before when Viking settlements were established here, in an era known as the Mediaeval Warm Period, when life would have been easier.

Which raises another line of questioning. That warming in the Middle Ages clearly had nothing to do with mankind – it was centuries before the Industrial Revolution, long before man-made greenhouse gases appeared. It must have been

**Oven-ready in the Arctic:** Ferdinand Egede and his family dig up spuds. Theirs must be the world's only potato patch with icebergs for a backdrop. Greenland has warmed enough to allow the first farming for a thousand years.                              *BBC*

part of a natural cycle of climate change, driven by shifts in the earth's orbit or fluctuations in the power of the sun.

So what's different about the warming now? Couldn't it also be the result of natural forces? Maybe we're witnessing a perfectly normal rise in temperatures which we have no hand in?

Carl pauses, preparing what will be a lengthy explanation. But Ferdinand wants to get back to work, the pilot is anxious to get moving, and I've never been so hot in a potato field.

I get a feeling I've had in previous jobs, a mix of awe, nerves and doubt, on learning of a development or a threat that sounds really serious. The neckhairs can tingle, a quiet descends and questions proliferate. In every subject I've covered, the practitioners have been well-rehearsed in scaring themselves to death.

In the 1980s, the generals I lunched fretted ceaselessly about our failure to prepare for the threat of an onslaught by Soviet forces: you know, they'd say, that we couldn't hold them for more than a few minutes. In the age of Gorbachev, intelligence types worried that his reforms were luring the West into a false sense of security: in a bunker beneath Nebraska, a US Air Force colonel, pointing to a picture of a smiling Gorby, warned that he could be the front man for a devious Communist plot. After the Cold War, analysts in Washington urged me to see that far worse than the Soviet Union was the limitless threat of Islamist terrorists equipped with anthrax and nerve agents. Even in Brussels, officials would hint darkly that disputes over anything from halibut quotas to the price of the euro could readily undermine the whole enterprise and risk seeing Europe slide back into its age-old state of uncertain peace and occasional war.

Experts in any field can get caught in a vortex of anxiety. And the news media are receptive, with an appetite for scares. Missile gaps, dodgy chemicals, creepily-modified food, monster asteroids – all can be big stories because editors think rightly that they'll fascinate readers and viewers. Stories about environmental dangers, above all climate change, have also long attracted the vocabulary of cataclysm. The challenge, I was realising, as with the generals and the spies, was to judge how to respond. As it turned out, the dire warnings about the likelihood of Russian tank columns racing for the Channel were wrong but the fears about attacks by Al-Qaeda were right. So what about global warming? Was it really plausible that Greenland was melting so fast that it was going to drown London?

In the hotel that evening, I'm knocked off balance once more. It happens to be seafood night with a buffet breathtaking for its range and total absence of political correctness: carpaccio of minke whale and smoked fillet of fin whale, which are delicious, and an Inuit dish that has to be attempted but is then best avoided – chunks of fermented cod which stink like shit.

I also come to hear of a tale that leaves me appalled. It may be entirely untrue. But when in the bar I recount my ordeal of our missed icefall, I wonder out loud how previous film crews have successfully focused on one particular section of ice and, in close-up, captured its collapse into the sea. I know now how difficult that is. If the cameraman stays wide, he has a chance of getting the break but it will only form a tiny part of the image; to get the close-up involves gambling on one piece of ice. When I raise this, I notice a few knowing looks.

And then, because the drinks are flowing, one veteran of the region comes out with a disturbing account of media trickery. He's heard a story of a film crew who were so determined to get the killer shot that they staged it. They got into position and then had the helicopter fly over the edge of the ice so that a crew member could drop an explosive charge into a deep crevasse. Once the helicopter was safely out of the way, and the camera was running, the charge was detonated by remote control, triggering a stunning collapse, filling the frame and achieving television perfection. And of course there'd have been no hanging around getting eaten by mosquitoes. Apparently, when challenged, they justified it by saying the ice was going to break off sometime anyway, so no big deal.

I go to bed, mind racing. We have done well, no question, even without high explosive, and we can fly back satisfied. But Steve's customary bottle of malt whisky, which has proved wonderfully calming in many other corners of the world, isn't quite working. I'm kept wide awake by images of dark ice, gelignite and the wrong trousers.

# 1

# Harm's way

I wake up with a jolt, a surge of anxiety. My head has cracked into the wall of our cabin and I have to brace myself in my bunk to stop it from happening again. It's just like being thrown, unprepared, onto a roller coaster. I'm on a whaling ship in the Norwegian Sea and it's rocking and heaving, not just up and down, and from side to side, but also in a vigorous corkscrew motion with irregular thumps and shudders.

My first reaction is confusion: the sea had been so calm when we'd turned in, cameraman Martin Roberts and I, neither of us even thinking about taking a travel pill. Now our world is being shaken remorselessly and my second reaction, one of overwhelming nausea, forces me out of bed, wondering whether I'll make it to the basin in time. I don't. Because I'm in the top bunk and Martin has the one below, he's already hunched over the basin by the time I climb down. I rush to the bathroom across the corridor and, between spasms, listen helplessly to the unlocked door banging behind me. I'm here to investigate Norway's highly controversial whale hunt but I'm little use to anyone right now.

Seasickness is always torture but this is a big assignment so I make a special effort to behave rationally. I stumble back to the cabin and swallow a couple of pills. I also tear open a packet holding a pair of special anti-nausea bands, designed to apply pressure to particular points on the wrist, and pull them on. I know the benefits will take a while to kick in and, because Martin is still hogging the basin, I head back to the bathroom, just in case. It's a wise move. I end up convulsed again, the unpleasantness compounded by the knowledge that the travel pills have been ejected and will have had no chance to settle things. Worse, during one violent upheaval, an unusually savage lurch by the vessel spoils my aim and a large sample of last night's supper ends up soaking one of the wristbands. I look down at the mess and can't begin to work out how to respond, how to clean up, what to do next. In an out-of-body way, I become aware of the extraordinary speed with which morale can collapse, and with which the clever idea of reporting on whaling can become detested.

With Martin immobile, and my attempts at medication failing, I grab some Arctic clothing and race up to the deck and the sanctuary of fresh air. It's about 3am but because we're so far north and it's summer, the sky is a pale grey. I grip a railing, gasp at the cold, keep my eyes on the horizon and watch the bow rising and twisting and plunging. For hour after hour. The clouds thicken and a light snowfall begins, gusts whipping the flakes into my face. I'm wearing gloves but the hand holding the rail is losing all feeling. I think about stepping back indoors but that's enough to have me leaning over the side once more. Eventually, the snow does drive me inside. The tiny lounge has a window facing forwards so I wedge myself between a table and a sofa and keep staring ahead, the waves now far higher than the boat, rolling towards the left-hand edge of the bow and crashing over it, spray blasting the glass.

Later, much later, and exhausted, I climb upstairs to the bridge. The skipper, Bjorn Andersen, takes one look at me and chuckles. The light never changes, grey night rolls into grey day and I lose any sense of time. I think back to the stable floor of the newsroom, and how I not only volunteered for this trip but actively pitched for it. I'd thought whaling might be one of the easier parts of the brief, one to chalk up early on. Now I'm beyond caring. At some point, the waves ease a bit as we sail into the lee of an island and I crawl into bed. Martin is groaning but sympathy isn't an option. For him or the whales.

Instinct tells me it must be easy to exaggerate environmental threats, that things can't be as dire as campaigners make out. And as with intelligence warnings, you can't always check if the doomsayers are right. Either the timescales are too long for a news reporter to keep up with the issue or the threat never materialises and those who warned about it can claim credit for heading it off.

There's also a question of trust. Nearly fifteen years have passed since Greenpeace hyped the hazards of an old oil rig, Brent Spar, but the newsroom hasn't forgotten and the incident is often recalled when an environmental group makes a claim that, to some, doesn't sound possible. And with spin such a feature of almost any aspect of public life, I assume, like many, that every organisation, every protestor, will be tempted to tweak their case to catch our attention. It's why, initially, I'm inclined to avoid the more obvious environmental themes: the rainforest, the ozone, the drying of the Aral Sea. Surely they're either hyped or old, covered to the point of boredom? But one editor, Kevin Bakhurst, is particularly interested in my doing a report on whaling. Not your classic piece with video shot by an environmental group, he says, but something first hand from one of the few countries where whaling is allowed. Norway seems closest and, sitting in his office, it's easy to say yes.

So I board the *Reinebuen* at the Norwegian port of Tromsø and unwittingly begin what will become one of the most unpleasant experiences of my life. My cabin is clean and well designed, the bunks wide and the reading lights sensibly positioned, and the sunshine glinting off the calm waters sparkles through a generous porthole. On a shelf above a writing desk, Martin and I arrange a little library – our trip could last about a week – and in the cupboard beneath the sink our stock of fruit and chocolate is something to be admired; we can't resist feeling house-proud, efficiently prepared for the work to come.

Our cold-weather gear, on hooks behind the door, is at the ready, gloves in pockets, spare batteries at hand, reserve camera charged up, new boots with their labels removed, thermals unpacked. I've learned my lesson from Greenland – when inside the Arctic Circle, no more chinos.

Up on deck, Bjorn is busy. He's supervising the fuelling for the voyage ahead and also dashing into his hi-tech bridge to answer calls from other skippers already out at sea, exchanging news about the best hunting grounds. In a brief moment of calm, I ask him to show me our likely route: out of Tromsø, hugging the coast, heading north between a line of islands and the mainland, up towards North Cape, the very top of Europe, on towards the border with Russia.

We'll be there in a day or two, he says.

I ask about the weather.

Pretty good, he replies, glancing at a smart screen displaying the latest forecast.

And then I raise the question I really want answered: how rough will it be?

Not too bad, says Bjorn, it's a good time of year.

It's May and, as we set off along the fjord connecting Tromsø to the open sea, the vessel is steady, the winds gentle. My mobile phone rings: it's an old friend, Paul Adamson, calling from Brussels, so I describe the scene to him, the snow on the peaks and the sky clean and bright, and as so often with people more office-bound than me, I'm berated in envious tones about the wonders of my new job. Paul was among those who'd urged me to accept it and, with the sun on my face and the promise of a vivid assignment, I have to admit he's right.

Then Paul asks what I'll do if it gets bumpy.

I've brought plenty of travel sickness pills, I tell him, and a pair of special wristbands.

How confident I sound, how ignorant of what's to come.

Up at the bow, we film Bjorn working on the key piece of equipment: a harpoon. In the winter, Bjorn and his crew fish for cod and herring, trawling nets from the stern, but when their quotas are filled and the days get longer they turn to hunting whales. Their target is minke whales, among the smallest of the many different species. The Norwegian government – better known for tirelessly labouring to settle international conflicts – has long endured criticism for allowing this hunt to go ahead. We've been given unusual permission to join a typical expedition to record how it's done. This season, there's a quota of 700 minke whales and Bjorn will hunt as many as he can.

I'd grown up with the campaign to 'save the whale' and remember collecting the stickers as a child. Whaling seemed so obviously wrong back then but I've given it little thought since. So I ask Bjorn whether he really thinks that killing whales is right.

We eat the cows, he says, so why not the whales? It's better than farming in a factory. And he adds what he hopes will be an overwhelming argument: whale meat is free-range, it's natural. You can call it 'organic'.

Organic, brilliant. I have to smile at the ingenuity of the pitch. How clever to exploit the language of green campaigning and then to use it to justify the very activity that led many people into campaigning in the first place. Bjorn looks pleased at my reaction.

Whaling, along with nuclear power, is one of the causes that launched the modern environmental movement. The strongest point in this debate is the unanswerable one of the threat of extinction: up until the 1960s, certain species of whale were hunted almost to oblivion. Even the whaling nations had to concede that action was needed, and the international ban eventually followed. Now, with some stocks recovering, the ban is fraying. Indigenous communities like the Inuit and some Pacific Islanders were always granted limited whaling rights (which included the whale I ate in Greenland), Japan claimed the need to catch whales for 'research' and Norway ignored the agreement.

Minke whales are among those regarded by the Norwegians as fair game; a Japanese official even suggested that there were so many minke whales that they were as numerous as cockroaches. Insisting that their slaughter is perfectly sustainable, the Norwegians say the process is no different to the killing of any other large animal. Critics say Norway's policy is driven by domestic politics, that the fishermen's votes are secured by allowing them to hunt whales out of the fishing season.

While it may be true that the minke population in this part of the ocean is relatively healthy, there is another fundamental issue, one which has continued to fuel the passion to stop whaling: that it's less about numbers and more about objecting to a practice that is simply inhumane, that it's immoral to kill these gentle, giant mammals in the high seas.

Bjorn breaks off from the conversation because he's having trouble preparing the harpoon. It's a complicated process, a bit like readying an old-fashioned cannon, a throwback to the days when the gunpowder and shot were loaded into the muzzle of the gun and then packed inside. What Bjorn has to do is insert a heavy steel spear, about a metre long, into the weapon. To ensure it flies out rapidly, it has to be a tight fit. Bjorn has to wrestle it in and, despite the cold, he's sweating by the time he's finished.

Next comes the fitting of the deadliest part of the weapon. The harpoon itself will penetrate the whale's thick skin but that won't be sufficient to kill it. So, at the tip of the spear, Bjorn fits an explosive charge, a metal canister about the size of a tin can, painted an innocent red. The size of the device is eerily similar to the cluster bombs I saw scattered and unexploded at Tallil airbase in Iraq after the Gulf War. In the desert light, the colour was so bright that the little bombs seemed almost toy-like, until we heard the boom of a detonation as someone trod on one, the weapon killing three people, their charred bodies lying near the pools of leaked fuel they'd been trying to collect. Now, when I thought I'd put military reporting behind me, I'm listening to the explanation of a similar type of high-explosive. This one, I'm told, has a very particular task: when the harpoon has reached one foot inside the whale, the canister will erupt with deadly force. Three small hooks on the end of the device are designed to latch onto the animal's skin and prevent the charge getting too far in.

I ask Bjorn where he aims the weapon.

The heart, not the head, he says. The skull is too thick.

How can you be sure of hitting it?

He admits that total accuracy can't be guaranteed. The whale only breaks the surface briefly, and the boat is always moving. It's real hunting.

The Norwegians say that in nearly all cases, this technique – a hand grenade exploding inside the heart – kills the whale instantaneously, that very few of the animals take longer than two minutes to die. The official line is that it takes one shot for a neat death with no pain, a claim that protestors have long dismissed as propaganda. That's why we're here, to record what really happens.

I mention to Bjorn that no less a figure than David Attenborough has written movingly of our inability to hear the whales suffering. If we could hear their screams, he wrote, there's no way whaling would be allowed.

He shrugs, you'll see, and leads us to supper.

We bunch round a table, Martin and I, and the Norwegians, four of them, while one stays on the bridge. It's an odd meal, given that we only left port a few hours ago: most of it looks like it's been cooked from frozen, pale with processed breadcrumbs and nothing green in sight, the sort of thing you'd expect after weeks at sea. Only the potatoes are fresh, small and fairly new, cooked with their skins on, and I watch amazed as these tough men of the sea painstakingly and delicately peel away the skins with their knives and forks, a fiddly task which goes on for minutes and brings to mind the daintiest of tea parties where politeness demands that no one should ever handle their food. To be polite, I mimic them, poking and scraping but wondering why they bother.

Conversation is awkward too: the crewmen obviously think we're in the way, taking up space, asking too many questions, challenging their way of life. Any mention of the anti-whaling movement produces a look of loathing, and the media seem to be hated too. I toy with seeing the effect of the word 'Greenpeace' but hold back. Bjorn's cousin, the friendliest of the lot, tells a story of two French journalists who once came on board. They were so seasick they had to be evacuated. The crewmen pause in their potato-peeling to laugh, and Martin and I feel obliged to join in.

Within hours, we'll feel like crying instead.


The note of the engine keeps changing – reversing, revving and then slowing. The rocking is still there, as is my nausea, but I realise the boat must be manoeuvring. I spring out of bed because I realise that this can only mean one thing: the crew have either just killed a whale or they're about to. I urge Martin out of bed too and we race upstairs to find that the worst has happened. We've missed the big event. If there's one thing more unpleasant than seeing a whale harpooned, it's being a news team that sleeps through the chance of getting the shot.

I'm furious that the crew didn't wake us, as they'd promised they would, and I'm even more angry when I think through the implications: without actually filming the harpoon being fired and seeing what we've come for, there's no way we can leave this purgatory. And, as that thought sinks in, the adrenaline of the past few minutes wears off and my innards remind me of the Arctic swell. Within seconds I'm hanging over the railing and notice that Martin is beside me doing the same.

This time Bjorn can't resist a jibe.

You English men, you are like women.

His crew roar approval, they're loving it. The media who so often give them a hard time are now humbled.

It occurs to me that we've ended up on a modern-day version of a longboat in the company of salt-veined descendants of Vikings. The only things missing are the horned helmets and a plan to pillage eastern England. Erik the Red would have loved to see a couple of Brits, helpless and heaving, women in a world of men.

I want to come back with a clever riposte, preferably something about the effeminate potato-peeling, but my mind, like my belly, is empty.

Another day passes, or maybe it's a night; the very idea of opening my diary to keep track makes me want to heave. In my wanderings to find a stable spot, I pass the galley and the cook shows me unexpected sympathy, urging me to eat a piece of crispbread. I also try more of the pills and they stay down longer than usual, along with some Coca-Cola, so I no longer actively want to die. Martin, sadly, is in marginally worse shape than me, too weak to curse the Norsemen, too sick to come onto the deck. So when I hear the battle cry go up, 'Kval', signalling that another whale has been spotted, I know it'll fall to me to do the filming. As I reach for our reserve camera, Martin valiantly rises from his pillow to explain how to set the correct exposure. I have to cut him short: how do you set it to automatic?

At the bow, Bjorn is gripping the harpoon, eyes scanning the waves. He occasionally twists round to shout an order at his cousin on the bridge to turn or alter the speed. The boat edges forward. Everyone is tense, the crewmen all poised for a sight of the whale. There's a flash of black off to one side and a lot of yelling. Frankly, I can't tell if it's a trick of the light. I switch on the camera and hope for the best. The sheen on the water is dazzling, the swell is still nauseating. I have no idea where to point so I choose the widest possible setting, including in the frame Bjorn and the harpoon and a big expanse of sea. Long minutes pass. I start to feel the cold. The hand holding the rail is protected by a glove but the one with the camera is bare – I'd had to take that glove off to manage the controls. I wonder how cameramen cope, and how long I can last. But when I think that failing to get this shot will mean staying even longer on board, the chill doesn't feel so bad.

Bjorn's shouts become more intense. I spot the rise of a black shape in the trough between two waves. Then there's a deafening bang and a cloud of smoke brings the whiff of high explosive. The boat quickly stops. Bjorn peers over the side. I move closer but he waves me back. I've no idea if the whale has been hit or not. But then I see Bjorn picking up his rifle. Earlier he'd told me that he only uses it if the animal does not die instantly. Clearly this one is still alive and injured. He needs to finish it off but it's somehow in the wrong position for him to open fire so the boat has to be moved. Time passes, and I imagine the whale in agony. I keep the camera running. Bjorn fires two shots, then pauses, before firing three more. The whole process, from letting loose the harpoon to the last shots, has lasted well over two minutes; the camera's timecode is the irrefutable evidence.

**Nauseous off the North Cape:** while a whale is dismembered I record a piece-to-camera before resuming my usual position of hanging over the side. You can see the animal's tail behind me. The grisliest butchery is out of shot.     *BBC*

The crew use long hooks to bring the whale to the loading ramp at the side of the boat. The harpoon is so deeply snagged in its belly that it takes two men to extract it. Bjorn had missed the heart. Ropes are lashed around the whale's tail and it's hauled on board by a winch. The animal is much longer than the boat is wide, so when its belly is on the deck, its head hangs over the side and, from its mouth, a stream of blood flows into the sea where a red pool forms. I notice a massive eye, staring lifeless at the sky. The gulls are gathering.

The crew are too busy to notice me so I move around to film different angles. It falls to the cook to handle the butchery. His first action is to cut open the whale's belly. It's a female, I hear, so there's a chance that it's pregnant. The knife enters the pale skin, just below the chest, and draws a fast red line down towards the tail. The skin parts and I'm staggered by the volume of intestines that spill out. There's no foetus, but the whale's belly is full of tiny shrimp, and the stench of this partly digested meal hits me hard. All the innards are dumped over the side and the gulls go crazy.

The cook then sets about carving out the fillets, the prize sections of the flesh, dark red and the size of logs or railways sleepers, the largest steaks in the world. Steam rises into the air. Blood is now flowing in small torrents, the crewmen's rubber boots sloshing through streams of red, and the scarlet pool in the ocean keeps growing. The steaks are laid on the deck to cool. The rest of the whale is unwanted. The ropes around the tail are loosened and as the massive carcase – with the long spine and the huge head – slides off the ship in one messy piece and crashes into the sea, I hope for a final sight of that massive, sad eye. But the gulls are swarming too thickly, and, anyway, within seconds the remains are sinking.

Bjorn is excited. This early haul will help offset his costs and, if he's in the right area, he'll land a lot more in a matter of days. His biggest worry is whether he'll have enough deck space to lay out all the meat. If it can't cool, it will spoil.

I ask him whether he feels anything for the whale.

Do you feel anything for a cow, he responds.

But what about all the blood, and the risk that the whale was in calf?

Well, it wasn't in calf, he says, and you get the same amount of blood in any slaughterhouse, you just don't see it.

But what about the length of time it took the whale to die?

It wasn't so long.

But, I explain, I timed the whole event on the camera.

Bjorn grimaces. You're right, he agrees, this time it took longer than two minutes, that's unusual.

There's nothing more he can say. The whale wasn't able to scream but the pictures will.

Our job is done and although Bjorn would love to be rid of us, he's also reluctant to leave this obviously rich stretch of sea. Initially he offers to drop us at some place a few miles away but when I check on a map and realise it's an island, I object: we'd need yet another boat to get us to the mainland, and I'd hate to have to explain that to Martin. So after much argument we settle on Europe's northernmost village, Gamvik, a wind-blasted stretch of cottages facing the North Pole. The crew, who never warmed to us, throw our bags onto the quay. Lying on the cold concrete, still queasy, we watch the *Reinebuen* race back to the hunt.

The whale meat is natural, no question, and this particular catch, if tightly limited, is possibly sustainable. But compared to the mechanised slaughter of an abattoir, this is hit-and-miss, a raw process requiring skill and luck. Sonar can't be used because it would scare the whales away so this is a modern version of hunter-gathering, the only difference being that the spear is fired by cannon and is tipped with a hand grenade. But, as in ancient times, aim is everything and what I witnessed was a bungled shot and a horribly slow death, an example of how whaling can genuinely be inhumane. After my report is aired, a minister quotes from it in a debate about whaling in the House of Commons; he describes the cruelty of a killing that took longer than two minutes. The Norwegians, used to this kind of criticism, are unmoved and actually increase the quota the following year, even though the evidence suggests that the hunt isn't worth it.

That's because Bjorn and the rest of Norway's whalers land more meat than Norwegians actually want to eat.

It's on sale in supermarkets but does not fly from the shelves. Plans to sell whale blubber to Japan were abandoned because it contained too many contaminants – the same winds that carry the soot that darkens the glaciers in Greenland also introduces into the Arctic food chain the deadly acronyms of modern industrial life, the PCBs and the PAHs, the toxic by-products of fossil fuels. So I wonder about the real motive behind the killing, about why this hunt is allowed. There's no single answer, but the national pride of a seafaring nation is definitely one factor; another is the need to woo voters in the fishing communities of the Arctic coast. It's certainly not about getting organic meat to Norwegian tables.

Martin and I are slumped on our bags, waiting for a lift to the local airport and the first of several flights to get us home. He's got some colour back in his face and has lots of questions.

He asks me whether I was sick in the bathroom the previous night.

As it happens, I wasn't. Apart from the very first night, I did all that kind of thing out of doors.

But Martin asks again, to check I'm sure, because he insists someone was being sick in the bathroom; the noise was unmistakeable.

We puzzle over this until a glorious reality dawns. If it wasn't him or me, then it must have been one of the Norwegians.

I look at the *Reinebuen* shrinking towards the horizon and, as I picture the steaming meat on the decks and the lifeless eyes sinking past the reach of the gulls, I at last have a riposte to Bjorn, too late, but cheering nonetheless: it isn't just Englishmen who are like women. Vikings get seasick too.

I've left the ship with relief and a sense of futility – wasted effort, needless cruelty, pointless slaughter. I'm also struck by the contradictions thrown up by whaling: how easily earlier generations of whalers so nearly wiped out entire species and how in more recent years the threat of extinction was used to galvanise international action to slow or stop the hunting. But how many environmental causes are that clear-cut?

The classic poster shot of ecological catastrophe shows the once proud fishing fleet of the dried-out Aral Sea. While the Norwegian fishermen are accused of being overactive and hauling the wrong animals from the ocean, the fishermen of Central Asia's lost sea have nothing to catch. Or even anything to float on. While whaling was the green issue that first motivated millions, the skeletal hulls stranded in the dust have long provided the most potent imagery of environmental ruin. What was once the world's fourth largest inland sea has for decades been shrinking because the rivers that feed it have been channelled into fields of cotton. Just as whaling is a deliberate act with serious consequences, so is the diversion of the waters that sustained a sea.

But this path is well trodden and every journalist likes to be first. With this one, I'm whole decades late. And what if the situation out there isn't that bad? Maybe previous reporters, under pressure to deliver a strong story, focused on the worst corner and ignored the rest. And what if the benefits of cultivating cotton – the thousands of jobs, the exports, the growth of a poor region – outweigh the damage? Maybe the environmental price was worth paying. England, for example, chopped down its forests to build a navy that went on to create an empire. Who are we to say that the wrong decision was made in Central Asia?

t's the strange white of the ground that catches my eye. We're driving through a dilapidated village in Uzbekistan, on our way to the Aral Sea, and beside the road a game of football is being played on a very rough pitch. The evening sun is low so initially I assume the light is somehow making the baked dust appear unusually pale. But when we stop and get closer, it's obvious that the land really is white, as if it's been very clumsily and haphazardly painted with great buckets of whitewash. I crouch down and see that the white isn't just on the surface but also reaches a bit deeper. A few children stop their play to watch me.

We ask around and people seem surprised that we should be interested in the colour of their ground. It's always that way, we're told. The village lies relatively close to where the shoreline of the Aral Sea used to be and the explanation seems to be that the land is laden with salts. As the amount of water reaching this area has dwindled, the salts have become visible and the result is that this playground and the unpaved lanes nearby have been bleached. The football continues, the children unfazed.

Further on, the road ends at what was once a thriving port, Munyak. This is our destination and to my relief we see that the famous fishing boats are still lying on their sides – I had worried that by the time we got there someone might have broken them up for scrap. Cameraman Tony Jolliffe climbs around to get the shots. The boats are falling apart and the ground is a dirty mix of sand, dust and scrubby grass, exactly what we've all seen in the pictures taken over previous years.

No one has exaggerated, it is a desolate scene, but I can't help feeling unimpressed, and I can see that Tony is having trouble making much of it – he's filmed all he can in just a few minutes. Partly that's because it's simply very hard to imagine that this arid landscape was ever under water, and also because these wrecked vessels look pretty much like any other boats stranded by a low tide. After days of travel, it's like making it to the Holy Grail and finding a small dull cup.

So we head into Munyak itself, and it's there that we find more telling sights. This isn't the first time I've seen communities in a state of collapse – when I was at university in Durham, the boarded-up terraced houses of the former coal-mining villages stood nearby, the reason for their existence closed beneath them. But this town's ruin is of an entirely different order. It looks utterly crushed. In this former super-power, the people are living like their ancestors would have done hundreds of years ago. The children are barefoot. I see two little girls struggling to carry water in old cooking-oil tins. The streets are like tracks, mostly dirt, and many of the houses are little more than shacks. Unkempt dogs pick over scraps. The heat is bewildering and the winds are constant, whipping up the endless dust so we have to shield our eyes. Dust gets everywhere – the children's faces, the few trees, the handful of battered cars. It's like a scene from science fiction, survivors of nuclear Armageddon. I'd come expecting stranded ships and we've stumbled into something worse.

The irony is that Munyak grew up beside the sea with plentiful supplies of water. Its role was to service a vast fishing operation – the haul from the Aral Sea was famous – and its processing factory used to be the Soviet Union's largest producer of canned fish. Footage from the Fifties shows jolly fishermen hauling in heavy nets and holidaymakers splashing in the waves. Now, with the sea too shallow and too distant to be useful, the factory has been abandoned. We wander into its empty halls, the machines and conveyor belts idle, the windows broken. There's a proud statue of a fisherman cradling what looks like a huge salmon, covered in dust. Thousands of people used to work here, it was the engine of the local economy, but now wild goats wander unchecked, picking their way over the rail tracks that used to deliver Munyak's tins of fish to the outside world.

The sea is said to be dozens of miles away. I'd like to see for myself how far it's retreated – but local advice is that even the toughest four-wheel drive will get bogged down either in the sand or the mud, the terrain too hostile. Warned of this in advance, we've managed to hire one of the few planes available. My heart sinks when I see it. For a start it's very old, perhaps not quite as decrepit as the dusty Afghan helicopters I saw in Tajikistan, but it looks like something Tintin might have flown in, a biplane with clumsy wings and dirty windows.

The aircrew, dressed in Russian military fatigues, are swaggering: they've taken a shine to my producer, Alex Milner, and her half-Greek looks. Once airborne, the pilot weaves the plane in a series of tight curves to impress her and he finds it hilarious when she feels ill. I try to exert some control – we are paying for this after all – but the plane is so noisy that it's easy to ignore me. Eventually, we get the crew to listen and to perform a simple task: fly as fast as you can in a straight line to the nearest stretch of sea.

I assume there will be a neat shoreline. Satellite pictures, which have recorded the rapid shrinking of the sea, give the impression of a sharp distinction between land and water. But after an hour of flying, covering roughly one hundred miles, what I see passing below us is mile after mile of confusing mess, of desert gradually morphing into pallid bog and then into endless shallows. The colours of the water, cobalt and turquoise, seem curiously artificial – I've been told that for decades the sea was on the receiving end of vast quantities of pesticides, washed down from the cotton fields upstream.

It's certainly unhealthy here: figures show that this region has the world's highest rate of cancer of the oesophagus. In the provincial capital, Nukus, we visit the hospital, stepping out of the fierce Central Asian sun into an airless cancer ward. Lacking the energy to move, the patients feel every chill so the windows are shut tight. The smell and the heat are overwhelming. The beds are old, the paint peeling and the men in here have the saddest faces I've ever seen.

The patients defer to the eldest. Dr Saparbay Kazahbaev introduces himself as a retired biologist who spent his career studying the Aral Sea, and tracking its decline. Too weak to sit upright, he lies with his head on his pillow, occasionally straining upwards to emphasise a point. His voice is rasping, almost a whisper, but he retains the classic style of a Soviet scientist, explaining things in a very orderly, if laborious, way.

He begins by saying he's pleased to be talking to the BBC; his fellow patients are listening intently. What follows is a short and very depressing lecture.

Dr Kazahbaev begins by listing the many types of fish which used to thrive in the sea, and then describes how the water used to have a favourable chemistry. Next he explains how the sea level dropped and how the little water that reached it carried toxic residues from the industrial-scale cotton projects inland. Then he makes the connection between the billowing dusts and the health of people living nearby.

First, he says, the salts get into your respiratory system. They're poisonous. He lifts his head to make sure my translator has done her job and that I've understood – poisonous.

Then the poisonous salts get into the plants and animals which we eat. He gestures by bringing his fingers towards his mouth.

And that's why I'm here, he concludes.

He can't have long. His eyes are determined but the skin on his face is dry and loose, and delivering his explanation has tired him.

When we step outside, it's time for lunch but no one is hungry.

What's dispiriting is seeing a civilisation slide. Back home, I'm used to a world in which new buildings go up, the streets get busier, people generally become healthier. Here, the land and its people have been poisoned and everything is regressing. In Soviet days, Central Asian cotton was a major export earning useful hard currency but the harvests were usually smaller than official statistics claimed and profits were siphoned off by a corrupt Communist leadership. Meanwhile the water diverted from the rivers was often wasted – the pipes and channels were badly built and poorly maintained and vast quantities of water were lost. And when it reached the fields, much of it was squandered through carelessness or overuse.

**Sands of time:** the dried-out remains of what was the Aral Sea near Munyak in Uzbekistan in central Asia. The dust apparently contains a toxic mix of old pesticides. I wash as carefully as I can afterwards. *BBC*

Is there a positive side? Some people must have earned a good living and a few will have become rich. And Uzbek cotton, cultivated under state control and with low wages, would have reached the world market. Its availability would have helped keep the price of cotton clothes cheap. Without realising it, I've probably bought shirts or trousers made of Uzbek cotton and been pleased at getting a bargain. The former Soviet Union initiated and managed an ecological disaster. But anyone wearing cotton grown there had an unwitting hand in it too.

Before we leave, we stumble across a curious historical footnote. Uzbekistan was always one of the Soviet Union's remoter republics and this part of it, Karakalpakstan, was so out of the way that it was used as a hot version of Siberia, a place of exile for the politically awkward. And as long as the cotton kept coming, officials turned a blind eye to what went on in this windswept corner. This allowed an artist to achieve something that could never have happened closer to Moscow: the discreet but efficient gathering of one of the country's largest collections of dissident art, paintings which for various reasons weren't appreciated by the authorities.

Now housed in a modern gallery, the works are at once disturbing and beautiful. 'Return of the Reapers', painted in 1927 when Stalin's grip was total, is Impressionist and shows a line of farmers walking, their bright turbans distinctly un-Soviet and the fields small, pretty and not collectivised. 'The Aral Sea Station' is a charming, warm scene, figures stepping off a train to greet their families, the men in conical Central Asian hats and the women in head-scarves, camels in the background, none of this the ideal image of a progressive Soviet Union. A vivid blue stripe on the horizon marks the sea itself, with two boats sailing on it. The railway is the only hint of the industrialisation to come, of devastation that will be visible from space, fill a cancer ward and turn a playground white. The painting is dated 1931, the calm before the ruin.

A prominent radio presenter calls to me across the newsroom and his colleagues stop to listen. Shukman, he says, you've got this extraordinary job: you go to these amazing places and tell us they're buggered.

News reporting is often grim but my role does seem uniquely pessimistic. It's actually in my nature to be quite upbeat and it is a relief when there are possible solutions to the problems I'm covering. In the Aral Sea, for example, there was a project to refill one part of it – I do mention it in my report – but the scale was tiny and even if it worked its effect overall would be negligible.

Sometimes optimism can be justified. In the late 1980s, scientists working for the British Antarctic Survey noticed a huge gap in the fragile layer of ozone in the upper atmosphere, a protective filter which screens out much of the sun's ultraviolet radiation. Wherever the ozone is thin or missing, the amount of UV light reaching the surface sharply increases, and the risk of skin cancers escalates. It was American researchers who worked out that the ozone was being destroyed by man-made gases known as CFCs. This was a major surprise: the gases, widely used in fridges and air-conditioning, were specifically designed to be harmless.

With satellite pictures showing the CFCs tearing a ragged hole in the ozone layer over Antarctica, reaching as far as New Zealand, Australia and South America, the international community quickly responded. The gases were to be phased out, first in the industrialised world and later in developing countries, a model example of the world tackling a self-evident threat. Problem over? Not exactly. The hole itself will take decades to heal and in the meantime millions of people live under it.

Punta Arenas, the town at the southernmost tip of Chile, doesn't have many celebrities but we've managed to secure an interview with one of them. Francisco Figueredo is an elderly musician and when we arrive at his house he's going through a selection of jazz records. He's due to present his weekly radio programme tonight so can't spare us much time. He wants to talk about his choice of music – a bit of Duke Ellington, others I haven't heard of – but he knows we're here for another reason: his medical history.

Not large but impossible to miss are the scabs and scars scattered across his face. A small plaster precariously covers the top of one of Francisco's ears. This is all the result of repeated cases of skin cancer.

The problem stems from his younger days, he says. No one knew about this problem, we were completely ignorant.

Punta Arenas is so far south that when the ozone hole appears over Antarctica every spring the effects are immediate. The fact that the town's climate is windy and cool is no protection from the ultraviolet radiation. After standing on the street for about five or six minutes I feel a tingling on my face and on my hands. The longer I'm out in the open air the more the tingling becomes a very mild stinging, nothing like a nettle sting, but more like the feeling when damaged skin is first touched by water, nothing severe but impossible to ignore. Initially I assume I've accidentally rubbed my face and hands with something acidic but actually I'm suffering from invisible sunburn. I ask the rest of the team if they're feeling anything and, yes, they too are getting the same sensation. It's uncomfortable enough for us to keep our filming short and get back inside.

On the NASA website, the exact position of the hole can be tracked as it rotates with the weather systems around Antarctica and today, at one of the town's busiest junctions, we pass an array of bright orange flags: it's a warning of 'high risk'. On the local radio, the information is given out along with the weather. What's strange is that in Europe UV warnings coincide with hot sunny days in summer; here the UV can be dangerous even when it's chilly and overcast. This threat can be felt but not seen.

The impact of the ozone hole is better understood now. One of the town's skin specialists, Dr Jaime Abaca, has set about gathering the data. By his count, the most dangerous form of skin cancer, malignant melanoma, is found here at a rate three times higher than the global average. And he is in no doubt that it's the result of the ozone hole.

The information is unsettling enough to send us scurrying for the nearest pharmacy to buy more sunscreen. I find the right set of shelves but think I must be mistaken when I can't see any creams or lotions with a protection factor higher than 10. I check with the manageress, Auad Jaihatt, but she confirms that no one wants to buy high-protection sunscreen, in fact very little of any kind is sold at all.

Most people, she says, just don't understand the risks of getting cancer, the message still isn't getting through.

Even more bizarre, as we drive around this UV-blasted town, we notice an incredible number of signs advertising tanning studios. One of the largest is *Cecilia International* with big plate-glass windows and a smart paint job.

I ask the owner how many customers she has.

About fifty a week.

I'm astounded. Fifty women, living in an ultraviolet hothouse, actually paying for an additional dose.

I'm introduced to one of the regulars, Evanella, a handsome woman of a certain age who reminds me of the air hostesses in early Bond films, with a careful hairdo and lots of make-up. And a very tanned skin.

She comes here about three times a week, she tells me.

I ask whether she knows the risks of so much tanning, particularly while living in a place that is already so vulnerable to the most potent rays of the sun.

She knows about the cancer, but this is a matter of personal choice. She feels better with a tan. It's too cold to go to the beach so this is the only chance we have, she insists.

I start to feel that it isn't my place to keep pressing her, to put to her the figures for skin cancer, to explain the NASA website with its images of the scarily large ozone hole right over her town.

She's made up her mind. A good tan, she concludes, makes my clothes look better.

What's a man meant to say? It's like being asked an ultraviolet version of the question, does my bum look big in this? I have no choice: the look of the clothes has to come first so I join the nods of approval from the rest of the salon.


Black snow, red sea, white soil and an orange face – there are some emerging connections. There are things that bring real benefits or pleasure in the short term. The Chinese soot is part of a process that generates electricity – which is badly needed. For the Norwegian whalers, a trickle of blood in the water is a small price to keep them employed. The white playground is the by-product of an industry that yielded valuable exports. And Evanella is happier seeing a tanned face in the mirror. But what about the longer term? Back in the 1930s, the man who invented CFCs, Thomas Midgeley, presumably thought he was doing a good thing, that his harmless gases met a genuine need and helped make refrigeration so cheap that it became available to millions. By strange coincidence it so happens that the same Mr Midgeley also came up with another invention, an idea for making engines run more smoothly: by topping up the petrol with a bit of lead.

# 2

# Heart of dampness

The brief dusk is over but a steamy heat remains and a lot of hysterical screeching begins. I know that's what's meant to happen in jungles but, after years of vaguely sympathising with the cause of saving the rainforests, I'm now uneasy being immersed in one. I'm beside a tributary of the River Amazon, near the town of Alter do Chao in Brazil, at a small hotel, walking along a covered path connecting my room to the main building. It's described as an eco-lodge, which means that very little of the dense vegetation has been disturbed, and that very little of what lives in that vegetation has been disturbed either, as I'm soon to see. An 'eco' tag has consequences.

Up until this moment, everything I know about the rainforest has been second hand and a bit stale – the singer Sting touring the television studios with the saucer-lipped chief of the threatened Yanomami Indians; the regular, almost monotonous invocation of Belgium or Wales as the area of Amazonian forest cleared by loggers every year; the wildlife documentaries with lingering beauty shots. One worry, which I keep to myself, is whether I'll find anything fresh.

Among the well-aired facts I've picked up is that one-third of all the world's different species exist here, making the Amazon the uber-hotspot for biodiversity. The only hitch is that biodiversity means all creatures great and small, a wonderful thing and vital for a healthy planet, no question, but some of those creatures are, let's face it, pretty revolting. You don't hear much in the conservation conferences about fighting for the tapeworm or that squirmingly malicious little fish, notorious in the Amazon, with a fondness for the odours of the urethra. Although it's apparently safe to swim on this particular stretch of river, I shudder at the thought, deciding that biodiversity is not always best experienced in person.

The walkway leads me towards the bar and I'm looking forward to a cold beer. I'm about to pass my cameraman's room and I had said I'd give him a knock to let him know when I was on my way.

I'm about to lean towards his door – but something large and dark on the ground in front of me catches my eye.

Right at the foot of the door is the largest spider I've ever seen. It's as big as my outstretched hand. It's thick and black, and is engaged in a curious and unnerving quivering. It shows no intention of moving but, because its body is pulsating, I assume that it's about to attack, and that I'm the nearest target.

At home, I trap spiders under a plastic cup and then slide a postcard underneath it but the same approach with this one would require a large bucket and a sheet of steel.

I call out, my voice raised by at least an octave. The cameraman on this assignment is John Boon, an agile Scot with a dry sense of humour.

I'll just be a minute, he shouts back.

But I can't let John emerge unprepared into the path of this beast. So I yell back that he'd better hang on, and explain why.

Just kick it out of the way, he urges.

Great idea, for someone who's a lot braver than me and isn't wearing sandals. No way am I going to start a confrontation. I wonder what WWF would judge to be the ecologically correct way to handle this problem. Given the rate at which species are being lost every year, I'd hate to be the one to have a hand in the demise of this one. Think of the headlines: 'Beeb man in extinction shock.' So I conjure up a line that any self-respecting environment correspondent might produce: that it would be wrong to intervene with this example of the Amazon's precious wildlife.

John is utterly disdainful, rightly recognising this as an excuse for cowardice.

But then I notice that he shows no sign of taking on the enemy either. And it is outside *his* door, after all.

So, realising that a couple of the BBC's finest are, frankly, stymied, I come up with a brilliant compromise. I'll bypass the monster and go to the bar but then, for John's sake, as a loyal colleague, I shall gallantly return later to see if his way is safe.

John utters some oath learned in a Glasgow playground but I'm away before I can make it out.

After twenty minutes, I convince myself I'm doing the honourable thing by keeping my word and returning. The spider has gone. John is liberated. But as we walk back to the bar, our laughter is nervous as we eye the restless shadows.


What everyone knows about the rainforest is that it rains, often every day, sometimes almost all the time, rather like standing in a sauna under a hot shower. A soaking is preordained, as is the resulting soupy mess of rainwater mingled with sun block and insect spray and lots of sweat. On my first full day, I realise that it's uncomfortable doing anything other than inhaling air conditioning and, if none is available, then fantasising about it.

But what no one tells you about rainforests is that they feature another form of rain as well: a gentle but constant precipitation of ants, bugs and assorted wrigglers tumbling from the dark heights. Whole ecosystems flourish in the canopies – their existence in the treetops is one of the wonders of the natural world – but, unfortunately, not all of them are very good at staying up there.

On our way to a research camp, riding on the back of a quad bike, I happen to glance down at my shirt. It's heaving with a mass of creatures, most tiny, but one particularly assertive ant seems the size of a paperclip. And because I'm looking down while I frantically swat these invaders, my neck is exposed and it becomes a landing zone too. I react with horror and manically flick and brush. Initially I seem to be winning this struggle to keep the Amazon's biodiversity at bay. But then I notice that a few of the pluckier arrivals have leapt onto my hands where they roam freely and untroubled over the sheen of insect repellent. And all the time, a fresh supply keeps descending.

We stop at a tiny clearing and try to shake ourselves clear. John films a few shots, his eye drawn to the occasional shaft of sunlight penetrating the gloom. Continuing my swatting, I wander off for a look around when suddenly I hear a loud yelp and spin round to an extraordinary sight: John is twisting in pain as Flavio, our guide, thrashes him on the back with his hat. I run up, confused. Has John caused offence? Has Flavio been in the forest too long?

The answer lies on the ground. Flavio reaches down and picks up a red-and-white-striped insect the size of a wasp.

It's a type of mosquito, he says. It was on John's shirt and trying to punch through. If it had stung him, you could forget filming for a few days.

He points out the insect's proboscis: it's thick and sturdy like a hypodermic needle, so out of proportion with the insect's body it's like a child holding a rifle.

We shudder, but time is short so we press on and set up for an interview. But we're shaken. Especially when there's another surge of primal fear as a familiar and scary black shape scuttles towards us: it's a scorpion, several inches long, tail poised.

It's OK, says Flavio. You only need to worry if it's got a red dot. Otherwise it won't actually kill you.

I can't tell if it has a red dot or not. All I know is that I'm sure the rainforests need saving in theory. But saving this bit, in practice, right this minute, every creature? Up to a point.


A bumpy track leads us towards what I'm told is a fresh example of deforestation. I think I know what it will look like – I've seen pictures of this kind of thing: the lone tree, the miles of bare dry soil, the forlorn trunk on its side. Deforestation has been in and out of the news for at least two decades so, as we lurch along in the heat, I'm almost resigned to merely grabbing the best images we can and moving on, filming what will be an essential scene in our coverage but not one that we have any hope of making distinctive. Can this new environment correspondent find anything new here?

But as we turn a corner, I enter a scene where I wonder how my assumptions could have been so wrong. Huge stumps lie in their thousands, many of them charred, and the red earth beneath them is churned into ugly ridges. The clearance is like a giant prairie heaped with junk timber. Nothing seems left alive. Amid the shattered trunks, their branches twisted, there are no birds. Countless wisps of smoke turn the sky grey and suddenly it feels hotter. None of the images I'd seen before remotely captures the enormity of this destruction. And there's something unimaginable in the Amazon: the insects seem to have vanished. Of course, I realise – there's no canopy for them to rain down from.

In one of my newspapers cuttings, a journalist had likened the deforestation to the horrors of the First World War, the fields ravaged by craters and trenches. Standing here now, I'm not convinced the writer had left his desk. The atmosphere, particularly the silence, reminds me more of urban warfare, battles waged in streets. The wrecked trees, even lying on their sides, are as tall as buildings and are grey like concrete. I recall the fighting for control of the scarred town of Gornji Vakuf in Bosnia. In a conflict with three opposing forces, this became a collection of ruins, a mini-Beirut, its inhabitants stunned after each spasm of violence. Like the destroyed forest, the town had thin columns of smoke twisting into the air, the whole place seemingly winded. What I'm looking at now resembles the same kind of carnage except that it wasn't caused by tanks and artillery.

It was bulldozers. Linked by chains.

I'm with an environmental officer, Ernesto, one of a small band of officials trying to stop deforestation: just seven men defend an area about the size of Britain and France combined.

The bulldozers, he explains, are brought in on trucks and at the edge of the forest the heavy chains are slung between them. The vehicles then advance side-by-side, in military formation, and everything in their path gets torn down. The trees are felled, the stumps uprooted. The wreckage is then set alight and eventually ploughed ready to be used for agriculture – either as pasture for cattle or fields for cultivating soya beans. From land that's dirt cheap, beef and beans fetch high prices.

But surely it's illegal?

Yes, says Ernesto, but there are loopholes. Virgin rainforest has the strongest protection in law but to retain that status it has to remain untouched; once it's been tampered with in any way, it's classified differently and enjoys less protection. So landowners encourage small-scale loggers to push into the virgin forest and extract the most valuable trees. When the work of the loggers is 'discovered', the landowner can exclaim in horror that his forest is no longer 'virgin' which just happens to mean, rather conveniently, that the penalties for any further deforestation are much lighter. And that's when the bulldozers are brought in.

Just as Ernesto is explaining this, we spot a truck in the distance, parked close to the edge of the remaining forest. He's immediately suspicious and we race over. Across the back seat I glance at John and see that he's as excited as I am: our report will fly if we can capture some action. In the front of the car is our escort, a policeman, who's armed. Confrontations can turn ugly. Local campaigners, including a priest in this very area, near the town of Santarem, have been warned to shut up on pain of death. In another region, an outspoken American nun was murdered for resisting the loggers. The land beneath the trees can yield so much money that it's triggered an equivalent to a gold rush, anarchic and unrestrained.

When we reach the truck, a battered old thing, there's no one around. But loaded onto it are four freshly felled trunks. I notice sap, almost colourless, dripping from one of them. I reach out and let my finger stick to it; it's surprisingly watery. I realise that while the massive scale of the deforestation is shocking, touching the life force draining from just one tree provokes a different sentiment: it's just plain sad.

The policeman reaches down to check his revolver and goes off in search of the loggers. He enters the forest, calling out, pushing through the undergrowth. We follow him, past a severed stump – the newly exposed wood seems unnaturally pallid, almost naked, and heaps of bright sawdust are scattered nearby. It's like stumbling into a crime scene just minutes after the act. We press on, the policeman's shouts echoing off the wood. And the din soon produces a result.

One of the loggers appears, dressed in a stained football shirt, a sheepish grin on his face. The game is up. The ringleader stumbles out too, hot and irritated, shirt slung over his shoulder, brushing flies from his bare chest. He's been caught red-handed and admits it. Two more trunks and his truck would have had a full load. Now he knows that the timber will be confiscated and that he'll be fined. He's so resigned to his fate that even the presence of a questioning British television crew doesn't faze him.

Do you know what you're doing here is illegal?

He nods, and Ernesto, translating, confirms that he knows the logging is wrong.

So why do you do it?

To make money, he says.

But what for?

He and Ernesto engage in a long discussion. It turns out the logger is trying to pay off a fine.

What for?

For a previous time he was caught logging.

So this is a way of life, and he's just one of thousands of men, pushing into the jungle, carving new inroads, paving the way for the big agro-industrialists. It's a march on countless fronts and seems unstoppable. It occurs to me that the standard comparison with Wales or Belgium underplays the point: the total area of forest cleared so far is about the size of three United Kingdoms.

Standing by the four dripping trunks, I think back to my cynical frame of mind as we arrived. Maybe the campaigning and the slogans and repetition of the chant, Save the Rainforest, have been around so long that I had tuned out. Hearing the same message over and over again must have left me cold. But talking to Ernesto, seeing his team in action – even just tackling the foot soldiers – suddenly strikes a chord. The statistics may be numbing but they're easier to grasp knowing our arrival stopped, or at least delayed, the felling of another couple of trees.

Ernesto instructs the gang to drive straight to the environmental police compound. The men look miserable.

The truck starts up in a cloud of smoke, the prized logs now a burden, and lumbers towards the main road for the two-hour drive to Santarem. It'll be dark by the time they get there and I surprise myself by feeling a bit sorry for them.

**A fair cop:** the moment an illegal logger is caught red-handed in the rainforest near Santarem, Brazil. Behind him is the armed policeman. The logger tells me he needed the money to pay a fine for… illegal logging. *BBC*

We meet again the next morning and watch the logs being unloaded and added to the collection of illegally felled trees. There are so many stored here that the mounds of logs are already several storeys high. The environmental police force has seized so much that its own yard is full and timber has to be stored on a nearby field; no one is quite sure what to do with it. But the officers know this is the tip of the iceberg, that most of it slips past them – that they're fighting a war which they're losing.

As we leave the compound, we emerge onto the riverfront and see one of the factors behind the deforestation. Beyond the whitewashed wooden ferry boats and the fruit stalls on the quayside is a structure that dominates the whole scene: a massive silo. This is where the soya beans, cultivated on what was rainforest, are brought for export. The store acts as a magnet for the farmers and traders. Long lines of trucks arrive laden from the interior and a huge conveyor belt feeds the beans into the bellies of the ships destined for the Atlantic. Amazonian soya is cheap and plentiful. Also, it's conventional in the sense that it's not genetically modified, unlike American soya, which makes it popular in Europe. Within a fortnight the cargoes will have crossed the ocean. Our aversion to GM is encouraging a soya surge here, and fortunes are being made.

The lurid blue of the swimming pool is glaring. I'm sitting in what could be the set of a crude millionaire sitcom, a Latin American version of Dallas. To one side is a grandiose, newly built villa, garish and screaming money – just a weekend place, my host explains. And in the shade there's a line of smart sports cars and upmarket four-wheel drives – just for fun, he laughs. This is one of the Amazon's richest businessmen, a soya baron, and I can't quite believe he's chosen to flaunt his wealth on air; I try to avoid catching John's eye in case we smirk too visibly. It's very rare that an interviewee pushes to be recorded in a situation that could hardly be more damaging to his case.

The soya man is proud of what he's achieved – he's a pioneering entrepreneur, he tells me, putting the jungle to good use, bringing development to the poorest part of a Third World country, doing what's right for Brazil. The soya, he says, creates jobs, boosts exports – nobody loses.

But what about chopping down so many trees?

We only use land that's already been cleared, he says.

So what impact is soya having on the rainforest?

Minimal, practically nothing.

His patter is slick and, as I find out, it's in tune with much Brazilian thinking.

On an internal flight, I hear the same views from fellow passengers, two smart men in suits who introduce themselves as sales representatives for a biscuit company. We make small talk until they ask me what I'm doing. When I explain, the tone darkens.

The forest is Brazil's, they tell me, and it's for us to decide what to do with it. Anyway, you chopped down your forests in Europe so who are you to tell us what to do?

I've heard that kind of thing plenty of times before but what follows is astounding: I realise, don't I, that America is planning to take over the rainforest?

When I splutter, amazed, the biscuit-men have an explanation ready.

Look at a map of Latin America, they urge me. Have I noticed all the American military bases set up in neighbouring countries, the build-up of forces in a near-circle around Brazil?

Yes, I agree, there are a few deployments of US personnel but they'll be supporting anti-drugs operations, any soldiers are there to bolster the fight against the drugs cartels.

Ah, they nod, and smile at each other. That's obviously just a cover. Of course the Americans say they're on a drugs mission. But we all know the truth, that they're preparing to do what outside powers have long plotted: to bring the Amazon under their control. And you British will help them.

I bite my tongue, there's no point responding. The very idea of invading the jungle, battling all that biodiversity, is exhausting.

Paranoia, it turns out, has a long history in the Amazon. Imperial attempts to undermine the country are a theme I keep hearing about. There was the British botanist, a century ago, who smuggled out Amazonian rubber-plant seeds and introduced them to Malaysia where the rubber industry was so successful that it killed off Brazil's. Then came Henry Ford who bought a vast tract of forest and set up a Utopian agro-industrial colony to produce rubber, only to see it crumble. Now there's Greenpeace, using the so-called cause of the environment to do the bidding of Western governments, interfering with Brazil's internal affairs.

I keep quiet when that last comment comes up. It's Greenpeace, with its well-organised infrastructure, to which most journalists turn in the Amazon. They know the best places to film and they've done impressive research. So even though I instinctively shy away from getting too close to campaign groups, it would be pointless to do so this time. Particularly since a British benefactor has given them an invaluable asset: a plane which allows us to get the aerial views that reveal exactly how much forest is being destroyed.

In fact one flight, over the main soya-producing area south of Santarem, shows me how vast fields are now the dominant feature of the landscape, the remaining green reduced to clumps and strips. We don't stay in the air very long – the violent thermals make the ride incredibly nauseating – but we don't have to go far to see what's happening, or to get the point.

Three years later I learn that, whatever the biscuit-salesmen think, the Brazilian justice system does know when to draw a line. Our poolside millionaire, it turns out, was becoming too brazen in his land-grab. The environmental police eventually brought a case against him and, to everyone's surprise, he was jailed. And in part that must have been due to mounting political concern within Brazil and abroad, to try to turn the tide of deforestation.

A magnificent black headdress tilts forward, a long black cassock sways and snags on the weeds. One of the world's great religious leaders, His All Holiness the Patriarch of the Orthodox Church, is marching into a field of Amazonian soya beans, long grey beard to the fore. Behind him are other black-suited Orthodox dignitaries, together with senior figures from other churches, bishops in bright purple, cardinals in white, officials and bodyguards, all crimson-faced under the Brazilian sun, while the whole holy collection is mobbed by a seething crowd of cameramen, photographers and reporters trying to record this unique spectacle.

The visit to the soya is the highlight of one of the strangest expeditions ever mounted in the rainforest. Known as the 'Green Patriarch' for his keen support for environmental causes, the leader of all Orthodox Christians is leading a symposium on the future of the Amazon in which about a hundred delegates from religions and universities and institutes all over the world are travelling up the river by boat. The rainforest attracts plenty of film stars but never before such a concentration of religious muscle.

Without saying so directly, the Patriarch is implicitly critical of the soya boom. This is a big story so media interest is intense. And vicious. A particularly aggressive photographer barges me into a sharp-spiked bush which allows him a better angle but costs me a decent position with the microphone, and also gives me a mass of painful cuts on my calves. There's no question in situations like this: revenge is obligatory, never mind the presence of His All Holiness, The Right Reverends and the rest. As the mob surges forward, my assailant raises his right arm to take a shot, which leaves his ribs vulnerable, a careless move, given that I'm equipped with a sturdy pole to hold the mic and its end is conveniently placed for me to execute a short, powerful but entirely accidental jab.

I get away with it unseen, which is lucky, because emerging from the throng is a man I need to interview, the senior British clergyman to join this bizarre event, the Bishop of Liverpool, James Jones. A silver cross glints on his chest. We find a quiet corner and explore a connection between his home city and the field of soya we're in. We've heard that the ships loaded up with soya beans at Santarem often make the crossing to the docks along the Mersey. There the beans are crushed and processed and added to animal feed. Some of that feed is fed to chickens. And those chickens end up as fast food. So ancient forest makes way for modern takeaway appetites in one country causing devastation in another.

The Bishop is clearly moved, describing how he used to watch the ships sailing on the Mersey without knowing what they contained. Next time I'm in a supermarket buying chicken, he says, I'll wonder how the animal has been fed, and if it was fed on soya beans that were grown here in the Amazon by chopping down the rainforest.

It's a powerful link, and raises a question I'd never really dwelled on before: how can we possibly know the true impact of a simple action like buying chicken?

And I learn that it may be more serious than simply losing trees. Emerging at the symposium is the latest science on how the clearing and burning could be altering the very climate. The smoke, wisps of which I've seen, contains greenhouse gases. And totting up all the smoke and gases from deforestation around the world produces an astounding figure: that almost one-fifth of all mankind's emissions come from burning up trees. The process I've witnessed in microcosm is actually a bigger source of carbon dioxide than all forms of transport. Surely this can't make sense?

Well, at the moment of my interview with the bishop, Greenpeace is capitalising on the crescendo of concern about this trade. Protests and pressure have brought the four largest soya producers to the negotiating table in Sao Paolo, the commercial capital of Brazil. As the Patriarch and his fellow leaders are being filmed in the forest, an agreement to limit soya's impact is being finalised. From the following year, the producers say they'll sell only soya grown on land that's already been cleared. A satellite system will monitor the promise of a moratorium on any new deforestation. It's a start.

An elderly farmer and his wife are sitting under a tree eating oranges, expertly peeling and slicing them in a way I haven't seen before. It's the hottest part of the day and the shade is welcome. Jose Amorin offers me an orange and I accept, along with a knife. I look closely at how they manage to neatly prise open the fruit and try to copy the same pattern of cuts. The Norsemen, fussing over their potatoes, might learn something too. But I discover early on that the task is impossible if you're holding a notebook and pen so I put them away though, even without them, I find it astonishingly difficult to carve my orange while standing and my attempts are so clumsy that rivulets of juice cascade over my wrists, and what I'd hoped would be a friendly and bonding activity disintegrates into an embarrassing mess. I'm here to learn about their lives as some of the Amazon's poorest and most vulnerable inhabitants but for the moment Jose's wife is staring at me with nothing but pity, and her grandchildren, barefoot and smiling, break off from their game of marbles to giggle at the stranger.

At last, cleared up, I get to the point. The previous year had seen an unimaginable natural calamity strike the region: the rainforest had no rain. For five long months one of the wettest areas on earth endured a drought that dried up hundreds of rivers, killed billions of fish and left countless communities isolated and hungry.

I ask Jose how he'd suffered.

Life became very difficult, he says, and he gets up and beckons me to follow.

Behind his one-room farmhouse I'm led into a lean-to in which there's a well. It's newly dug. Previously, I'm told, there's always been enough rain, there's never been a need to tap into the water supplies underground. But after nearly half a year passed without rain he was forced into this drastic and unprecedented step.

What if there are more droughts?

He shakes his head. I'll stay but many others will leave.

I ask the question because of a warning from British climate scientists. Their computer forecasts show that if global warming intensifies, the Amazon could experience drier conditions which could, incredibly, turn the rainforest into arid savannah later this century. Climate change could achieve what the loggers are trying to, but on an infinitely larger scale.

One of those scientists, with me in the Amazon, is Richard Betts of the British Met Office's Hadley Centre for Climate Prediction, here to take part in the Patriarch's symposium. When he first noticed how the computer models were forecasting a drier Amazon, the results were ridiculed, particularly in Brazil. So he ran the models again but got the same outcome. A few other climate modelling centres then started to detect a similar effect – that a warming Atlantic could draw rain-laden air away from the rainforest, leaving it dry and, ultimately, without trees. Still, the idea seemed too ludicrous to contemplate. How could mere computer predictions possibly be right?

But then came the drought of 2005. Images emerged of rivers transformed into muddy ditches choked with gasping fish, villagers unable to manoeuvre their canoes, faces turned to the cloudless skies, the foundation of life here vanishing. The computer forecasts suddenly seemed more plausible and Brazilian scientists were among those now convinced that global warming could lead to something as unthinkable as the death of the rainforest.

Hunched with Richard over his laptop, I'm watching his model running. It shows a counter flashing as the decades advance, and a map of the world with the continents and oceans superimposed with twitching patches of colour – red for hotter, orange for warmer, blue for cooler. Viewed at face value, it's a horror story. A small blob of orange appears directly over the Amazon in the middle of this century, and then turns red and rapidly expands. By the end of the century, the computer is saying, the world's largest rainforest will be finished. Part of me wants to dismiss this as grown-up guesswork, a game on a laptop. If weather forecasters have trouble with what'll happen the next day, what chance is there of being accurate about the rest of the century?

Richard admits there's no certainty about this, and that the drought of 2005 may be a one-off. But he says it's a taste of what may come.

There are lots of reasons why his forecast may be wrong. Maybe the calculations have missed a key factor or unforeseen natural processes will kick in, the great forest responding in unpredictable ways. But I can't help thinking about Jose and his well, and what more drought would mean for him, what life would be like if his bit of the map turns red.

We're all on edge. I've long since learned that whatever the story nothing focuses the mind like the approach of the first live broadcast. We're 1,000 miles upstream on the banks of the Rio Negro in the heart of the rainforest in the Jau National Park and a key test in our assignment is approaching, our first attempt to go live on air. Our location is so remote that if something fails, there's no backup.

But we're nervous for another reason as well: the unpacking of a particular equipment bag. The afternoon light is failing and the insects are gathering but no one cares. From the bag comes a mass of tough material, about the dimensions of a family-sized tent, which we spread out. The crew of our boat are on hand to help us, tough-faced Amazonians curious about our over-excited shouts. I'm reminded of a Victorian adventure story for schoolboys, with eccentric explorers rigging up some improbable technology in a faraway land and local people who think they're crazy.

The object at the centre of our attention is a big balloon under which we'll hang a small camera. As helium flows into the material and starts to shape it, the tension mounts. The idea is the brainchild of television engineer Martin Doyle, his face flushed beneath his sun hat, working feverishly to see if the thing will fly. In a planning meeting a month before, he'd asked the very sensible question of how we were going to convey to viewers the scale of the rainforest. It'll be no use just having a camera at ground level pointing at you, he'd said. You've got to get a camera above the trees as well. And he'd found a firm that specialised in dangling cameras from balloons. Producer Mark Georgiou and I had winced at the time. We knew Martin was right but we also knew we were already straining the budget. With breath held, we'd written a begging email to an editor who saw the potential and approved extra funds so the balloon could join our baggage. One small challenge was left for Mark: how to source eight industrial-sized canisters of helium in the middle of the Amazon.

Now the balloon is straining at its tether. Mark had found helium in an industrial area of Manaus and, on a boat designed for fishing expeditions, it had made an unusual cargo. Gently, the material filled, we watch the balloon rise a few metres above the clearing, not confidently and not straight up either. We're like anxious parents watching a child go solo on a bike. An evening gust catches the balloon and pushes it perilously close to a very thorny tree. We yank it back and urge it higher. But it's too heavy for its load. So Martin strips away the safety tethers, leaving just one, and also removes a BBC logo, and this gives the balloon just enough lift to clear the trees and park itself high in the evening sky. It's a fantastic sight. We rush to the monitor that's connected to the airborne camera and the picture is electrifying, a panorama of vivid forest and gleaming rivers, a rolling ocean of billions of treetops stretching out to the horizon.

**Our proudest moment in the Amazon:** the BBC's balloon camera starts to rise above the rainforest in Jau National Park. Sadly it wasn't able to fly any higher until the logo was peeled off to reduce weight.                    *Mark Georgiou*

When we go live on air, my earpiece is filled with the amazed voices of producers and editors back in London. I had worried that we may be accused of using a gimmick, of wasting money on a boys' toy. But then it occurs to me that this is almost certainly the first time our audiences have ever had a live view over the top of the vast reaches of the

Amazon rainforest. And the feedback later reveals how viewers appreciate the immediacy of live broadcasting, of having this ridiculously distant spot beamed into their living rooms, a process that allows actions on the one side of the world to be visible on the other.

As the days pass, the insects become less irritating and the landscapes more fascinating: the evening light turning the forest gold, the tributaries so wide they may as well be seas, the leap of fish and the rustle of caymans. By getting used to the heat I'm more comfortable, less threatened and more sympathetic, and two episodes confirm it.

The first involves a Finnish aid-worker, an energetic man who's set up an animal sanctuary. Even under a fan he's dripping with sweat and so am I, as everyone usually is, but he suggests that we join him in, of all things, his sauna, specially constructed in the middle of the forest. I can't imagine anything less pleasant and tell him. But he keeps asking. So one night we give in and try it. A motorised canoe speeds us through the moonlight to an island. I'm already bathed in sweat as we reach the man's house but there's the sauna so in we go, a picture window offering a view of the dripping creepers, the heat so intense I can hardly breathe. I last about five minutes. Outside I stand under a shower that's fed from deep underground: the water, the coldest I've felt for days, is blissful and I can't imagine why I ever felt ill at ease.

The second episode comes when our broadcasting is complete, the phase of any assignment when the shoulder muscles slacken. We're crossing a stretch of river famous for its pink dolphins and nearby there's a village where they're attracted by gifts of fish. Most visitors stand on a jetty to watch them rise from the river, their pink heads and antics almost comic. That's where I first put myself, content to be a spectator. Also, who'd willingly get in the river knowing its lurking terrors, especially the fish with the power to have us cross our legs whenever it's mentioned?

But our guide at the time keeps calling me.

It's safe, David, honestly. You've got to do it.

What he's doing is sitting half underwater on a ledge, legs apart, holding a piece of fish out over the river, feeding the dolphins.

Maybe it's his pressure or the heat or a genuine curiosity, but I end up joining him, the water warm, my knees apart. At first the river surges a little. Then an enormous snout rises right in front of me, jaws open to show dozens of tiny teeth. As instructed, I reach out one hand to gently press against the dolphin's throat, the other is holding the fish. The dolphin grabs it and sinks underwater. My heart is pounding, the experience exhilarating. Maybe there is something worth saving here.

# 3
# Hot air

We're an odd collection, five of us thrown together in a car travelling through the strange landscape of the 'big island' of Hawaii. Our destination is the top of a mysterious mountain where we'll see an instrument that's become a fountainhead of knowledge in the science of global warming. In the world of those who most worry about climate change, we're on the equivalent of a pilgrimage, a grinding journey towards truth. The problem is, things are a bit tense.

It's hot and heavily overcast – that doesn't help. We've just set off from the town of Hilo and pass depressingly battered homes, scruffy cars and public buildings whose whitewash is stained by the tropical heat. Outside a row of dilapidated shops there's a group of teenagers, obese and slouching, clothes and scowls copied from a big-city ghetto. This is the underbelly of Hawaii, a long way from the palm trees and hula skirts that tourists come for, a place of poverty amid what's famous as a paradise.

The road rises through suburbs, the sky murky and the conversation tricky, partly because the road is twisting and partly because of who's in the car: this overheated SUV turns out to contain a microcosm of a political battle over global warming and I've strayed into the firing line.

With me and cameraman Steve Adrain, veteran of Greenland, there are two people from the American government agency that deals with weather and climate – what's called NOAA, the National Oceanic and Atmospheric Administration. It's the official body tasked with providing forecasts not just for the next few days but also the coming decades. NOAA has nothing like the profile of the space agency NASA but it did feature in the climate disaster movie *The Day After Tomorrow* – Dennis Quaid playing a rugged scientist whose warnings are ignored by an oil-crazed White House.

As we drive into the highlands, NOAA is, in real life, facing similarly intense pressure. Its scientists are being paid by government funds to research global warming while their ultimate boss, the then president George W. Bush, is openly unconvinced of the problem. And right now a tiny part of that conflict is being played out on the back seat with me sandwiched in the middle.

To my left is NOAA's top specialist in carbon dioxide. A lean, energetic Dutchman, Pieter Tans has made a career out of measuring the gas and developing ways of ensuring the accuracy of readings made all over the world. Not for him any easy assumptions about global warming. From conversations on the phone before the trip, I know that Pieter can be impatient with my sloppy phrasing and glib questions. He's rigorous about gathering data on carbon dioxide that is as robust as possible. I also know that he's anxious that a wider audience should hear what he's been finding out.

To my right is one of NOAA's press officers, Kent Laborde, a smiling stocky figure with a rather military bearing. His role, he says, is to make sure that everything goes smoothly, that we get the shots and interviews we need. Sometimes press officers can get in the way; Kent seems pleasant and cooperative. But I'm also aware that he's been sent all the way from headquarters in Washington DC to keep an eye on things – in particular to watch what Pieter says. With the White House at this stage questioning man-made global warming, it would be extremely tricky for NOAA to have one of its top people step out of line.

As we climb into the hills above Hilo, past vivid green plantations, the clouds vanish and the sun becomes penetrating. I can sense the simmering discomfort across the back seat. For Pieter, it's an affront to have a 'minder' despatched to monitor what he tells me. He believes that it's the duty of any researcher to be as open as possible about findings – especially those that could affect millions of people. And since it turns out that Pieter is an admirer of the BBC's independence, he's urged me not to be discouraged by any restrictions Kent may impose.

In a chat with Kent, he's explained that his job is merely to remind Pieter to keep to the facts about his research. Pieter's role as a federally funded scientist, Kent says, is to study carbon dioxide and no more – certainly not to announce to the world what the US government ought to do about it. And he cautions me not to lead Pieter down that path.

So it's not just the two of them in this drama: I've been given a part too. And two years later the episode will feature in an investigation into how the White House interfered in climate science.

As we talk, the hills become mountains and I start to feel a bit car-sick. Pieter has a lot to tell me and Kent leans closer to keep track of what's being said so I feel claustrophobic – also that I've slipped back in time. I haven't been in a situation like this – with whispers and confidences and knowing looks – since going on a school trip on a bus when I was about ten years old.

I look out of the window. We've been driving for two hours and I wonder how much more I can take. We've left behind the trees of the lower slopes and are now amid dark fields of lava on the approach to the summit of a volcano,

Mauna Loa. The air is getting thinner as the road snakes through jagged rocks and black dust. Mauna Loa, quiet today, is active, occasionally venting and spewing fresh lava. Reaching an area covered by a recent flow, sinuous shapes creating a new landscape, we stop so that Steve can film some views.

I stroll away, needing a break from the in-car politics, and also to pee. The terrain, all black, seems utterly barren. I find a suitable spot and to my surprise notice that down by my boots, rising from fissures in the rocks, are tiny fronds of bright green ferns, life's first colonisers. I like to think I'm helping them.

**Higher and higher:** Pieter Tans of NOAA describes the rise in CO2 every year since 1958. We're at Mauna Loa in Hawaii, more than 11,000 ft above the Pacific, where the longest set of measurements has been made. *BBC*

As I look up, I see the summit of Mauna Loa. It doesn't have the classic cone of a volcano but more the shape of a rounded hilltop. And up on a crest to one side stands a small collection of white buildings, the laboratories we're heading to. At 11,000 feet, I feel lightheaded as I arrive. The sun is fierce but the air is icy: I'm in the middle of the Pacific but cold. And the simple task of pulling the tripod from the car leaves me out of breath.

In this spectacular setting, Steve has a lot to film – unbounded vistas towards the ocean, boiling layers of tropical clouds below us, the silvery domes of observatories, masts swaying in the breeze, instruments that spin, lenses that glint in the light. But Pieter points out what we've come for. It's a slender tower, one of the dullest sights here. Steve is going to struggle. At the top of it, there's what looks like a cluster of drainpipes – very ordinary tubes, a couple of inches in diameter, sticking up into the air. Most of us wouldn't even notice them or, if we did, we'd assume they were something to do with the plumbing.

But these are pipes we've travelled some eight thousand miles for, pipes that, I'm told, will provide answers to the most troubling questions about global warming: how can we be sure we're causing it? How can we be certain that we even have a hand in it? If it's such a big deal, where's the smoking gun?

Of all environmental issues, climate change is the hardest to grasp, and I'm wrestling with it.

Felled forests? Obvious, I even touched the fresh sap, no quibbling there. The hole in the ozone layer? No debate needed, the fridge gases did it and I saw the cancer scars on an old man's face. Soot in Greenland? You couldn't miss it, the dirty fingerprints of pollution carried by the wind. And I have no problem with the idea of the climate changing – it always has, as the earth's orbit wobbles or the sun's output alters. I even remember some of the patterns of the Ice Age from my geography classes, the seas rising and falling, the ice sheets advancing and retreating.

But it's a much bigger step to say that the warm period we're in now is actually being made even warmer by us.

Is the invisible carbon dioxide that we're releasing seriously leading us towards death and destruction? Are the quantities really large enough?

It's a question that keeps coming up. And generally, because I'm an environment correspondent, people assume I must be a green convert. An old friend of my father's, while dismissing global warming, smiled pityingly as he described me as 'a believer'. And some campaigners do indeed invoke near-religious fervour in their calls for action on climate change. But I find myself resenting these assumptions. It's rather like people judging which political party I might vote for.

The fact is that I've come into this job as a bit of a doubter, and certainly suspicious of some of the more doom-laden claims. Do I think global warming is killing millions of people right now? No. Is London going to flood tomorrow? No. Will all the polar bears die on Tuesday? No. A year or two into it and I've seen how environmental campaigners have been right about some things – but this one? It's a very big, very difficult idea to accept.

I keep asking: how can we be sure we're causing it? And everywhere I go, I find people with the same question, including my colleagues at the BBC in London.

I tug open a heavy soundproofed door, feel the chill of air conditioning on my face and peer into a temple-like gloom: this is the holy of holies of broadcasting, the focal point of the collective energy of hundreds of people every day, a place familiar to millions: the studio. With the lights down, the innards of television are in shadow, the presenter's desk surrounded in the dark by hulking cameras, cables snaking over a grey floor. I've come to prepare for a live appearance. We have forty minutes to go.

Emerging from the black is the floor manager, headset perched over her hair. She welcomes me with a smile that's friendly but also detached – like someone trying to talk while also watching television, she wants to engage but is also listening to instructions from the studio director. I'm used to it. And, from previous visits here, I know she's interested in environmental issues. As she helps me to get ready, she asks about my story tonight.

It's about the threat of the sea rising, I say, while carrying out the first task of preparing for studio reporting: gripping my moulded plastic earpiece and trying to twist it into my ear. Dangling from the end of the earpiece is a plastic tube which the floor manager clips to a cable that she delicately feeds inside my jacket – as a colleague once admitted, it's a pleasant process not unlike being fussed over during the fitting of a suit. The cable slots into a little box on my belt. This is 'talkback' which allows me to be in touch with the studio director in the control room. I hear his voice and I too become a little detached as I try to maintain our conversation while listening out for anything he might tell me.

For the moment I'm not needed. So I explain that the British government has published a report into the risks of flooding in the coming century and it concludes that large areas of the country look vulnerable.

Sounds bad, the floor manager says. She's clipping a microphone to my tie, and does a bit more tailor-like rummaging inside my jacket to run another cable down a second box clipped to my belt. I'm now fully wired. The control room can hear me. Our interrupted chat is public.

Cables sorted, I explain that the study is by a team set up by the government's chief scientist and explores different scenarios for sea level rise and how they could affect our coasts. In the worst cases, it finds, large parts of eastern and southern Britain could be overwhelmed.

As I come out with this, it sounds more dramatic than I'd expected – it's quite something to say that 'large parts of the country could be overwhelmed'. Maybe it seems worse because we're standing in the dark with the tension of a bulletin approaching. But the floor manager appears shocked – until another figure appears from the gloom. It's a cameraman, who's been in a distant corner adjusting controls, and he wants to join in.

What do you mean 'could be overwhelmed'? His tone isn't aggressive but it is forceful. He wants me to be more precise.

I'm having to get used to this. My reporting attracts plenty of comment and criticism but nothing provokes challenges – and abuse – like global warming.

So I explain what I know, that as the seas get warmer, they expand in volume – it's a physical fact that water takes up more space if it's warmer. So in coming years the sea levels could keep rising.

The floor manager is nodding sympathetically.

But the cameraman shakes his head. How can they blame that on global warming? How do they know there isn't some other, perfectly natural reason for the sea level to change?

He's right to ask. But before I can answer another voice joins in. It's a lighting man. The lights have now been switched on and he's reaching up with a long pole to adjust the angle of one of them. The presenter's desk is now bright, as viewers would recognise it; what they won't see are the scuff marks and chipped paint, hallmarks of a busy studio.

The lighting man says that the sea has been rising and falling for millions of years. What's the fuss about now?

The cameraman wants an answer to that too. And to another question: if it's happened before, how can it be our fault this time?

There's no hostility in any of this, more a determined curiosity, so the floor manager feels the need to come to my aid. It's because of all the greenhouse gases, she says.

The cameraman rolls his eyes. That's what they always say. But how can anyone know that? How can they really know that what we're doing is having an effect?

I take a deep breath, this needs careful thinking. I've been in this kind of spot before. Over the years the people who work in news but aren't directly involved in the journalism have often challenged stories which are confusing or don't seem plausible. This can be difficult but it's a healthy process and always valuable because theirs are the views of extreme common sense, unswayed by the interests and excitements of the newsroom – and useful preparation for the audience feedback that may come later.

I start by saying that it's not me saying these things about the dangers of flooding, I'm merely reporting them. I'm not a scientist and I'm certainly not a campaigner – I don't have an agenda – so please don't pin all this on me.

The floor manager, consciously or not, has edged closer to me.

Yes, I say, the world has got warmer and cooler in the past, and the sea has risen and fallen, no question. But from what the scientists say we're now seeing something bigger and faster that apparently seems to be linked to our greenhouse gases.

I use the word 'apparently' to give myself some distance. And I can hear that my voice has become more strident. It's not just the result of having one ear blocked by the ear-piece – it's the giveaway clue of someone trying to cope with uncertainty. I'm reminded of an episode that one of America's ambassadors to London once described to me. While delivering a politically-awkward speech to the Russians, he noticed how in the margin beside a tricky passage his aide had scrawled an instruction: 'weak point, speak louder'.

What I do feel confident about is the study itself – it's by the chief scientist's so-called Foresight team, it drew on the work of the country's top experts in this field, and its conclusions are soberly written. It's not just a press release rushed out by a pressure group. But it's one thing to cover a government study into the dangers of future flooding – the scenarios for a rising sea can be plotted fairly straightforwardly on a map. It's quite another to buy into what are said to be the causes of that flooding. What the authors are suggesting with their scenarios is a series of links between man-made greenhouse gases and the warming of the air and oceans. And that's where I start to feel just a little uneasy.

The lighting man shrugs and leaves. It's twenty minutes to air time and he has other tasks. But the cameraman pushes once more on the point that goes to the heart of the whole issue of climate change. It's about whether it's definitely true, beyond reasonable doubt, that we are involved, that our greenhouse gases really are heating us up, that this problem is as genuinely bad as people keep saying it is.

He sums it all up with one pithy observation:

They don't really know for certain, do they?

I'm interrupted before I can answer. There's a commanding voice in my earpiece.

Sorry to break up your little chat, the director is saying. We've all been enjoying it because it sounds like you're getting quite a hard time in there.

I can hear laughter in the control room.

He asks me to move to a designated spot beside one of the big screens. Maps and other images are to be played in live behind me and there can easily be glitches, particularly problems with matching the timing of my script to the moves of the graphics. A run-through is essential. And we're on air in fifteen minutes.

I'm guided to a little cross of black masking tape on the floor and I can hear the director calling out to all the different teams to check they're poised – graphics, sound, lighting, vision.

As I wait, I wonder. Is it really plausible that our way of life is cooking the planet and threatening to flood our cities? Are we really sure about this, that it's not some reinvention of a hippy ideal to yank us back onto horse-drawn carts or a newly branded version of the age-old struggle against capitalism? Greenpeace and others may have a point about the whaling but are there hard reasons to drive less, stop flying on holiday, avoid the Kenyan beans in the supermarket?

The director starts his countdown. He must sense that my mind is elsewhere because he tells me sharply to look up into the camera. I'll get my cue any second.

Back in the thin air of Mauna Loa, the pipes we've travelled so far to see run from the tower, along the ground and then into a small laboratory. We step inside to see what they connect to, and the answer is as visually disappointing as the pipes themselves: a few electronic boxes sitting on a simple rack of shelves. Is this it – the foundation-stone of all the fears about global warming, the motivation to wean the world off carbon fuels? A very ordinary metal frame houses a set of unremarkable gadgets. It's no more impressive than the kind of music system I'd have been proud of as a student in the 1970s. Can this really be the climate-equivalent of the ancient Greek Oracle?

I'm feeling dizzy. After the mountain winds, the room is stuffy and the view through the windows is dream-like, stretching towards the island's other big volcano, Mauna Kea. Jet lag combines with the toil of handling the Pieter-Kent business to leave me feeling confused, actually slightly deranged.

But time is short and Pieter is eager to explain things, how a researcher in the 1950s, Charles David Keeling, picked this high-altitude spot to start measuring carbon dioxide. The air up here isn't the purest but it's what scientists call 'well-mixed', distant from the pollution of heavy industry but not totally isolated from it – in other words, it's typical of much of the air circulating round the planet. Back then, few understood why Keeling was bothering to haul his instruments up this remote mountain or why it might matter, and he faced constant battles to secure funding.

Pieter tells me how Keeling devised new techniques for measuring the amount of carbon dioxide in the air, a difficult task because there's so little of it. In fact at first he thought something was wrong. For a start, the level of carbon dioxide was recorded as being higher in the winter than the summer – that couldn't be right. Also, it kept climbing every year – also unexpected. The chances, back in those pioneering days of this kind of science, were that the instruments were faulty. But Keeling persevered and Pieter shows me the result of half a century of measurements, a graph that has become known as the 'Keeling curve'.

Kent stands at a discreet distance.

The slight dip every summer, Pieter says, is because the plants of the northern hemisphere are growing and sucking a lot of carbon dioxide from the air. In the winter, they take up less of it so the graph rises a bit. So, the measurements have been shown to be not only sound but also highly sensitive.

Pieter points out that Keeling's first reading up here was 315 parts per million – that's 315 molecules of carbon dioxide for every million molecules in the air.

I ask for the latest reading.

Pieter consults the instruments. It's 378 ppm – 63 ppm higher, a huge increase in less than 50 years.

Kent just listens.

Pieter goes on to explain how at the start the carbon dioxide was climbing by less than one part per million every year – about 0.7 ppm a year. But it's now jumping up at more than two parts per million, sometimes closer to three. So the rate of increase has trebled in fifty years.

The most striking thing, he says, is that we've seen an increase in carbon dioxide levels every single year since 1958. And at 150 other sites around the world, they've been getting similar readings.

Kent nods. These are hard numbers, you can't argue with them, Pieter's just doing his job.

But next comes the more controversial question: how do we know the rise is man-made? Back to the cameraman's challenge in the studio: how can they know for certain the increase is because of us?

We move outside to record Pieter's answers on tape. Steve picks a spot for the interview, with a backdrop combining laboratory and panorama. We're side on to the sun and I can feel it burning my left cheek.

Pieter begins. First, the rise in carbon dioxide is so large that it can't be explained by natural causes.

Next, if we add up all the coal, oil and gas burned since the nineteenth century, you get a number that's roughly the same as the increase in carbon dioxide observed in the air and the oceans – what we've burned matches what's been added to the atmosphere and seas.

Now look at where the carbon dioxide is emerging fastest – the northern hemisphere. No coincidence that that's where most of the fossil fuels are used, in the big industrial heart-lands of Europe, China and America.

Finally, there's a chemical fingerprint too. Fossil fuels lack a variety of carbon called carbon-14 – a radioactive isotope – and levels of it in the atmosphere have been declining. Less carbon-14 in the air suggests more burning of coal and oil.

Kent doesn't react, he's unreadable, a professional.

Pieter has given quite a performance and he concludes it very emphatically: in my opinion, he says, all of these observations add up to one thing – they nail it, that man-made greenhouse gases are adding to the warming.

It's been a long interview. The sun has been unrelenting and the left side of my face is sore.

I'm too lightheaded to weigh things up. Instead, as I gaze at the pipes and try to picture the invisible molecules drifting into them, I'm moved by a sentimental and utterly unscientific idea: that Keeling began this task in March 1958, two months before I was born, so his graph's inexorable rise has occurred almost exactly during my lifetime. His data, gathered on a cheap set of metal shelves on top of this remote volcano, show a clear trend during events and changes that I have lived through.

So I trace the numbers and match the dates.

When I was born in 1958, the level stood at 315 ppm.

As a young boy in the 1960s, when Europe was just starting to follow America into a consumer boom, the streets of my home town, Oxford, had very little traffic and our kitchen had few of the appliances and lights that we expect today. By the time I was five, the level was up by three parts per million to 318 ppm.

When I watched the moon landing in 1969 and compiled my own Apollo 11 scrapbook, thrilled by an era of unrestrained technological optimism, the Mauna Loa reading jumped to 324 ppm.

In 1977, while teaching in a mission school in India before starting university, I remember roads full of bicycles rather than cars and often going to bed by torchlight as the country struggled without enough power: the level was 333 ppm.

Eleven years later, when I was back in India with my wife Jess on our honeymoon, the traffic in Delhi was becoming more intense, we enjoyed air-conditioning, industrialisation was gathering pace around the world and back home we had two cars. The level stood at 351 ppm.

The following year our first child, Jack, was born, the Berlin Wall fell and China was about to start its breakneck race for development: the mountaintop instrument reached 352 ppm.

In 1992 when our second son, Harry, arrived, the United Nations held its Earth Summit in Rio and the countries of the world promised to work towards avoiding the worst effects of global warming. Low-cost air travel was catching on. The carbon dioxide level stood at 356 ppm.

By 1994, when our daughter Kitty arrived and we needed a much bigger car, it was 358 ppm.

In 1997, when the first agreement was signed to try to limit the rise in carbon dioxide – the Kyoto treaty – the graph was nudging 363 ppm.

When I started this job in 2003, it was 375 ppm.

At the time of writing, it stands at 388 ppm.

Our descent back to Hilo feels much quicker and it's certainly better tempered. Kent and Pieter got through the day without clashing and, filming over, I can relax too. But around this time there's a scandal about White House officials doctoring climate research to emphasise the doubts of climate scientists, the uncertainties of their conclusions. It's also alleged that journalists are being denied access to the key researchers, some of whom are being barred from going on air. A not-for-profit organisation, the Government Accountability Project, later launched a detailed inquiry and investigators contacted me about the Mauna Loa experience.

In a phone interview, asked to recall Kent's behaviour, I racked my brain for anything that might have smacked of censorship or distortion. It was certainly true that between applying to interview Pieter and actually being allowed to do so, nearly five months had passed and it probably would have been longer if I hadn't pestered – that may have been an attempt to suppress reporting of his findings. But in the end, the trip did happen. The investigator asked how it went. If Kent had publicly constrained Pieter or intervened during our interview or prohibited any discussion of the causes of the rise in carbon dioxide, it certainly would have fitted a pattern of official attempts to smother evidence of global warming – and the report later concluded that that was certainly the intention. Kent himself was named as having cancelled one scientist's appearance on a television programme on White House orders.

But with me, up on that mountain, it didn't happen. A footnote in the report records how I found NOAA public affairs to be helpful, which is true in that Kent was always pleasant and that my day on Mauna Loa was not blocked. It's nothing much to brag about but I was the reporter the oil-hungry White House did not try to muzzle.

The episode prompted a series of thoughts. First, the key findings were not censored: the world's most detailed record of carbon dioxide in the atmosphere is plain for all to see. Second, that beneath the noise of campaigning are the still, small facts of science – so, although we're not all going to die from climate change immediately, the Keeling Curve showing carbon dioxide's steep rise doesn't look too healthy either. Third was a personal lesson: that if I was to report on this topic, with all its controversy and bitterness, I must anchor everything on original research – that I should get to the frontlines of the science. On a journey of bizarre locations and strange encounters, Mauna Loa was just the beginning.

# 4

# Shaken and stirred

The bar is like so many in underfunded British academic institutions – a few sad bottles on the shelves, spotlights to add a touch of sparkle – except that resting on the polished wooden surface of the bar itself is an utterly unique feature: a huge jagged lump of what looks like the purest, dazzling crystal. It's a chunk of ice the size of a small boulder and it's so clean, so flawless, that it's as alluring as a jewel. I'm in a small crowd happy not to do much except gawp.

But we're not allowed to admire it for long: the ice was brought here for a purpose and a man in a kilt, dressed in full Scottish rig for a special evening, raises an axe and, to our cheers, smashes it down with a flourish. There's a minor explosion: fragments fly across the room, splinters glittering in the light, a mist of tiny diamonds cascading to the floor. We flinch and then surge forward to scoop the debris into our glasses.

We're drinking whisky and, although Scots usually react vehemently (and tediously) to the treachery of adding ice to their precious drink, the figures in kilts here actively encourage me, making an exception for two reasons: this is no ordinary ice – cleaved from an ice sheet, it's reckoned to be a mind-blowing one million years old – and we're in a place too remote for any other Scots to see us: Antarctica. With a South Pole gale tearing at the roof, the rules, just this once, can be bent.

I'm at Rothera, Britain's largest Antarctic base, a community of fewer than a hundred which this evening is turning its back on the wild world outside to focus instead on the serious business of Burns Night. We may be a six-hour flight from the Falkland Islands, one thousand miles south of the southernmost tip of South America, a faint dot on the edge of a largely unexplored continent twice the size of Australia, but because this outpost attracts so many Scots certain rituals must be observed: Issy the cook is pulling haggis from the oven, Paul the boatman is puff-cheeked with his bagpipes and Linda Capper, the press officer, is diligently reminding me of the dance routines for a ceilidh.

We're in the base canteen and, as I look at the rows of flushed faces and listen to the rising din of the conversation, I realise that the excitement is partly because we're at the equivalent of the end of a school term. It's January, which in Antarctica means late summer, so with the approach of winter when temperatures will plummet and the winds accelerate, most of these people will soon be going home, the main research season over; only a hardy band, a dozen 'winterers', will remain to endure the unending night ahead. Everyone has a reason to let rip – those staying and those leaving – and, across the table, I catch cameraman Tony Fallshaw's eye. An engaging Londoner, face creased with smiles, he's a master at making the most of any situation, however unfamiliar, and I can tell that we're both thinking the same thing: our companions, who've been unfailingly amiable and supportive so far, are now charmingly unhinged. In the week we've been here, we've never heard laughter so raucous or seen drinking so enthusiastic. And one sight is pure gold: one of the most senior scientists has turned out in a dinner jacket, startlingly smart in this untamed wilderness, but his feet are clad in the researchers' favoured indoor combination of heavy socks and sandals.

Of all the things I'd expected in Antarctica, an overheated party in a modern building wasn't one of them. I'd imagined having to cope with something rougher – not with the full-strength misery of the early polar explorers, eating their dogs and enduring blizzards under canvas, but with conditions that might at least connect with that heroic age. Reminders of their exploits do adorn the walls – black and white photographs of the haunted faces of the hungry adventurers, Ernest Shackleton's ship Endurance being crushed in the ice, men in tweeds surviving on a diet of tinned meat and fresh penguin. But ignore the pictures, as it's easy to do, and you could be in any transplanted corner of provincial Britain.

If I pick up a phone, I'm automatically routed to a switchboard at the headquarters of the British Antarctic Survey in Cambridge. There's a reasonable Internet connection so I can check my emails. There are hot showers. The cupboards in the canteen contain cheering, very British supplies of Branston Pickle and Marmite. And one throwback to an earlier era, when the Royal Navy sent expeditions into Antarctica in the 1940s, is curiously comforting: in addition to breakfast, lunch and dinner, a fourth meal called 'smoko' is provided mid-morning, not just tea and biscuits but heartier fare like steak-and-kidney pudding or a bun crammed with roast pork. I love it. And in case that isn't enough, a large box is kept topped up with chocolate bars and one day, after a full lunch, I absent-mindedly grab one and minutes later realise I've eaten it without even noticing. A ceaseless appetite is a fact of life in Antarctica.

In a pause in the Scottish reels, I move to a window and wipe away the condensation on the double glazing, the outer shell of this centrally heated British colony. The midnight sky is pale – it won't get dark for several weeks – and I can

just make out the Union Jack, buffeted by the storm, cling-
ing grimly to its flagpole. Streams of snow twist and surge
in the gusts. And looming above the base, beyond the wind-
scoured runway, is the vast grey-blue cliff of the Antarctic
ice sheet. In places, it's two miles thick, layer upon layer of
ice, a hidden realm unimaginable in scale. I watch the gale
stripping away the snow exposing the towering reaches of
ice beneath.

Right now, it's a hostile and unforgiving landscape,
reminding me of polar veteran Rob Swan's blunt summary
of survival here: 'Antarctica wants you dead.' But in gentler
conditions, with the sun shining, this same terrain can also
appear far more inviting, far more spellbinding, than I'd
thought possible. The mountains, as big as the Alps, rise
straight from a bright sea into air so clean that islands that
look close at hand are in fact more than a dozen miles away.
And the views are made all the more astounding because
they keep changing, not only with the shifting light but also
because the icebergs that fill the bays are constantly moving,
structures the size of villages manoeuvring in the winds and
currents. I look one minute and see an intricately sculpted
wall of the deepest blue, next there's a vast white dome; ten
minutes later and they're replaced by other fantastic shapes
– a temple with massive columns, a gargantuan animal, a
futuristic building.

The ice exerts a lure, far beyond the views and the glint
of our boulder on the bar-top. For generations it's promised
an exotic combination of danger and beauty, the enticement
of exploration and conquest in an alien land. It's what originally brought the pioneers to struggle for the Pole and, in
Captain Scott's case, to make it but perish on the return. The
beauty remains and the dangers continue but now the ice
holds a different kind of fascination, its myriad layers worth
exploring not in a race to plant a flag but to understand how
they might shed light on a modern concern, one that never

troubled Scott or his companions, about whether the world is warming and why.


Most environment correspondents seem to get to Antarctica at least once in their careers and when I landed the job I wasn't quite sure why it was expected of them. I was drawn by the idea of visiting such a unusual place – similarly inaccessible and apparently weird as, say, North Korea – but I doubted that the weeks of travel involved would be worth it for the likely news coverage. Was anything new really going on?

The reporting I'd seen before occasionally seemed clichéd and, although I've always thought television news can provide a useful window on obscure parts of the world, the sight of researchers in orange suits camping on the featureless snow often left me with an uneasy suspicion: was this of any relevance or interest to our viewers? Like millions, I've long admired the staggering footage of the Attenborough documentaries and I've relished the tales of the relentless polar hardship. But wildlife programmes and history books are one thing, news reporting is another, and I kept wondering what would justify a visit by a news team. Ultimately, I didn't want to be away for ages just to produce another feature about penguins.

Normally I'd try to keep thoughts like that to myself. But the truth has a habit of being blurted out and, on this occasion, it happened during my first visit to the most glittering event in the calendar of British science: the black-tie soiree held every summer at the Royal Society, the country's oldest scientific body. It's billed as a unique chance to mingle with a selection of research teams but I arrived mildly irritated at having to dress up and also sceptical about whether this was the best format in which to discover anything useful: was this really the kind of event an experienced newsman should bother with?

I toured the stands, wine glass in hand, and gradually began to see the point. I learned about new research into nanotechnology, next about an innovative technique in astronomy. And then I found myself beside a display board explaining the work of the British Antarctic Survey. The only visitor at that moment, I was accosted by the press officers, Athena Dinar and Linda Capper. They demanded to know why, unlike every other environment correspondent they'd ever met, I hadn't been clamouring for one of the rare spaces on a trip south.

It wasn't the place itself, I explained, I'd love to go. But I was wondering about the time required for a trip compared to the likely value of the news stories, given that, well, how can I put it, not much new was going on down there.

This produced a very stiff reaction.

Of course there's news, Linda insisted. Haven't you heard? We've got a lot of top people down there. And they're digging out the key evidence about climate change.


I've got a harness round my waist and thighs, crampons on my boots and more ropes than I can keep track of. I'm fitted with a radio mic and I've strapped on a safety helmet. Tony has fitted a miniature camera to one side of it, with a cable running down to a recording unit deep in my anorak. He wants the camera to capture the reporter's-eye view but the cable has the effect of tugging on one side of my helmet, making it lop-sided, and it's just one of many things distracting me, the worst of which is the thought of what we're about to try.

We're high up on the ice sheet looking down on the tiny buildings of the base at Rothera. Eighteen months after my evening in black tie, I'm wearing three layers on my legs and four on my upper body. Tony and I had collected the clothes during a briefing visit to the British Antarctic Survey in Cambridge, one hot summer's day. In a vast attic room, we'd been ushered down long rows of shelves, arms outstretched, being heaped with fleeces and jackets, hoods and gloves, and trousers made of heavy, old-fashioned moleskin material that reminded us of something Shackleton might have worn. All this was crammed into enormous orange kitbags which, like all the heavy equipment and stores, were then loaded onto a ship for the long trek south. We weren't to see them till we arrived by plane six months later, novices reunited with unfamiliar clothing.

Today we're very glad of it, well-clad and shielded from the wind. We're on the ice sheet to go through a safety training course for all visitors to the base and this session is the most strenuous. Although I'm standing on what looks like perfectly normal snow, it's only a covering for the massive blocks of ice below. And nearby is a feature that makes this terrain especially hazardous: a crevasse, a chasm in the ice. Crevasses are the great terror of polar travel – fissures, often as large as ravines but disguised by snow, and the graveyard for many an explorer.

Now we're about to descend into one. Trained earlier today to abseil and taught to kick the sharp points of my crampons into the ice, I edge into position. Behind me is a small hole in the snow. It's impossible to imagine that this tiny entrance could lead anywhere threatening but I'm about to find out. Doing this as a normal visitor would be unnerving enough but because this is television we've added whole layers of complexity: while descending I must find things to say and Tony, additionally burdened with the camera, must try to film me.

We begin with a short scene at the surface. I explain where we are and where I'm about to go while shuffling backwards through the snow towards the hole. I feel I'm being fairly coherent until I feel one of the ropes pulling on a leg and ending up entangled on a crampon. I free it and we start again only for the same thing to happen. A third time, all goes well but the mic has worked loose and Tony is hearing too much wind noise. We're getting tired and we're only just starting. Our guide, an experienced mountaineer, makes the very rational observation that we're working 'with too many variables' – snow, wind, ice, crampons, words and video. But television is far from rational so we persevere. And Tony, realising that the biggest problem is caused by one particular rope, shouts above the wind: just stop that rope from getting caught around your arse.

**Abseiling and talking at the same time:** Tony Fallshaw shoots my descent into a crevasse in the ice-sheet near Rothera in Antarctica. The place is so beautiful we spend hours exploring it before filming a frame.                    *Linda Capper, BAS*

Rope adjusted, the words and the filming flow and we record a segment which takes the viewer as far as the actual descent. At this point, Tony has to get ahead of me, climbing down into the crevasse himself so he can film me from the inside. This involves detaching myself from the main safety rope, my gloves fumbling in the cold, so that Tony can attach himself to it instead. He then vanishes from view. Minutes pass and I hear nothing. The problem is that when he's down the hole and I'm in the wind up above we simply can't hear each other. So I shuffle towards the hole and bellow. Eventually after much yelling in both directions, he tells me he's found a position a few metres down and that it's my turn to go.

It's more awkward than I thought it would be. In the training room, abseiling was surprisingly straightforward – feet against the wall, lean back and gradually feed out rope. It was even enjoyable. But in the narrow confines of a snow tunnel, descending at an angle, I don't have room to lean back and also find that I'm having trouble releasing rope to allow me to slide down. I lose track of how many attempts I make but I get a rough idea from the exasperation in Tony's normally patient voice. At last we manage to record another segment, as I leave the bright air of the surface and enter the snow layer below.

Tony descends still further, dropping out of view and then suddenly shouting. A stream of obscenities rises from the depths.

You won't believe it, he shouts.

I don't. As I follow him down, what I see next is beyond comprehension. From a world of black and white and grey, I slip into an utterly different reality. The crevasse, narrow near the surface, opens into a magical cavern in the ice, startlingly bright, a frozen aquarium with an infinite variety of blues – it's a bit like diving inside the ice-boulder on the bar, as vivid as a coral reef, alive with colour. The light penetrates from above, from the sides and even – somehow – from below so that the ice takes on endless hues. There are giant icicles like stalagtites, twinkling but lethally tipped, and wonderful alcoves and curves in the walls and floor. To one side, a narrow gap twists down to another cavern which, though deeper, is even brighter.

I reach out to a crystal wall and slide my gloves over it – it's incredibly smooth. There's so much to take in: below me is a luminous frozen pool and, to one side, what appears to be a miniature temple that's lit from within. A glowing pathway leads to an arch beyond which is a natural chute that we clamber down into another glittering chamber. And this crevasse is just one fissure in one corner of an ice sheet as thick as a mountain. I try to picture how many other caverns and lakes and mysterious features exist unseen within this lost domain.

Tony and I can't stop swearing in amazement and our guides grin at us sympathetically – they've seen this kind of four-letter disbelief before. Later, when we view Tony's footage, it sounds like I'm babbling.

We try to get our bearings, and it takes time, we're in such an outrageously unusual place. Gathering material for a television news report often follows a pattern – filming the main activities, interviewing the key people, recording a 'piece to camera' – but down here we're so amazed, so excited that hours pass while we not only work out what to do but learn how to do it: every step involves kicking the crampons into the ice, every move means checking we're hooked onto the correct rope, every turn opens up new sights that prompt another foul-mouthed exhalation.

One spectacle is especially riveting: one of the dozens of giant icicles stretches right down beside me, like a slender tree trunk, so I find I can get a really close look inside it. The ice seems more ruffled, more disturbed than the Burns Night boulder and eventually I work out why: locked inside it, reminiscent of the tiny flecks of soot I saw frozen in Greenland's ice, are hundreds of little bubbles, gems floating within a giant crystal.

Our guides explain that these pockets of air are like time capsules, miniature samples of the atmosphere, trapped when the snow falls around them, becoming compressed and turning into ice. Opened up, they'd release that air and provide a chemical record of the weather at the time of their capture. So what looks to me like a chamber of incomparable beauty turns out to be a treasure trove of key information. Just as Dave Keeling's instruments atop Mauna Loa provide a record of carbon dioxide levels over the past fifty years, the bubbles I'm looking at now could form part of a record on an infinitely longer timescale.

We finish our filming and climb back up the tunnel, the blue light turning grey. I assume my watch is wrong when I see we've spent five hours in the cavern. It felt like an hour at most. We're so late that a radio call is made to the base to see if there's any dinner left. There is, but I know it won't be enough.


I'd never thought of science as heroic. But experiencing what's involved in studying the ice sheets changes that – in Greenland and Antarctica scientists have braved the most absurdly awful and hostile conditions. My afternoon in the crevasse was just a taste, comparatively benign, of the grit required for polar operations. Toughest of all have been the projects to drill deep into the ice to extract cores, great lengths of ice marked like tree rings with the stripes of each year's accumulation of snow, within which are found the precious bubbles of each year's air.

One operation reached deep enough to bring up a record stretching back 400,000 years, another went down even further, extracting ice formed as long ago as 800,000 years. And each one has required forbiddingly daunting arrangements. While I found it hard enough struggling in gloves to deal with my ropes in an Antarctic summer, the drilling teams endure the full cycle of polar seasons to deliver massive loads of equipment to the bleakest spots imaginable. One European project, EPICA, involved convoys of snow tractors crossing 1,000km of ice just to reach the right place. Then the drilling rigs have to be assembled and operated, during long years of toil in blizzards and darkness, to ensure that the ice cores reach the surface, their dainty cargoes of ancient air preserved unscathed.

The results are among the most compelling of any scientific investigation: analysis of the bubbles reveals the patterns of the Ice Ages with the temperature falling and then rising with the onset of the warmer periods in between. And matching this record of temperature, almost in step, is the level of carbon dioxide. In a few places the temperature rises before the carbon dioxide but generally if the gas increases then the temperature follows. Over the aeons of time exposed in this record, the climate changes dramatically – cold to warm and back again – and all perfectly naturally, no hint of a man-made influence because mankind was non-existent or tiny in number. I trace the rise and fall of the carbon dioxide – that also obviously happened for totally natural reasons.

My immediate thought is that our current obsession with carbon dioxide is out of context: the level of the gas has fluctuated on a huge scale without any hand from us. Sure, the carbon dioxide looks like it's driving the warming but all as part of a natural cycle of change, one that ebbs and flows like a tide. But then I look at the figures more closely. For a start, the record shows that the climate not only changes – a word which implies a gradual, gentle process – but it also soars and crashes. There are savage surges in warming, precipitous collapses in temperature, in an ugly series of shifts some of which occurred not over centuries but over decades. Whatever caused them, they would be not easy to live through.

Still more revealing are the numbers themselves. I run my finger along the ice-core data for carbon dioxide over the past 800,000 years: with all the natural changes, the Ice Ages and the warm periods between them, its level never got above 300 parts per million. I think back to the Mauna Loa record: in 1958, the carbon dioxide level was already higher, standing at 315 ppm and it's risen every year since. Now it's

388 ppm. Nothing in the normal cycles of the planet over nearly a million years has ever taken it remotely close to that level. I'm hit by an obvious conclusion: whatever natural forces are at work, we seem to be adding quite a lot too. The rise in carbon dioxide since the 1950s is pretty dramatic but set in the context of the ice-core record it's startling.

We've edited our video reports and Tony has successfully sent them by Internet to London so the next stage is to prepare for what will be the first live television broadcast from Rothera. We've no idea if it's possible. In theory, the 'footprint' of one particular satellite, hovering over Brazil, will stretch far south enough to reach us. So we pick a spot just beside the hangar where there's a source of power and a phenomenal view over the icebergs to a line of low hills on a far headland. If we're lucky, the two big satellite phones we've hauled along will have the strength to beam their signals to the invisible spacecraft just above the horizon, and on to the newsroom.

I try to help but the truth is that Tony is faster working alone. He assembles the two phones – four panels slotting together on each device to form a flat dish – and connects them to a small video box. In turn, cables run from that to the camera and a lot of other wires snake around in ways that are not entirely clear to me. At one point Tony gets me to stand in position, earpiece installed, wired up, to listen out for London. Time after time he dials to no avail. I really can't see this working. But Tony keeps trying, switching everything off then on, reconnecting all the cables, dialling again and to my amazement I suddenly hear an engineer in one of the control rooms calling out to me – he can see me and hear me and I can hear him. Even over such a fragile connection I can tell that he's thrilled: voice raised, he calls out that he can even make out the icebergs behind me, a live view of a lost continent. We test the line, check the speed of the connection and generally congratulate ourselves – it works. So, in a few hours' time, when we're due on air, we'll just step back into position, switch everything on and go for it, no problem. What could possibly go wrong?

So confident are we with this early triumph that we decide there's even enough time for a short expedition, something long planned and potentially fascinating. Down at the boat-house, we don thick rubber survival suits and life jackets and set off by boat under a blue sky for an island called Leoni. A researcher there is studying how plants are adapting to the twin changes of warmer temperatures and the increase in UV radiation because of the ozone hole. She's been trying to persuade me for a few days to make the trip but it's taken me a while to see the point: that in this great continent of ice, there are bursts of green where there used to be white. This part of Antarctica has warmed by three degrees Celsius in the past fifty years – far ahead of the global average – and lichens and mosses have somehow colonised the rocks. So we weave through the icebergs, land on Leoni, and film a few quick scenes – we haven't got long, our live satellite slot is looming. But the island itself is serene and sheltered, the air gentle, the tender plants softening an otherwise harsh land-scape with the result that we stay far longer than planned. When we spot a little hut, a refuge in case of storms, Tony and I even joke that we should have brought a picnic hamper and a decent bottle of wine.

The journey back seems quick and soon the jetty is in sight. But as we approach it looks strangely different and in a moment I see why – it's very bad news. In the two hours we've been out, the wind has changed direction and all the icebergs that bobbed around us so prettily on our trip out are now bunched up blocking our path back. Jostling together, like pieces of a clumsily attempted jigsaw, the white lumps and blue blocks are crammed against the harbour wall and our inflatable, which suddenly feels very puny, has no chance of forcing its way through. At the controls, Paul reverses and scans the ice for an opening but we're facing a blockade that's not only solid but also razor-edged. A scene that was enticing is now full of menace. More to the point, we're screwed. If we can't get out, it won't matter how well our satellite phones connect with London or how much the newsroom is looking forward to a broadcasting 'first' – we'll be stranded in a boat going nowhere.

We run through the options and my heart sinks: keep hunting for an opening (but that looks hopeless); kill some time doing more filming in the hope that the wind will change (not great either); radio for help (but the only vessel big enough to force open a path is three weeks' sailing away); turn back to Leoni and sit it out in the hut (fine, because there are emergency supplies there, but disastrous if you're due on the news in an hour). This is far worse than being late for a flight – a nightmare combination of overconfidence and bad weather. I glance at Tony, his face grim. Time always seems to haemorrhage with the approach of live television and never more so than now.

In the end, without warning, there's a twist in a current or an imperceptible shift in the wind – I really don't care which. But it's enough to clear a narrow channel through the ice so that we can gingerly nose our way through, reaching the dock with 30 minutes to go. We get a lift straight to the hangar and Tony races to plug up all the wires, punching buttons and telling me to get ready. Naturally, none of it works. Nothing. No connection, no signal, no little lights blinking as they should when the satellite is found. There's silence in my earpiece and the crushing sense of failure on our shoulders. We must have cursed out loud because a large seal sleeping on an ice floe not far away briefly raises its head, glancing in our direction. At this moment, Antarctica doesn't want us dead, it just wants us to be quiet.

But Tony won't give up, dialling and redialling. One phone gets a weak signal but then drops off. Then the other hooks up at full strength but only for a minute. We need both to work to give us the bandwidth for a video image. I think back to the extraordinary luck of the ice parting to let us through and wonder what other weird chain of circumstances will make a connection with London. And then it happens, all lights are blazing, and once again excited voices are relayed from 9,000 miles away, the news presenter Huw Edwards tentatively announcing that he hopes we can cross live to Antarctica and I'm on, a blurred figure reporting on a message from the ice.

Straight afterwards, we rush to shake hands. Tony can't stop grinning. In a business that's so fleeting we've made some history and the buzz is amazing. If I wasn't so immobilised by wires, I'd even hug him.

**Finger trouble:** during a very chilly live broadcast from Rothera I struggle to operate my laptop – it's too fiddly with gloves on, too cold without. The edge of the ice sheet looms in the background. One listener says the line is so clear she doesn't believe I'm in Antarctica. *Linda Capper, BAS*

Most of our filming has revolved around the work of the scientists at Rothera. But in our last few days, the pressure receding, we spend more time with the support staff, the people who make the place function, and learn how they maintain a healthy sense of humour about the science, calling the researchers 'beakers', after the scientist character in The Muppets. I only discover this when I ask one of the pilots what he thinks about global warming and he holds up a firm hand and declares that he's not going to talk about that kind of thing at all – because that's beakershit.

Other details are surprising too. When out camping on the ice, the warmest layer to sleep on isn't some hi-tech foam mattress but traditional sheepskin. Containers for equipment are made of old-fashioned wood rather than plastic, which apparently breaks more easily. During the winter, when the waters are motionless, diving under the frozen surface of the sea is like swimming through glass, the visibility virtually limitless. A female researcher and a male assistant fell out at the start of an assignment but were trapped by a blizzard in their tent for three weeks without a break, a polar purgatory. Antarctica is so huge that the distance from Rothera to the South Pole is about the same as from London to Istanbul. The photographers accompanying the early explorers couldn't afford to have their few shots spoiled if perfectly positioned penguins wandered off so the birds were simply nailed to the ice. And if those pioneers ran out of candles during the hellish night of winter, they'd collect penguin chicks, behead them and insert a wick into their oily bodies – apparently this yielded enough light to read by.

A radio operator describes one of the worst accidents at Rothera. A plane carrying four people, on a journey to the interior, had stopped to refuel and then took off but didn't gain enough height to clear an iceberg floating near the end of the runway. The aircraft crashed onto the ice and caught fire. Because icebergs often capsize without warning, as melting changes their centre of gravity, it's a British Antarctic Survey rule never to venture onto one – in any circumstances. So within full sight of the base the plane burned and no one was able to respond – no boat could risk getting close, no one could have climbed onto the ice anyway and the base has no helicopter. Those there at the time must have watched in horror. One person thought that they saw someone climbing from the wreckage but amid the flames they may have been mistaken – and the others hoped that he was.

On a rocky hill above the base there's a memorial to the four victims – three Canadians and a Norwegian – and to others who've lost their lives here: two men sledging over sea ice, three men vanishing in the 1950s. But the most recent is the most poignant. In 2003, a young biologist, Kirsty Brown, was snorkelling just offshore as part of her research into ocean wildlife when she was seized by one of the most ferocious creatures in the Antarctic: a leopard seal. Possibly mistaking her for a smaller seal – as a dark shape on the surface – it dragged her deep underwater but then let her go, maybe confused by the taste of her drysuit. By then, however, she had drowned and could not be revived. To a tight-knit community, even one with calamity etched into its history, her death was a particularly heavy blow.

On the day I visit her plaque, low clouds are hurtling over the mountains, shadows flicker on the icebergs and, below the cliffs, a small launch with divers on board is bouncing across a bright grey sea. She loved this place, I'm told, and was passionate about understanding its changes. Bewitching and brutal, Antarctica has a lot to tell us, but at a price.

# 5

# The ground beneath my feet

Time for my own scientific discovery: if you share a tent with someone for several days and neither of you can wash properly, it may not be comfortable but it doesn't become offensive because – and here's the revelation – you both become smellier at exactly the same rate. I have long empty hours in which to speculate about the science involved: the decline in hygiene must somehow be synchronised with the recalibration of the nostrils, our odour receptors adjusting imperceptibly but in unison. Maybe someone should follow this up.

All I know is that for much of the past week a cramped orange tent has been home to cameraman Rob Magee and me and, while I haven't noticed any particular stench rising from him, he hasn't complained about me either. So far. At least not publicly. Which prompts another line of thinking: maybe Rob, being a calm, good-natured Irishman and unfailingly polite, wouldn't say anything however badly I smelled. So maybe I do stink, he isn't telling me, and my theory is nonsense. Except that the producer on this trip, Kevin Bishop, is a no-nonsense Cornishman who wouldn't mince words if there was a problem. He's wangled a tent on his own next to ours and I watch his reaction as we emerge each morning: nothing unusual, his nostrils must be adjusting too. Maybe the theory is right. One thing about this rambling is certain: I've got too much time on my hands.

I'm in Greenland, on a return visit to the ice, and the trip has gone on far longer than planned. We're in a tiny camp to report on the work of a team of researchers and we'd arranged to stay for 24 hours. But day after day we wake up to bad weather – a white sky blending seamlessly with the snow on the ground – so that the helicopter that brought us cannot fetch us. Being late May well inside the Arctic Circle I'm under the same unchanging pale sky that framed my nightmare with the Norwegian whalers; the distinction between day and night is irrelevant, the sense of isolation complete, and clothes brought for one day are still in use after four.

One of the few daily rituals is the attempt to talk to the helicopter company about getting out. Morning and evening, Kevin plods out into the snow, switches on our satellite phone – a chunky thing the size of an old-fashioned mobile – extends the aerial and starts the laborious task of trying to get through. If he succeeds, he's asked if he can see the horizon and each time he has to say he can't, which means the pilot won't even to try to pick us up. Rob and I stand nearby but don't need to be told what Kevin has heard: he usually just sighs, rolls his eyes and snaps the phone shut. A further part of the ritual is that we then take it in turns to ring our wives, the calls becoming more awkward each time, the polar weather riding roughshod through our flight bookings and domestic plans, the most important question, about when we'll return, unanswerable.

Frustratingly, as the crow flies, the helicopter is based only about 50 miles away in Ilulissat, one of the larger settlements on the west coast of Greenland, a pretty village of fishing boats, huskies tethered outside brightly painted houses, sealskins drying in the wind. But between this bastion of civilisation and our camp lies the edge of the ice sheet with a fearsome field of crevasses. I saw the giant cracks and cliffs as we flew in, row after row of ugly great scars, and even the most experienced explorer would shy away from trying to cross them. So we have no choice but to wait.

Though funded by the American space agency NASA, the camp is not exactly space age. From the air, it looked like a few dots against the vast expanse of white; I hadn't realised how well I'd get to know them. Two semi-permanent huts, each the size of a caravan and half-buried in snow, and a line of small orange tents for sleeping, for five scientists and the three of us. In one of the huts, there are a few desks with computers and at first sight this could be a field office anywhere, lights dangling, piles of equipment, heaps of notebooks. But the room is exceptionally cold and I soon see why: filling most of the space beneath one of the desks is a block of ice, crystal-clear, which has accumulated over the years and encased the hundreds of cables connecting the gear. If it melts, the ice will cause real damage so it is left untouched and unheated, a constant chilling reminder of the vulnerability of working in this polar wilderness.

Next door is the kitchen and dining area with a simple cooker, shelves crammed with food and a small table just large enough for the eight of us to squeeze around. There's one small gas heater and a single plastic window looking out into the permanent pallor. Beside the cooker stands a large dustbin filled with snow, the first stage in our water supply. Nothing is easy here. The longer we stay the more we become used to the task of dragging the bin outside to keep it filled. The job of then melting the snow is a slow process – the tent is never very warm – so we all lend a hand, standing over a metal pan, stirring snow over the heat. But even then, there's one more stage before the water is fit to drink. Ironically, because it's so pure it lacks the minerals the body needs to rehydrate so every glassful has to be dosed with powdered flavouring. Water that I'd thought would be the most delicious in the world ends up tasting like a cheap canned drink that's lost its fizz.

An old wooden crate acts as a lobby for snow boots and anoraks from which a ladder brings you up to a trapdoor and the outside world. And that's it, what's known as Swiss Camp, a rough little settlement, primitive but practical. The NASA connection had led me to think we'd be in lunar modules on the ice, maybe like those hi-tech Japanese sleeping pods, or something left over from the moon landings. Instead this place is less Sci-Fi and more Wild West, a frontier post, a place for rugged pioneers. At the very least I'd assumed that the agency that sends men into space might provide some ingenious polar plumbing. And, as it happens, when we first arrive, it's me that first needs to ask: where do I go?

I'm at a literary festival at the Royal Geographical Society and an audience of several hundred is asking questions about polar travel. The gold-leafed roll of honour at the entrance lists the greatest names in exploration including Scott and Shackleton and it's here that some of the most daring expeditions have been planned and supported, the beating heart of Victorian Britain's restless venturing to map the globe. I'm the last of a panel of three speakers and had expected to be nervous – a polar reporter amid genuine experts, a hack among professionals. But by my turn a topic has come up which has lowered the tone. Someone has been brave enough to ask what I suspect everyone wants to know about: bodily functions in the world of ice and snow, and my fellow panellists do not shy away from giving answers.

From my very first polar trip, this has emerged as something people seem endlessly curious about: do you have to do it in the open? What about the cold? Don't you worry about getting frostbite, you know, down there? If I'm feeling impatient, I just kill the theme stone dead by describing Rothera and its perfectly normal arrangements: lots of porcelain and an efficient sewage plant like anywhere in Britain, no big deal, next question. But I have seen that this is disappointing, that people are eager to be appalled. So to the serried ranks at the RGS I decide to explain how it worked at Swiss Camp. The clue, I emphasise to them, is the word 'camp'. So I describe what happened when I, as a new boy, asked the inevitable question.

Head up the ladder, one of the scientists tells me.

I assume he's going to direct me to a tent or some other structure that I haven't noticed, but I'm wrong.

Look down the hill straight ahead of you and you'll see a pole, it's bright orange, you can't miss it.

Ok, then what?

He looks at me oddly: well, if you can do it standing up, do it right there.

And if not?

If you can't do it standing up then look for the shovel. Just dig a hole, do what you have to do and cover it up.

The great hall of the RGS is silent as I describe walking through knee-deep snow to the edge of the camp and finding a forlorn orange stick standing amid a featureless plain of ice and snow that stretches without so much as a tree or rock or any kind of shelter for a thousand miles. I can almost hear the audience weighing the full horror of such an utterly exposed scene.

I'm tempted to provide more detail but can't quite bring myself to tell them that the wind that so chilled my ankles on my first trip to Greenland feels a lot worse if your trousers are wrapped around your ankles instead.

Nor do I explain how, in all my time there, living with seven others in that tiny community, there seemed to be an unspoken protocol under which I neither saw anyone any-where near the pole nor was aware of being seen myself. And this during a time of constant daylight and no one leaving the camp. Was it luck? Or some instinctive sense of decorum? I wonder whether NASA, planning missions for astronauts sharing a far smaller space, might learn something.

Swiss Camp is the brainchild of a towering figure of Arctic science, Konrad Steffen. Originally from Switzerland, 'Koni', as he's known, is director of the envi-ronmental science centre at the University of Colorado and couldn't have been more accurately cast for the role of polar specialist: tall and lean, thick beard, hair flopping towards sharp eyes, heavily lined face ready to break into a smile at the smallest irony. Our prolonged stay, for example, which is obviously a burden to his small team, becomes a running joke. The hardships of camp life – the pole, the bin of snow, the ice-filled work-room – are dismissed with a laugh. The effect of the weather on Rob's cameras is a constant source of amused sympathy – the main camera packs up on the first day, the reserve breaks down on the second, leaving the small last-resort one which is the kind of thing people take on holiday. For Koni these misfortunes are mere fodder for a great sense of humour, minor challenges to his determin-ation to see the lighter side of a treacherous land.

During one of our long evenings together we urge him to recount some of his experiences. He's modest, maybe even shy, but eventually relents. And we've picked our moment: the wind is battering the little window with crystals of ice, what sound like fistfuls of gravel pummelling the plastic. Steam is rising from mugs of tea and another load of snow is subsiding into a pan on the stove. And so Koni begins, in his Swiss-German accent.

On one expedition, he was woken in his tent by the anguished howling of one of his huskies. He looked out to see a terrifying sight: the dog was being chased around the tent by a polar bear. Koni couldn't possibly get out and all he could do was hope the bear was too busy to think of coming in.

Weren't you scared?

Maybe a bit, he says, gazing into the distance. But it was also funny, and he's actually chuckling at the memory.

On another occasion, camped on an ice floe, he realised that it was breaking away from a much larger section of ice and that his route back to land was disappearing. With the crack widening and the ice at risk of carrying him on a current out into the ocean, he reckoned that he had one means of escape: to jump onto his snowmobile, rev it up to full power, aim for the gap and, like a stuntman, try to speed over the gap.

I made it, he says, and he laughs some more.

What seems to motivate Koni is the desire to gather the most accurate data he can. In the 1980s, he set himself the task of answering one of the hardest questions in polar science: how much solar radiation is actually reflected by snow. Getting this right is essential for calculations about how rapidly the world might warm if the amount of snow cover changes. The answer might seem straightforward – a bright white surface surely reflects most of the sunlight reaching it. But for Koni that wasn't enough: he wanted to know how much was being reflected at different times of the day, the amount varying with the angle of the sun. And the only way to arrive at a genuinely accurate result, he believed, was to set up his instruments, make sure nothing got in their way or knocked them over, and then keep a constant watch for the full 24 hours of an Arctic summer's day. Without a break.

That was hard, he admits, keeping awake for so long. Again, he's smiling.

This grit is really impressive. One of the junior researchers had told me earlier that Koni never seems to feel the cold. We'd been preparing to join a short expedition by snowmobile, a notoriously cold form of transport, and I'd seen Koni donning only a flimsy anorak and fur hat so I asked the researcher for advice on what we should wear. He replied with great seriousness: 'everything you've got'. But even with every layer, the extreme chill of riding over the ice at high speed left us numbed. Koni, though, seemed untouched.

What's striking is that this senior professor, at the top of his field, with the equivalent of a proud war record, continues to put himself at the frontline of research. At this stage of his career, he might readily have done what so many others in his position do: despatch juniors and students to do the fieldwork for him. But that's not Koni's style and he returns to Swiss Camp for a month every year to keep the instruments and equipment going. One morning I climb out of our tent to find him repairing one of the snowmobiles. Engine parts are lying on a tarpaulin, his hands are black with grease and he couldn't have looked happier. And the sight makes a mark. This hands-on science doesn't mean that his findings should be any more reliable than those of a more delicate lab-bound figure. But I can't help feeling that a readiness to brave the polar world adds credibility to what Koni says, that his steady, deliberate, cautious words must carry weight.

For the past twenty minutes the tent has filled with an intoxicating and utterly improbable smell. The largest pan, the one normally used for melting the snow, is brimming with, of all things, lobsters and standing over them is one of Koni's closest colleagues, a senior scientist with NASA. Just as I was amazed to see Koni stripping down the snowmobile, so too am I amazed to see the man in charge of one of NASA's most expensive missions, a polar monitoring satellite called IceSat, gently checking that each claw is submerged, that the pan still has enough water.

And for someone brought up to expect NASA scientists to look like they did during the moon landings – carefully parted hair, white shirts and dark ties – the man calmly taking his turn to handle supper couldn't look less likely: he has a mischievous grin and a diamond stud in one of his earlobes, and he talks about climate science with real animation. This is Jay Zwally and during our stay we've learned that he's a formidable cook – his halibut steaks on our first night were worth talking about for several days afterwards, all the more surprising after expecting to be eating space food out of packets.

As the lobsters are readied, Jay and Koni talk about the value of repeatedly visiting this strange little settlement, how the data patiently gathered over the years has led to a string of discoveries.

When Swiss Camp was first set up, they explain, the aim was to study the snow, ice and weather and one of the first tasks was to plot its position as precisely as possible. The assumption back then was that the ice sheet, that great structure of ice covering Greenland, was so vast and so cold that it was essentially immobile, that the ice crept downhill towards the coast but too slowly to worry about. Under the camp itself the ice is a mile thick – an eerie thought – and it's hard to picture something so huge moving at all. But Koni describes how his early measurements showed that the camp was actually inching along at a rate of about one foot – 30 centimetres – every day, not exactly high speed but enough to raise questions about how the ice would behave if Greenland got much warmer. He's also found that the temperatures are rising, that the area of the ice sheet where there's melting every summer is expanding and that the summer season itself – the period of the year when melting is possible – is becoming longer.

This is important, says Jay, a key factor in how much ice may melt into the ocean.

He breaks off to serve up the lobsters. For a few minutes we all fall silent, there's a job to do, shells to be cracked open. The taste is outstanding. The last time I ate lobster was in Brussels and I wonder what the moustachioed Belgian waiters would make of this surreal gastronomic outpost.

Once the largest pieces of meat have been prised out and we're tackling the claws, Jay picks up the narrative.

The GPS satellite devices that track the position of the camp revealed something else unforeseen. For most of the year, they detected that the creep of the ice is at a fairly regular pace but during the summer months they found that the ice doubles the speed of its slide towards the sea.

Doubles in speed? That sounds far-fetched. How, I ask, could ice a mile thick actually accelerate?

That's what the readings show. During the summer, the camp's position moves not at one foot every day but at two feet a day.

Jay is emphatic on that and Koni nods in agreement.

So how could that happen, how could the warmer air of summer have any effect on an ice sheet so heavy, so thick?

By now I'm going back over pieces of shell in case I've missed anything.

What seems to be happening, I'm told, is that when the temperature gets above zero – as it's doing for longer periods each year – the upper layers of snow and ice melt and form large pools. These dot the surface of the ice sheet and many linger until the freeze of winter. But some of this meltwater suddenly disappears, draining violently through cracks in the ice, descending through the crevasses and chasms down to the base of the ice sheet. There the water forces itself between the ice and the rock it's resting on.

I think back to the blue light of the crevasse in Antarctica. This ice sheet too is riddled with unseen chambers and passages.

We clear the plates and Jay explains how the water, which melts on top of the ice sheet, flows down through it and ends up under it.

And? The idea of torrents surging through this uncharted terrain is fascinating but I don't see why it might matter. The picture is clear but not the point.

So Jay spells out the next stage. That water down there acts as a lubricant, it helps the ice slide over the rock. The more water that reaches the rock, the faster the ice sheet will move. That's why it accelerates every summer.

And the summers are getting longer, Koni adds, so there's more time every year for the ice sheet to move faster.

Which means that what was an infinitely slow conveyor belt of ice is picking up speed so that more ice is reaching the ocean and breaking into it.

Greenland has long been studied because the water locked up in its ice sheet would, if melted, raise the global sea level by some 6 to 7 metres, about 20 feet. It's the kind of statistic easily bandied about by campaigners and the very use of it can imply it might happen immediately. But what's obvious from talking to Koni and Jay is that there's no question of that amount of melting soon – Greenland is still a very cold place and it would take hundreds of years to melt its mass of ice. But what's also clear is that they have found a mechanism with the potential for rapid change, so that relatively small rises in temperature can have extraordinarily large effects, with something as apparently minor as a longer summer leading to more ice reaching the sea and adding to the risk of the flooding of distant cities.

The lobster long finished, I'm attacking a packet of crackers. With the great food and a bottle of wine, this has had the air of a dinner party, but one of the strangest I've ever attended. Not just because of the pale light of midnight seeping through the little window but also because the tents, the table, the instruments and everything else are being shifted at a rate of about one inch every hour. Slowly but remorselessly, during the course of the evening, the stirring leviathan of ice has carried us about four or five inches closer to the sea.

**Splendid isolation:** Rob Magee and I are stuck in a NASA tent on the ice sheet in Greenland but the researchers' skilled cooking keeps spirits high. At this stage, we think the delay will only last one day at most.                    *Kevin Bishop*

One morning we wake to a slightly clearer day. The horizon is just visible so the helicopter is on its way for us and our bags are heaped a short distance beyond the tents. We hear the drumbeat of the rotors and strain for a sight but the sky is still white and although we can tell that the helicopter is approaching we can't see it. The noise raises our spirits until, to our frustration, it recedes – the pilot still can't see enough. We have no choice but to shuffle back to the tents, deflated.

Jay is on hand. Don't worry, he says, tonight we'll have sushi.

I pound around the camp, boots creating a pathway through the snow, past the instrument tower, past the snow-mobiles, round again and again. Rob joins me but leaves after a few circuits, bored by the repetition and probably mildly uneasy at my obsessive need to keep going. The air has warmed and I'm soon down to one layer and sweating but it takes a long time to feel calm.

Hours later the helicopter does manage to land. The pilot is in a hurry and keeps the rotors turning, whipping up a blizzard, too loud to talk, our previously tranquil camp stirred into a maelstrom. The loadmaster, a robust Inuit, takes charge, urging us to keep passing him bags to stow, not to dawdle, bellowing in the din. We shout our goodbyes, Koni once more chuckling behind his snow-flecked beard – he knows how relieved we are to be getting away. We climb inside, the door slams shut and soon we're airborne, the crevasses stretching ahead of us towards a yellow sky above the coast.

I look across at the pilot. His face is taut with concentration. But I notice something else about it as well, something I'd watched for in others during our long days at Swiss Camp but never seen: the man's nostrils are twitching.

I shrink back in my seat. My theory is right. We all stink but have adapted.

And over the intercom the pilot confirms it, with a polite but clear statement of the facts: you did not have the chance to have a shower.

There comes a time after every assignment – however surreal, challenging or delayed it's been – when you return to the normality of the newsroom, to the unchanging sandwiches of the tea-bar, the colleagues working regular shifts, the editors constantly weighing the stories they'll put on air. There's usually some curiosity about how things went, though questions rarely go on longer than they do when someone returns from holiday – we want a few headlines but not too much detail. After this latest polar trip, there's also a bit of debate about how much more coverage of ice anyone can take. One editor says that he may soon suffer from 'ice fatigue' and suggests that I 'give the icebergs a break for a while' while another wonders if there aren't any other important research projects worth reporting on, maybe 'a few hotter ones'.

I try to explain that all I'm doing is what any news reporter should do – react to the key events and keep track of the major developments, and that it's not exactly my fault there seems to be so much research in the polar regions. I point out that climate scientists had first forecast back in the 1980s that the Arctic in particular would warm first and fastest, and that week after week the top scientific journals, including *Science* and *Nature*, carry the results of ice studies, like those by Koni and Jay, many of which increasingly strike me as worth exploring.

As I see it, these are not findings dreamed up as campaign slogans. Researchers like those at Swiss Camp have gone through the mill gathering data, writing up their findings, seeing how they fare under the microscope of peer-review and then waiting to see if they're accepted for publication – that's a thorough set of filters. Of course there's no guarantee that what's published is always reliable – a Korean stem-cell scientist was among those whose work was printed in journals but later found to have included fabricated data. But the scrutiny is meant to be tough and should help distinguish between what some people say about global warming and what's actually being found out, which is often different. The cry that dangerous change is happening right now is not the same as the more nuanced conclusion that there are processes capable of dangerous change and that there may be early signs that they are starting.

For years, for example, there's been concern about the fate of the permafrost, the vast tracts of frozen soil stretching around the Arctic but mainly in a great arc across Russia. Every summer the upper layer of the ground thaws, a normal seasonal process which releases some greenhouse gases including carbon dioxide and methane. So a ready assumption is that the whole lot will melt, release even more gas, and make global warming even faster. This would be what's called a positive feedback loop where one change triggers another which in turn speeds up the first. According to papers published in *Science* and *Nature*, a team of Russian and American researchers conclude that if the thawing of the permafrost became widespread it would certainly have the potential to cause dangerous feedback – though they also make clear that it's too early to say for sure that it's actually under way.

I check with editors whether they want this covered; I think it's well worth investigating. It will mean returning to the Arctic but, I assure them, won't involve any icebergs or even much ice.

The best thing – cameraman Duncan Stone and I are firmly agreed – is that after our overnight flight from Moscow to Russia's Far East we should keep going all day, drink plenty of water, get our filming done and then aim for an early night. Above all else, we should politely but firmly refuse all offers of drink. We've got a lot to do and the last thing we need is friendly locals opening bottles which, by ruinous custom, must be finished once started. We've both done plenty of reporting in the fringes of Russia and, as we arrive in distant Yakutsk, the smiling Asiatic faces are reminders of how readily firm intentions can collapse in the face of ebullient, smothering hospitality.

In fact every time I return to the former Soviet Union I remember the lobotomising effect of a grubby and unlabelled bottle produced by the colonel of a tank regiment. In the break-up of the country in 1990, his was the first unit to switch allegiance from Moscow to Ukraine, times were tense, and his invitation to join him in multiple toasts was more an order than a request. On an empty stomach, after a day's filming in the cold, the effect was almost hallucinogenic and I watched myself merrily drinking to the future friendship of the new Ukraine and the BBC. And when a junior officer arrived bearing a large wobbling lump, wrapped in old pages of the military newspaper *Krasnya Zvezda*, which turned out to be an entire ox tongue, tendons still attached, I was impressed to observe myself readily accepting a roughly cut inch-thick slice – the colonel had done the carving with his penknife – and not knowing or even minding whether the tongue was cooked or raw.

So the seven-hour flight from Moscow, sleepless, in a crowded old jet with 'free-seating' – which in my case meant a seat whose base and back were freely collapsing – triggers plenty of memories. It also takes us into a time zone nine hours ahead of London, to a region, Yakutia, so far away that it's actually beyond Siberia, and into a state of mind best dealt with, as Duncan and I keep concurring, by being sensible. So, after a quick shower, we head out into Yakutsk for our first filming.

I'm looking for signs of something I'd heard about, permafrost damage, where the solidly frozen ground gives away in the summer thaw. They're not hard to find. A major road near our hotel is closed because a hole the size of a large car has opened up in the tarmac – the ground beneath has thawed causing what looks like bomb damage. Old houses tilt at crazy angles. And a gang of labourers is hurriedly strengthening an office block to stop it collapsing – I crouch down with Duncan to see them toiling in the gloom, stooped under a narrow gap between the foundations and building itself.

I ask if this is normal.

Sure, every summer this kind of thing happens.

Are you seeing more of it?

Maybe. The summers do seem to be getting longer.

I'm with a group of local Yakuts. They're friends of our translator, Mimi Chapin, an American scientist and former guide in this region. A formidable figure, with a regal head of white-grey hair, she's made a numbingly long journey to be here, right round the globe from her home in Alaska.

Her friends are sculptors who work with ice in the winter and, when they can get it, the ivory of mammoth tusks.

Would we like to see a mammoth tusk?

Of course. I'd read how this region used to be home to the magnificent woolly mammoth and how in the summer thaw the remains of these extinct great beasts are occasionally unearthed.

A rickety staircase leads us up the outside of an old apartment block to an artist's studio. Leaning in a corner is one massive tusk, a lathe holds a smaller piece, intricately carved ornaments lie on a workbench. The ivory is expensive stuff to work on, I'm told, but when the snows retreat, the mud usually reveals some and prices fall.

We're offered tea. We've more filming to do but I accept, glancing at Duncan. I know he's determined to keep going, but he's as tired as I am and soon the table is brimming with food – plates of smoked fish, a dish of cream cheese with wild strawberries, a local blood sausage. Bowls of onion soup appear. Mimi explains that the onions are wild, the brief summer offering wonderful natural bounty. More tea is brought. And then I hear a sound I'd been dreading, the crinkling, snapping twist of a metal cap being removed from a bottle, the starting gun to a lost afternoon.

I pretend not to notice what's happening but glasses are being filled and passed around.

It's just to welcome us, says Mimi.

I'm back in the colonel's office, at the same crossroads of what's rational and what's reasonable, the choice between duty and decency.

A toast begins, Mimi translating, this one to friendship and we all raise our glasses. I know what Duncan is thinking and don't want to catch his eye – I've got us into this.

The vodka slips down.

Thank you, that was wonderful, but really one is enough for me, that was perfect.

Mimi relays my thanks and excuses and the bottle retreats. But only for a while.

Soon our glasses are refilled for a toast to Mimi's good health.

How can we not drink to that?

This time I look towards Duncan and he's smiling benignly. Maybe this stuff is doing us good. I look at my watch and in the time it takes me to work out that it's dawn in Moscow and the middle of the night in London my glass is filled again.

When it's my turn to make a toast, I'm delighted to find that I'm neither lobotomised nor hallucinating. Instead I feel curiously levitated, even optimistic, my counting of time zones miraculously sharp, our failed attempts to be sensible so misguided. We may even have found a cure for jet lag. The result is that we're more than ready for our afternoon's filming, at an establishment few towns can boast, Yakutsk's famous Permafrost Institute.

At first sight, for such an unusual place, it's a disappointingly standard Communist-era building, with heavy double doors, scowling receptionist and light fittings without bulbs. We've arranged to film here but, as so often happened with assignments in the old Soviet Union, someone insists the correct permissions have not been given. Mimi does battle, eventually wins and we're led to the top of a long concrete staircase.

We're told to dress up warmly before being led down into the basement. There, another door leads to a lower level, a dark flight of steps descending through frozen ground. Crystals of ice glint amid the soil and stones. This is permafrost – I'm actually in it. The institute's unique feature is that its laboratories are underground, cut into the permafrost so that researchers have immediate access to it. The earth is rock-hard to the touch, spindly filaments of ancient roots curl inside it, a natural deep freeze.

Our guide, a stern, robotic woman, starts reciting her lines. I tune out, assuming it'll be a list of the institute's virtues but then I listen more closely. Since studies began in the 1950s, she's saying, the summer thaw has been gradually reaching deeper into the soil every year, and that the area that's thawing is getting larger too, extending further to the north.

I ask how sure she can be of this.

She's rather affronted, and lists all the monitoring stations scattered across the region that gather the figures.

And why is the thaw getting larger and deeper?

Natural cycles, there are natural cycles.

It's the answer I'd expected. Russian scientists are prominent among those unconvinced of man-made climate.

I look again at the frozen walls, at the intricate weave of soil, rock and plant. I don't press the point about the possible causes of the warming. But on our way back up, we pass a frozen cascade, a giant icicle flowing down the steps, the result of an event no one had thought possible here: a warm spell had triggered a flood, running water where there's usually just ice.

Siberia and the lands beyond it are notorious as regions of ice and exile. But no part of Russia's Far East had a more forbidding reputation than Kolyma, named after one of the great rivers running to the Arctic Sea, the route along which thousands of prisoners were ferried to the worst gulags. This was the outer fringe of the Soviet empire, a dumping ground guarded by hostile terrain, far beyond the reach even of the Trans-Siberian railway. Yakutsk, already 4,000 miles from Moscow, is just a staging post to Kolyma. Getting to the region's main town of Cherskii is another 1,200 miles north-east, across a mountain range, well inside the Arctic Circle, a smudge of dirty concrete beside the gleam of the river. Distance is just one obstacle; Kolyma remains a so-called 'closed' region and our visit involved a wait of several months to get permits.

Although Kolyma was a byword for the nightmare of Stalinist rule, Cherskii itself used to be perversely popular. Released prisoners sometimes stayed on and others chose to move in, attracted by exceptionally well-paid jobs and local authorities prepared to be lenient. Life in the land of the camps could, ironically, be a little freer than in the rest of the country. And in Communist days, Cherskii was well connected. It merited a daily direct flight to Moscow. But by the time of our visit the runway is out of action and the airline lays on an enormous helicopter, baggage and cargo heaped between two long benches without seat belts. Duncan notices that none of his gear is weighed; the aircrew check if they can fly simply by taking off and hovering for a few minutes above the ground to see how things feel. I wish he hadn't told me: we're starting a two-hour flight over empty terrain to a destination on the very edge of the map.

Sergei Zimov is a great showman, all bushy beard, wild ambition and astounding stories. His wife Galina is calm and elegant, the efficient one, alternately smiling and frowning at Sergei's boasts. Together they make one of the most appealing couples in polar science. It's a tribute to them both that their tiny centre, the North East Science Station, has attracted interest from around the world and that their work in collaboration with others has featured in the top journals. The permafrost research I'd read about in *Science* and *Nature* was carried out with scientists from the University of Alaska Fairbanks, where Mimi works, and she's very warmly welcomed.

**Armour-plated research:** Sergei Zimov at the controls of his BMP armoured personnel carrier. He says it's the best way to negotiate the melting permafrost of Siberia. My face tells a different story. *BBC*

We've come in September, the tail end of summer. According to Sergei, life is easier in winter when you can drive over the frozen rivers and the ground is solid. Now, with the endless mud and bogs, even a four-wheel drive can't cope so, he says, you need a special form of transport.

You mean the hovercraft? I'd seen a very decrepit-looking machine down by the river.

No, not hovercraft. Stronger. Tank.

Tank? A scientist in a tank?

He's right, though it's not quite a tank but more an armoured personnel carrier, a massive vehicle with tracks called a BMP. Its guns have been removed but it's still the regulation military green – Sergei bought it directly from the factory. I recognise it immediately. In my days covering defence, intelligence officials would worry about the hordes of BMPs poised along the Iron Curtain. In the closing days of the Cold War, I saw them on the streets during the unrest in Georgia and Armenia. BMPs, designed to carry infantry into battle, were Moscow's vehicle of choice for repression.

I'd stood close to them but never been in one, until now, when the engagingly eccentric Sergei dons a tank driver's cloth helmet and invites me to climb in. It's like riding in a speedboat, the immense vehicle powering over the curves of the ground, saplings crushed without effort, the clanking tracks surfing over the mud. I'm standing on the commander's seat, my head poking up through a hatch, my only handhold the armour-plated cover. Sergei is grinning at the controls, whatever he's saying overwhelmed by the roar of the engine, a war machine in the service of science.

We halt beside a lake, one of thousands that dot the landscape in summer. Sergei explains that satellite analysis shows that over the last 30 years the number of lakes has increased. This matters, he says, because rising from each one, in spasmodic bursts, are streams of bubbles containing methane. The gas is produced by the thawing of the soils beneath the lakes, long frozen bacteria warming up enough to become active, digesting the organic material in the ground and emitting the methane as a result.

The bubbles surge to the surface and burst. And the methane, I'm told, is 23 times more potent than carbon dioxide as a greenhouse gas. So a big effort has gone into developing new ways of assessing how much gas is escaping, one technique being to survey the lakes in winter and measure the bubbles of methane trapped in the ice. Duncan films the bubbles with an underwater camera, quicksilver shapes drifting up through the dark green water. They make a powerful image.

Sergei uses a home-made device, rather like a small plastic umbrella, to trap the bubbles just below the surface, the methane then passing into an old soft drinks bottle. When Duncan is in position, Sergei releases a small jet of gas and lights it, its pale blue flame spluttering in the afternoon breeze. Analysis of the gas itself, Sergei says, reveals the age of the organic material that's thawing – and that shows how much permafrost is no longer permanently frozen. The most recent study of the methane shows that it's no longer just the beds of the lakes that are thawing – soils deep beneath them are as well, ground that has remained frozen since as far back as 40,000 years ago is now stirring. Just as the guide in the Permafrost Institute told me, the thaw is reaching steadily deeper.

As well as the methane, carbon dioxide is emitted and Sergei wants to show us the process of measuring that too. A long boat trip takes us to an extraordinary series of muddy cliffs, a forlorn spot known as Duvanny Yar. Here the permafrost is exposed. Amid the great banks of solid brown earth are curiously shiny blocks and lumps – this is ice, yet to melt. When it does, whole chunks of cliff collapse, a close-up view of the process under way in Yakutsk, the thaw suddenly undermining the surface. And all the time, as the soils melt and make contact with the air, bacteria are kick-started into action, the resulting gas this time being carbon dioxide. Sergei deploys a gadget to record the amount – the numbers on a digital display surge in just a few minutes.

I ask why the soils here are so rich, so laden with organic material.

One reason, Sergei says. Mammoths. This vast terrain was home for hundreds of thousands of years to woolly mammoths, bison, deer, all kinds of grazing mammals. It was one of the largest single ecosystems on the planet and ranks as one of the best fertilised: think of all the incredibly rich manure dumped on it over the millennia. Add to that the grasses, roots, trees and shrubs and there's layer upon layer of material, a giant dungheap.

While we're talking, one of his colleagues lets out a shout. He's been digging in the mud and his shovel has hit a huge bone. Gingerly, he extracts it. It's like a great white log, part of a thigh bone, and when I hold it the weight is startling. I suggest that this place by the river must have been a graveyard for mammoths. Sergei shakes his head: the whole region is a graveyard.

Mimi explains why this matters.

As long as this stuff – the mammoth poo and the rest – is frozen, it's out of the way. But if it starts to thaw, there's a lot of potential greenhouse gas in there.

In fact, she says, it's a ticking time bomb.

Time bomb? Isn't that a bit strong?

If I'd heard that kind of phrase from someone carrying a placard outside a climate conference I'd have ignored them. But here's a steady, mature, reliable figure who's studied the data and is prepared use that phrase on air. That makes me pause. As does the fact that she's not saying the bomb is going off right now; instead that it's lying there, ticking, ready to explode.

I ask why Mimi and Sergei are prepared to use this kind of language.

It's because the numbers point that way, they say, and they run through them.

Already there are more than 700 billion tons of carbon in the atmosphere, in the form of greenhouse gases. If the frozen soils are as rich as they think they are, then the carbon dioxide and methane that could be released from them would add another 900 billion tons. That's more carbon than is in the air right now.

So, whatever the Mauna Loa instruments are measuring? More than double it. The readings from the most recent Antarctic ice cores? Twice as high.

I need to check what this means.

You're not saying this is happening right now?

No.

You're saying this *could* happen?

Yes.

It's like trying to assess those warnings from the generals in the Cold War. We're not saying the Russians will invade, they'd say, but if they did we wouldn't stand a chance. Technically, I'm sure they were right. And in the same way, I have no reason to doubt the assessment of the potential release of gases from the permafrost. The question is, will it happen?

In the science station's guesthouse, Duncan and I edit our reports. This time the Internet link is unusable: an ancient line, it carries only one kilobit every second – a decent connection would be hundreds of times faster. So Duncan fixes up two satellite phones – smaller versions of the ones Tony used in Antarctica – and points their dishes to the southern horizon. Amazingly, they work and our video material makes its long slow way to London.

We wake early the next day. We're due to fly out in the afternoon. But before that we'll try some live broadcasts, the pattern on these distant trips. Being eleven hours ahead of London, we'll go live into the previous night's *News at Ten*. Duncan wears two watches, one set to London time, one to Cherskii, to avoid confusion. I think it adds to it. As he prepares the gear, I step outside. It's a cold morning, the sky grey, and the few flurries of snow in the air give me a line: on air, I'll refer to the first snows of winter. The connection holds up, I mention the snow, the editors love it and Duncan and I feel triumphant. Galina has prepared a breakfast of pancakes and caviar. All we have to do now is pack and catch the helicopter. Things may just be going a bit too well.

I'm sorry, Sergei announces. There's no flight today.

Why? We're shocked. If we don't get this one, we'll miss our long string of connections – Sredno-Kolymsk, Yakutsk, Moscow, London.

Weather, he says. The snow. They can't fly.

Duncan shoots me a look of deep irritation. And I do feel partly to blame, as if I brought on the snow by mentioning it.

So we unpack and hang about. For the rest of that day, and the next, in fact for four days in all. It's like Swiss Camp all over again: the blurring of the horizon, the never knowing, the phone calls to our ever-cheerful travel agent Dave Bristow, usually expert at extracting us from out-of-the-way spots, but stumped by the polar weather.

Sergei's attitude is just like Koni's. It's the Arctic, what do you expect?

One attempt to reach Moscow, he told us, took him two whole weeks as he reached various air strips only to be held up some more. His son almost missed his own wedding because of the weather. He's trying to reassure us but it's not working and we're determined to find some other option. What about using Sergei's boat to travel up river to Sredno-Kolymsk, the next airport? Too dangerous, Duncan's gear might overload the vessel and the river can get rough. The trip might also take 12 hours and there wouldn't be enough fuel to make it. Or we could take enough fuel but then we'd have to leave the gear behind. What about driving to the next town? That's possible but not advisable at this time of year: there are very few roads that aren't overwhelmed by mud. In winter, no problem, you'd just drive over the ice but the freeze is still several months away. And even if you made it there's no guarantee of getting a flight. The armoured personnel carrier? Hasn't got the range. Can we charter a plane? No, there's nothing here. Sergei has a small aircraft but he admits that he's modified it, apparently rearranging the engines, and Galina, the sensible one, won't hear of us going near it.

Gradually we become resigned, taking it in turns to be resilient, exchanging fantasies of some Western jet making an unplanned stop and whisking us home. As in Greenland, I find a circuit and pound round it, this time following the lanes around the camp, through a landscape of stunted trees, old women in headscarves stooped over bushes picking the last berries of summer. Duncan settles into a thriller which, by coincidence, is one of my favourites: *Kolymsky Heights* by Lionel Davidson, involving a Canadian Indian called Johnny Porter, whose polar features mean he can pass for a Russian Chukchee, an Arctic James Bond. Smuggled into Cherskii by the CIA, his target is a secret laboratory beside a dark lake – as it happens, this fictional lake is in exactly the same area where we filmed the rising bubbles. Like us, Porter has to get out. Unlike us, he gathers enough spares to assemble his own jeep and drive away, crossing the frozen sea dividing Russia from Alaska. His escape is inspiring. I know Duncan to be a wizard at electronics. But building a car? From spare parts? We wouldn't know how to start.

Our wait leads me to wonder about another extraordinary escape, this time a true one, involving another David Shukman, my grandfather on my father's side, who was in Siberia more than a century before me. He was sent not as a prisoner but as a conscript in the Russian Army, deployed to fight the Japanese in their war of 1904–05. While I fret about my delayed flight, he was one of the first people to ride the newly opened Trans-Siberian railway, a journey that would have taken a month, the soldiers crammed into a goods wagon, sheets of felt the only insulation, the immensity of frozen Lake Baikal crossed on foot. Here I'm fed stewed moose and barbecued sturgeon but he would have endured rations of black tea and bread. I have a satellite phone and can ring home every day. When he fought in what was then the world's largest battle, at Mukden, and was wounded, news of his injury took months to reach his family. While I race over the mud in a BMP, he'd have waded through it, cursing the insects.

So what would he have said to a grandson not merely volunteering for Siberia but actively pressing to make the visit? And this interest in the permafrost? As an infantryman, he'd have loathed the rock-hard soil, his arms jarring with the shock of trying to dig a trench. And what about this curious job of mine, working for a medium that hadn't been invented, covering a subject that hadn't been thought of? In a poem, my brother Henry pictures our grandfather, a tailor, appearing in his hotel room and watching his overeducated, fumbling attempts to sew on a button, expertly taking on the task himself with his 'big-nailed fingers, strong as a fiddler's' – 'leave that to me, you've better things to do.' Would he puzzle over my interest in Russia's mud and lakes and bubbles, and gently suggest I needn't bother – why not leave Siberia to him and find something better to do? And what is this global warming anyway? Bandaged, chilled, and shaken on the painfully long journey home, he might have yearned for some warmth – who in their right mind would worry about too much of that?

# 6
# The wrong kind of weather

With his smiling open face, Wilitie Van Wyk has the looks and manner of a younger version of the actor Will Smith, an elegant figure welcoming us to the family farm on the edge of the Kalahari Desert in South Africa. We've reached his place after a bumpy journey down a lane that became a track which petered out in a blaze of baking sand and, as we leave the air-conditioned refuge of our car, Wilitie politely hurries us to the shade beside the farmhouse. In the breeze of the afternoon heat, the ground utterly dry, puffs of dust are whipped into the air. In fact there's dust everywhere: on the walls of the single-storey buildings, on the cars, on our clothes, life here precarious, on the margins of what's possible.

Looking around, the dominant feature is sand, the first impression vulnerability. In fact, the word 'farm' doesn't feel quite right; I can't see how anything would grow or live. A fenced paddock is nothing but sand, and towering over the scene is an immense dune. A few splashes of pale green turn out to be tangled bushes of thorns, no use to anyone. This could be a scene from the American Dust Bowl, but it must be yielding some income. Wilitie is now at college and, back for a break, translating his parents' Afrikaans, their upbringing too poor for much schooling.

They moved here because land was cheap but the key to their lives is rain. If there's the right amount, grasses grow on the sand and provide enough nutrition for animals to graze on. But after a run of very dry years, I'm told, the grasses die out and the cattle don't make it.

Cattle? My mental picture of cattle has them shuffling contentedly over a thick green English meadow, ankle-deep in lush grass.

Leading me into the furnace of the sun, Wilitie points out the reality here: a few bony shapes at the foot of the dune, their hooves sinking rhythmically into ripples of sand.

But what do they eat? All I can see are the thorn bushes.

That's why we need the rain.

Everything hangs by a thread, year after year. If the grasses don't grow, Wilitie's parents won't raise enough cattle to make enough at market to have enough cash to support him and his brother.

So how have the rains been the past few years?

Not good, you can see.

I ask Wilitie about his future. Brought up on the farm, he's shared his parents' toil, minding the livestock, safeguarding precious water, fighting the sands. But at the same time, his education has opened his eyes to a life in town, maybe a job in an office, where the dust can be vacuumed and the pay doesn't depend on whether the rains come.

So, will you stay, and others of your age?

Wilitie grins. He's embarrassed, maybe he feels he's letting his parents down.

But his answer is emphatic: no.

And he justifies it: if it becomes more windy and there's less rain it might become difficult for the next generation.

And then, intrigued by us, he asks what brought me here.

I explain that we're reporting on new research into how climate change could affect the Kalahari Desert.

You mean global warming?

Yes, but the warming is only part of it, and I tell him what I've picked up, what the studies are saying: that climate change isn't as simple as the temperatures rising. It's messier than that, a lot more complicated. In Africa, for example, the forecasts say there could be less rain in some places but more in others. Or more rain but in such concentrated bursts that it falls in a deluge that runs off wasted. Or, if there is more rain, the warmer air means it could evaporate faster. And there could well be more of something Wilitie himself has just mentioned: stronger winds.

A professor from Oxford University, the holder of a distinguished academic position, descends to his elbows and knees in the dirt of the desert to do his research. It's not a sight one might expect but this is how David Thomas, year after year, has measured a feature of the natural world most of us wouldn't think of: precisely how much sand is shifted on a dune for a given speed of wind. He counts individual grains. Literally. One device of his, a cylinder with holes at regular intervals, is fixed into the dune and traps airborne sand at different heights; the samples are then weighed to see how much sand is moving at different altitudes. Another gadget electronically records the impacts of individual grains of sand, 'pings' registering the height of the grains as they fly through the air, each one part of the process of moving an entire dune.

Just as Koni patiently stayed awake all night to measure how much Arctic light the snow reflects, or Dave Keeling maintained his carbon dioxide monitors in Hawaii, David Thomas has made a career out of patiently monitoring sand. Dunes are very rarely static, he tells me. Over the millennia, the Kalahari Desert has expanded and contracted as the dunes have advanced or retreated and one determining factor is the wind speed. Too fast a wind and too mobile a dune and plants can't take hold. And there's really only one way to investigate that properly – to study the billions of building blocks of a dune and find out what it takes to shift each one.

**Every grain counts:** devoted to accuracy, Professor David Thomas drops to his knees to check an instrument in the Kalahari Desert. I'm impressed by his search for hard numbers not abstract slogans. *BBC*

Naturally, the answer varies – there are different types of sand, different moisture conditions. But as a broad conclusion, David says, if the wind reaches 15 mph or more then the tiny components of a dune will be lifted into the air and begin the process of moving the entire structure. Lands that are marginal now will become useless.

Once again, I'm struck by the diligence of the research, the attention to detail, the reluctance to leap to a seemingly obvious conclusion. One could so readily assume that global warming will make the deserts bigger. But without understanding the systems at work, we can't really know how the dunes will respond or whether some deserts will get bigger but others smaller, let alone how that might affect the dune looming over the Van Wyk farm.

Using his knowledge of the grains, David then applied it to three different computer models of climate change in southern Africa.

So what do the results show?

That by 2040 the dunes at the southern edges of the desert could be 'activated' – hit by winds fast enough to shift them – impacting the Van Wyks in South Africa and people in neighbouring Botswana and Namibia as well. By the sounds of it, Wilitie will have left long before then anyway. By 2070, dunes further north and east in Angola, Zambia and Zimbabwe may start to move, too, and by 2099 the full extent of the Kalahari basin, half of which currently has some plant cover, will be desert.

Or could be.

Everything rests on the computer models. And how can we know if they're right for the Kalahari or anywhere else? They may say the desert will expand and the Amazon rainforest will get drier and the world warmer. But is it conceivable that they can be accurate?

Don't touch anything, our escort warns us, as he unlocks a large door and lets us into the inner sanctum of the UK Met Office in Exeter. The air is cold and there's an industrial hum from banks of electronics. This is the new supercomputer, a device that carries out billions of calculations every second, a dozen rows of wardrobe-sized cabinets invisibly churning through scenarios for the future climate, a machine whose results are helping to shape government policy.

Visually, it's a damp squib, a few flashing lights, very little to film, nothing like a Pentagon supercomputer I'd once seen at a US Air Force research lab in Colorado. That machine was so fast, so showy, it was cooled by the same plasma fluid used in battlefield first aid, liquid fit for humans bubbling through the glass display of a robotic brain, its task to plot the myriad possibilities of a Soviet missile attack.

The computer in Exeter is designed to explore a longer-term threat. The modellers, from the Met Office's Hadley Centre, start with what they call a 'storyline', a narrative for the coming decades of how emissions of greenhouse gases may rise, how the oceans and the ice and the forests could respond, how mankind itself could react. By definition, the details about a possible future must be estimates or even guesses. Who can be sure how the world will turn out in thirty or seventy years' time?

No wonder that of all environmental questions, computer-driven climate forecasts are the most contentious. An obvious criticism is that if the forecasters can't get the weather right for tomorrow, what hope for the climate in decades' time? One answer, which I've found helpful, is that there's a crucial difference between them. The weather is what you experience day by day – and all kinds of things affect it, hour by hour. But the climate is the *kind of* weather you get over 30 years, the span of a typical generation. As I try to get my head round this, I think of the example of southern Spain. Its climate is hotter and drier than Britain's. But if you fly down there for a week's break you could find yourself in weather that's colder and wetter. And as a child in Oxford I remember the canal freezing so solidly that we could safely play on it. A generation later, my own children have seen the canal iced-up but never thickly enough to walk on. Climate forecasts aren't about exactly what will happen, but about what could happen in more general way.

But that still leaves the key question: whether the models will get things right, even in more general terms?

This matters hugely because models are the basis for the whole issue, the foundation of the projections and for an explanation of the basic problem. If I ask scientists why they're sure that we're having a hand in the warming, they point to the models. If, they say, you add up all the natural forces at work – the sun, the earth's orbit, the oceanic patterns – these factors don't produce enough warming to explain how temperatures have risen in the past century. You also have to add the effect of our greenhouse gases, they explain, because the natural causes of warming can't be sufficient on their own. That's what the models show, believe us. And that's why this subject is so hard: it involves an element of trust.

Unlike David Thomas counting his grains, climate models are based on assumptions. The modellers themselves admit there can be no certainty, only a range of probable outcomes, differing likelihoods of various futures. But for validation they point to other climate centres – in the United States, France, Germany and elsewhere – whose models have different parameters and designs but yield results that are broadly similar, at least agreeing on the core point that more greenhouse gas inescapably means more warming.

Modest and well-intentioned, the modellers are eager for their findings – and their limitations – to be understood. On my Amazon assignment, Richard Betts of the Hadley Centre went to great lengths to join our filming so that he could explain his research and how it was coming up with its improbable conclusion: that the rainforest could get less rain. Listening to Richard's descriptions of what could be a century-long drought, and to other modellers' similarly scary scenarios, I wonder about the strange nature of their jobs: coming into work and watching a virtual copy of our world fry in furnace-like temperatures or drown in perfect storms, and then going home in the evening.

I ask Richard and others if they couldn't all be wrong – scientists have made plenty of mistakes in the past, after all.

Maybe, I'm told, but we've run the models backwards in time and they're pretty good at replicating the past climate.

If we're getting the past right, surely we can have some confidence we're on the right track for the future?

But is that really proof of how accurate the forecasts will be? That depends.

The modellers accept that some forecasts are more robust than others, that the odds of being right about how temperatures may rise are better than those for estimating future rainfall. Plotting which areas may get wetter or drier – and what kind of weather there'll be at which times of the year – is the hardest challenge. It's one thing to say that warmer air can hold more moisture and therefore lead to more rain, quite another to know where that rain may fall or when. But it's the question Wilitie and his family most need answered, and so many others.

A class of neatly dressed twelve-year-olds is sitting on the dried grass of southern Kenya, marshalled into tidy rows, the girls in pink-checked dresses with wide white collars, the boys in pink-checked shirts and black shorts, all waiting patiently for what this sweating visitor from England has to say. The school is called Nado Enterit which means 'red soil' though with the rains a month late the soil is a pale brown. I'm near the town of Kajaro and the people of this part of the country are mainly Maasai, the parents tall, proud, resplendent in bright colours. Tradition dictates that a child must bow his or her head to an elder for them to touch; the shy ones keeping their eyes to the ground, the cheekiest grinning at the strangers and running off laughing.

The teacher tells the class that we've come from England and that we're reporting on the drought.

I say that I've heard that the usual rains haven't come for five years running now and that I'd like to ask what it means for them.

Polite and nervous, the children remain silent.

Then, with the teacher's help, they start to offer a few stories.

One boy, who gives his name as Onesmus, says the drought is frightening and his father has become sad.

A girl says her family lost two of their cattle and that they started to be hungry.

I ask for a show of hands. How many of you have lost cattle in the last year?

In this class of nearly thirty, almost every child throws an arm into the air. I look carefully and count only two that do not.

Cattle are the currency here, the main source of income and of status, a Maasai family's standing judged by the size of a herd. A man without cattle is considered 'dorobo', nothing better than a backward hunter-gatherer. But the ability to sustain animals depends on a good supply of grass and that, in turn, hinges on the rain. And a recent run of dry years has proved devastating. On average, the farmers in this area have lost two-thirds of their cattle in the past few months. At the market, the price for a single animal has collapsed from a typical 20,000 shillings to a few hundred. It's nothing new to have bad years but so many in a row proves overwhelming and forces radical change.

In the fold of a gentle hill, we're taken to meet Karariet and his wife Mary, both dressed in the classic stripes of red and yellow and pink. He's sombre and strong – the archetypal Maasai warrior – and keeps hold of a long stick. She's wearing an elaborate necklace of bright beads and also has a piece of polished bone hanging high at her throat. It's an impressive display for a poor family; producer Nora Dennehy, who's spent time with the family before our filming, says discreetly that she suspects the jewellery has been brought out in our honour.

Theirs is a story of desperation and hope. The last drought killed off twenty of Karariet's cattle leaving him just four. He faced a choice. Give up completely and drift to the slums of Nairobi to search for work; try to rebuild his herd; or stay but approach life differently, adapt to the new conditions. With the encouragement of a charity run by the Anglican Church, Karariet chose the last option, which must have been hard because it must have appeared so undignified.

Instead of minding – and struggling to keep – a large herd, the plan is for the family to cultivate crops. As we talk, Mary continues her weeding, stooped over long rows of cassava, not what a Maasai wife would normally be expected to do. She's convinced it's the right move, telling me that the first harvests have helped keep them going and even pay for some roofing for their hut. He doesn't seem so sure, standing aloof, watching his last emaciated beasts; but maybe he just can't face being filmed on his knees in the earth.

Up the road, not far away in Nairobi, I'm on a different planet. The first conference session has ended, delegates are streaming from the hall, and queues for lunch are forming, lured by the smell of barbecuing meat: climate diplomacy may be slow but it'll never be hungry and there's no shortage of food. Great mounds of beef are sizzling and there's more waiting in the marinades. I watch amazed. No one seems to object. Less than a hundred miles from Mary, Karariet and the children of Nado Enterit primary school – people stricken by seeing their cattle starve – the UN compound is hosting the annual climate negotiations, and one of the official themes is helping Africa to cope with drought. An unofficial theme seems to be helping yourself to beef. I've rarely seen so much on offer, the irony as rich as the aroma of the spices. It tastes rich as well: yes, I take a plate, too. I've never been good at sustaining outrage.

Some 6,000 officials and observers have gathered in Nairobi to continue a process that began with the Earth Summit in Rio in 1992, what's called the UN Framework Convention on Climate Change. A year earlier, the talks were held in Montreal and in 2007 it's Bali. As I watch the suits jostling with their plates, I wonder if anyone realised that climate change would create not so much a single band-wagon as an entire wagon-train, a convoy of well-meaning people flitting from continent to continent, a new mobile industry created in the name of tackling global warming. And I'm following the flock too, duty calls, but I'm uneasy that my plate is just as full and my carbon boot print as heavy.

Montreal's achievement, confirmed after ill-tempered talks which lasted all night, was the breakthrough of agree-ing to keep talking, not in a 'process' – the Americans objected to the word as too laden with commitment – but in a 'dialogue'. So Nairobi one year on is just that, another dialogue. The German environment minister asks the ques-tion many have in mind: what's the use of us all being here? The most tangible advance, the one African countries most need, would be to find ways of raising funds to help them, to make the tiny investments that convince a Maasai warrior to switch from cattle to seeds. But even that proves elusive, money is tight and no one can settle on how to manage it.

In the shade of a marquee, during one of many breaks in proceedings, I meet some of the members of the climate 'community', the world's newest profession. There's an immaculately coiffed blonde Californian representing the state's Republican governor, Arnie Schwarzenegger. I ask about Arnie's recent announcement of radical laws on green-house gases – isn't he now at odds with much of the rest of his party, certainly the president? She sidesteps the question but not before firmly correcting me – it's the 'governor', not

'Arnie'. A senior official from the state government of South Australia has made the long trip. He urges me to report on the drought afflicting the Murray and Darling rivers and sounds apocalyptic about future choices on water – do we let the farmers have it to grow us food or the cities have it so people can wash?

And there's a trader from the newly created carbon markets, his well-tailored suit evidence of the boom in deals involving 'reduction permits' – the system where a factory that cuts pollution, and has the cut measured and verified, can then sell a credit for it. Other companies that can't or won't cut their emissions can buy the credits, in effect buying the right to keep polluting. I'm struggling with this: so, I ask, you're trading in an absence of greenhouse gas? You're buying and selling missing hot air? He explains it again, but my mind wanders back to Nado Enterit and a forest of pink-checked arms rising from a parched playground.

As with anyone reporting a subject that becomes high profile, I start to get my share of hostility. Climate change seems particularly explosive. One letter-writer to a local newspaper, complaining about green taxes, describes me as 'that seething shite'. A friend helpfully shows me a link to an American message board inviting responses to the question, 'Is David Shukman the greatest cause of global warming?' A few viewers regularly send me reports of bad weather – above-average rain in Devon or snowstorms in China – as if to suggest that these events prove that global warming is wrong. Complaints accuse me of doing the government's bidding by hyping climate change to make it easier for ministers to punish motorists.

And several are galvanised into action by the anti-global warming thriller, *State of Fear*, by Michael Crichton, the author of *ER* and *Jurassic Park*. Crichton's output automatically gets global publicity, so this plot, in which environmentalists stage disasters to hide the fact that climate change is a hoax, provokes plenty of comment, some of it aimed at me. Which makes an invitation from the US Embassy in London particularly appealing: would I like to join the author for lunch? He was to die of cancer a few years later but, on that spring day, he's on impressive form.

Six foot seven, like something from the canopy of the rainforest, Crichton is ushered into a room of a dozen British academics and science journalists, bearing a presidential aura. His voice steady like that of an astronaut, his manner gracious, he listens attentively and when he casually mentions that he was lucky that *ER* made him 'financially secure', it's pleasing rather than objectionable. He's not in hostile company – we're not green activists of the sort he targeted – and I'm not alone in having enjoyed parts of the book. There's a great scene where a wealthy and very fashionable eco-campaigner tries to justify her gas-guzzler by pointing out that she makes her maid drive a Prius. Crichton's eye, best displayed in his autobiographical collection *Travels*, is wonderfully sharp. So there are some fans in the room, though most of us have read a lot of the science of climate change and think that, on balance, he's dismissed it a little too readily.

Over our starters, Crichton explains his perspective. He's as environmentally aware as the next man, he says. When his children were babies, he and his wife used cloth nappies instead of throwaway ones. But, more recently, studying the research papers on carbon dioxide and warming has left him unconvinced of the link; the evidence, as defined by the usual rules of science, isn't there. He sets this out with great calm, no fanfare, just stressing the point that the case, in his view, is far from proven.

As the main courses appear, we're encouraged to ask questions. One veteran science correspondent puts it to

Crichton that so many different branches of science are now reporting signs of climate change – the coral analysts, the tree-ring specialists, the atmospheric physicists, the oceanographers – that surely there comes a point where the balance of probability tilts one way?

He's not persuaded. During his training as a doctor, he saw how certain conditions are given priority status, that research and funding are directed towards them, that it becomes a mechanism for securing finance and for advancing one's career. It doesn't mean it's all wrong, just that judgements become skewed.

When it's my turn, I try to engage him on the theme of scientific diligence. I have in mind *Jurassic Park* – a far better book than a film – which praises the role of empirical enquiry, of gathering fact and testing a theory. I describe how I've seen so many researchers go about their work in the Arctic or Africa carefully and methodically. These aren't campaigners, they're genuinely interested in discovering the truth. His answer is similar to the one before: in effect that climate change has become such a guiding principle that researchers can be unwittingly distorting their findings.

What I don't get the chance to say is that scientists may well be labelling their grant applications as climate related in a bid to win funding. But what matters is what they do with the money once they get it. Assuming the measurements aren't faked, the result should be that more fieldwork is carried out and that more evidence – either way – is gathered. Surely we're learning more?

Standing for our coffee, my neck aching as we chat with him, Crichton jokes that he'll agree he's wrong if the global average temperature rises by another 1.5 degrees Celsius by the middle of the century – except that none of us is likely to be alive then to check. And Crichton himself, a model of civilised discourse, rare for a Hollywood contrarian, was only to be around for another three years. Looking back, I wish I'd steered the conversation away from climate change and onto other environmental problems, challenges that are more immediate and obvious. After all, a common theme in his thrillers – whether it's recreating dinosaurs or self-replicating nanomachines – is the idea of science taking a wrong turn, of progress being unpredictable and dangerous. I kick myself for not asking one question in particular: if, as a parent, he was concerned enough about the environment to shun disposable nappies, what other, more tangible, ecological threats might trouble him?

# 7
# There is no away

In the infinite black of a Pacific night our plane descends, the propellers droning, the cabin lights so dim they may as well be off. Through the window there's no view except a pale outline of my own puzzled reflection – we could be anywhere. There's a bump as we land, and in the distance I see a handful of lights, the first after five hours of flying. This is without doubt the darkest place I've ever turned up. Even arriving in the poorest corners of Africa the airports have floodlights, yellow jackets gleaming on the ground crew. But at this one, there's no one to be seen, ours is the only plane, a few red lights mark the runway, a single floodlight shines from a vast hangar, and a jeep's sidelights show where we should head. I take care on the unlit steps of the aircraft leading to the potholed concrete. Even that's dark.

This is Midway Atoll, a speck of coral right in the middle of the Pacific Ocean, two thousand miles from the nearest continent. On a map, amid the sweep of endless blue, it's almost too small to find, a dot beside the International Date Line, the definition of remote. The air is warm and ahead of me are the eerie silhouettes of a few people waiting for us. The scene is dreamlike, made more disorientating by the eleven-hour time difference from London. To one side, what I take to be a tall clump of trees turns out to be a building. The hangar with the one floodlight is far bigger than I'd first thought, its roof so high it's lost in the night.

And there's a smell unusual for an airport: a mild but pervasive stench. Amid the dark I can't see much but I can hear cooing and rustling, flapping and squawking, the island alive with sound. Nothing loud, nothing as sharp as in the jungle, this is the gentle murmuring of a multitude of birds, not threatening but not soothing either – there are too many for that, invisible but unmistakeable.

I enter the hangar, an empty building designed to handle thousands of personnel, still bearing the markings of the US Navy from its massive operations during the Cold War. I'm among a dozen passengers in an echoing monument to American military might. As I look at the stencilled instructions and picture the lines of uniforms waiting for orders, I see this as a film set: the giant metal columns, soaring into the shadows, are post-apocalyptic, and us few survivors live amongst them.

War, birds, darkness. Hitchcock would have loved it.

I need to sleep.

Midway is now run by the US Fish and Wildlife Service and the manager, Barry Christenson, approaches to welcome us. The floodlight is behind him so it's impossible to see him properly. The introductions are friendly but the event is surreal: darkened faces, occasional flashes of light on an eyeball, voices raised amid the hunt for baggage, torches flickering uncertainly, and all the time in the background the subdued but incessant presence of the birds.

Barry explains that it's because of the birds that the landing has to take place at night. Midway is home to the world's largest colony of Laysan Albatrosses and to reduce the risk of hitting one, or disrupting their lives, the US government's weekly charter flight from distant Honolulu is timed to arrive well after sunset. In addition, the lights are kept low because another species of bird, the petrel, is nocturnal and artificial lights confuse them.

Leave a light on and the curtains open, Barry warns, and you'll soon hear a petrel slam into the window. It can kill them.

This is a nature reserve and the overriding message is that the wildlife comes first. We must try to stand back, we're told. But as I'll come to find out, whatever we do here, there's a human menace from far beyond these shores.

We load up a convoy of golf buggies – the main transport on the island – and set off in a cloud of dust. Everyone drives slowly, the track bumpy, the headlights too weak to see much. In a dip up ahead there's a brown bundle. From this distance it could be a bag; in Africa you'd assume it was a pile of elephant dung. But as we get closer, I can see the bundle has feathers. It's an albatross chick, the size of a very big hen, tucked into a dusty hollow, stubby wings twitching as we inch past and disturb its sleep. It's the season when the chicks are growing but can't yet fly and are at their hungriest. Over the next few minutes our buggy will twist and turn to avoid many more.

I ask how many albatrosses live on the island.

At this time of year, says Barry, we have something approaching two million. No wonder the smell never lets up.

We're taken to the old officers' quarters, another flashback to the US Navy in the 1950s, all whitewashed concrete walls and plumbing borrowed from a battleship. I draw the curtains for the sake of the petrels and lie down – we've been travelling for three days. It's like being at sea, isolated and so far from land, except that I can hear a muted warbling and clattering of beaks. The albatrosses nest everywhere including the grassy area just outside my window. The sounds should be soporific – and I want to enjoy them – but I can't settle so reluctantly reach for my earplugs.

Dawn on Midway is very similar to the Amazon at dusk: every creature crazily trumpeting its presence, the din outrageous. The earplugs are useless. I part the curtains and watch an incredible scene. The grass, the tracks, the dusty areas for parking – they're all covered with albatrosses. There are birds snug in potholes, others half-hidden by shrubs, many more perched openly on patches of grass or concrete. As I look around, there isn't a single view – up different roads, between buildings, towards a dune – where there isn't at least one albatross. Barry's remark last night that there are two million of them is suddenly manifest. With just sixty of us on Midway – wildlife officers, support staff, a few visitors – humans are ridiculously outnumbered.

The brown chicks are awake, unable to move but excited. And the adolescent albatrosses – splendidly white – are engaged in elaborate and noisy flirting. In twos or threes, they face each other and perform an energetic and synchronised bobbing of the heads, up and down, so fast and so violent it's almost wrenching. Then, on some secret cue, they'll stop the bobbing and dramatically tuck their beaks under a wing. But not for long: the final act in the play is for the beaks to be lifted vertically – all at the same time – for a loud, long hooting. That over, it starts again.

A path takes me right through all this. A few adult birds eye me as I pass but most are away scouting the ocean for food, their trips ranging over hundreds of miles of ocean and lasting days. The younger birds hardly react as I pass. They have their own agenda and a sleepy-eyed British reporter isn't going to bother them. Sadly, Midway's history hasn't always been so kind. In the late nineteenth century the albatrosses were decimated by raiding parties, boatloads of sailors landing for easy and lucrative plunder: the white of the birds' eggs fetched good money for use as a coating on photographic paper and the long white feathers were in demand to adorn ladies' hats. The colony came close to being wiped out.

Later, the first trans-Pacific cable was laid via Midway – it was the route for the first round-the-world telegraphic message. The construction teams wouldn't have thought twice about clearing away the birds. One worker brought his pet canaries which then escaped and on my way to breakfast I see a descendant hopping on a fence, its yellow body tiny beside the vast albatrosses. In the 1930s, aviation came to Midway, a runway was laid and the albatrosses shifted well back – at such a vital stop, no one could risk a bird strike, particularly given the calibre of the passengers involved. Pan American Airways was using the island to refuel its luxury Clipper flying-boat service between San Francisco and Japan. Only the wealthiest could afford the tickets – Rockefellers, Astors and Vanderbilts were among those making the trip. The hotel built for them has since been demolished but the hangar to house the plane still stands.

A decade later Midway became pivotal in the Second World War, the Americans fearing the Japanese would seize it as a staging post for attacks on the US mainland. Buildings including a concrete command centre still carry the scars of bomb damage from an air raid. Footage filmed during the attack captures an amazing sight: amid the explosions and carnage, the albatrosses stay remarkably calm. The film-maker John Huston, on the island at the time, used the shots as a symbol of defiance against the invaders – the Japanese attack failed and the birds live on. It's possible, given their life span, that some of the albatrosses that survived the bombardment are around today.

Barry shows us the memorials to the war. There are chicks nesting between huge polished guns and at the foot of a long wall etched with the story of an epic struggle. The Battle of Midway, fought offshore, was a turning point. The US Navy, outgunned by the Japanese, somehow surprised the Emperor's fleet and managed to sink three aircraft carriers, a blow that stemmed the Japanese advance. Three miles down, the wrecks still litter the seabed.

Then, in the early days of the Cold War, before spy satellites could keep watch over the Soviet Union, Midway became a key base for surveillance. Relays of patrol planes were kept airborne on a track between Midway and the Arctic to spot the approach of Communist invaders. At one stage the island supported a community of 5,000 people. Faced with the threat of global conflict, nothing could be allowed to halt the operations on the runway: the albatrosses were ruthlessly kept at bay. Known as 'gooney birds' for their clownish appearance and huge webbed feet, the birds were popular but had to be tightly controlled.

Pictures from the time highlight the attractions of Midway as a posting for a serviceman and his family – the beaches and clear waters. In one, a naval officer's wife poses in a fifties one-piece swimsuit. In her hands is a large glass ball, and she's smiling. The balls were used by Japanese fishermen to float their nets and this one, like many, broke free and drifted across the ocean from Asia. Barry has one beside his fireplace. The balls were treasured finds, beautiful objects with a fascinating story. But the fact that they were carried so far was a clue to a problem that was only just emerging back then. If a fisherman's float could make the journey, so could a lot of other things, objects only just being invented.

We set off along one of Midway's blisteringly hot beaches and convention dictates that, as correspondent, I should carry what are called 'the legs', the cameraman's tripod. They vary in weight and design and I'm convinced that this one is the heaviest yet. It comes with a handle which makes life easier until it bangs into my knees; others have a long strap to pass round your neck which I never like because if you stumble, the load swings forward and then back into your hip. So I'm doing what I normally find easiest: a fireman's lift, the tripod balanced over my right shoulder. This is tolerable for a short distance but soon the angular metal components start to grind into the uppermost point of the shoulder bone and I have visions of an X-ray revealing a shockingly deep groove.

The thought lingers as my boots sink into the soft surface of coral sand. Our team is strung out, it's far too hot to talk, and we haven't brought enough water. We started much later than planned so the sun is almost directly above us, making the sand so glaring that I'm squinting even through sunglasses. Being here on holiday, this scene would no doubt seem very different – vivid turquoise sea, deep blue sky, hardly another soul for hundreds of miles. I fantasise about ditching my load to enjoy the place but I know – as with every time I've had this thought over many years – how this will jeopardise the filming; cameraman Rob Magee's look of scorn wouldn't be worth it.

I recall an assignment to Turkey where in similar noonday heat I'd struggled with a tripod up a long flight of steps to the home of the Bosnian ambassador, an elegant, unruffled figure. To my irritation, he'd been waiting for me at the top and had followed my sweating progress very intently. When I'd made it, and he took in my pallid, strained face, he announced that the sight fascinated him because it brought back memories. He'd once worked as a foreign correspondent for Yugoslav state television– and had enjoyed it – until reaching an important personal decision: that tripod-carrying wasn't really suitable for a man beyond the age of forty. As I stumble over the baked sand, I'm about to turn fifty.

So the trudging continues, head bowed, and because I'm looking down to avoid the sun I unwittingly study the beach more closely. The sand, which had appeared clean, is in fact laden with rubbish. There are lengths of rope, shampoo bottles, the casings for computers, industrial-scale plastic sheeting, fragments of artificial white and blue. In one spot there's even a torn net from a tennis court. In itself, this isn't unusual: I've seen this kind of mess on beaches all over the world, and often worse – condoms, sanitary towels and turds are all too common. But this place is so remote it should surely be pristine.

Most numerous are disposable cigarette lighters. Two or three inches long, they mostly come in blue, orange, red and yellow. Mauve and green seem rarer. A few have markings on them, phone numbers or labels in Japanese and Cantonese, occasionally English. One bears the name, 'Happy Garden', a motel in Taiwan. I bend down every few paces, one hand steadying the tripod, the other grabbing a handful of lighters. I stuff them in my pockets until I feel them leaking seawater into my trousers which would normally be embarrassing but I'm too hot to mind. And after a short stretch, I stop to do a count: I've gathered sixty-two. If I brought a sack, I could fill it with cigarette lighters in under an hour. There must be thousands.

I turn to Matt Brown, a tall, genial figure from the US Fish and Wildlife Service.

He simply shrugs at my collection: it's normal, sixty-two in a few minutes, no big deal.

And at the top of the beach, he shows me something more shocking.

An albatross lying on its back, dead, its wings splayed. With a white belly, it's one of the adolescents. Fully grown, its wingspan would have reached a magnificent two metres across, what should have been one of the greatest spectacles soaring above the ocean. But this one never made it.

Matt explains that at this time of year the parents, constantly trying to feed their young, often mistake rubbish for food. They see plastic items, on the beach or out at sea, and pick them up. In particular, to their eyes, the cigarette light-ers look remarkably similar to the albatrosses' staple food, squid. As it happens, the body of a squid is lying nearby, for some reason unwanted. A dark pink, the size of a small cigar, it is virtually identical to one of my leaking lighters.

Matt crouches down beside the bird and uses his pen-knife to gently prise open its belly. It's mostly decomposed, the feathers masking a hollow skeleton and there's hardly any smell. Any insects have long since devoured the flesh and moved on. So Matt finds it easy to part the rib cage. It takes me a few moments to comprehend what I'm seeing: inside the cavity there's a yellow cigarette lighter, along with a worn orange toothbrush, and a fragment of red plastic that looks like it came from a broken cup. A snapshot of everyday modern life turned deadly.

Matt tells me what must have happened:

The albatross chick was fed the plastic objects because the parents assumed they were food. The plastic took up space in its stomach leaving less room for real food just when it most needed to grow. Gradually the bird, denied enough sustenance, became malnourished. Eventually, a failure to thrive will have become an inability to survive.

How many albatrosses, I ask Matt, will have eaten plastic?

Oh, every one of them. Every single one, he says with emphasis. The ones that make it are the ones that don't eat too much of it.

How many die of it?

Who knows, maybe hundreds every year, he says.

The birds are protected by the legal status of a nature reserve but can't be defended from eating our waste which, by a quirk of geography, is delivered to them from thou-sands of miles away.

Midway, seemingly isolated, in fact lies in the path of a great oceanic flow of rubbish. Rather like Greenland being the innocent dump for an airborne stream of industrial soot, the island lies in one of the world's largest currents, a circular river of seawater known as the North Pacific Gyre. Acting like a whirlpool, it sweeps down from Alaska, past the urban sprawl of California, right across towards the great cities of Japan, up past the industrial heartlands of coastal China and round to Alaska again. Rubbish dumped in rivers or storm drains, caught in floods and winds, thrown from cars and ships, finds its way into the ocean and what's now known as the Great Garbage Patch.

The waste isn't easily seen because most of it floats just below the surface. But I talk to the skipper of a yacht which has docked at Midway for repairs and he tells me how he sailed through nothing but plastic for an entire day. And Matt says that however much they try to clean up, the waves and the birds bring tons of fresh material every week.

If people don't take it away, he warns, it'll still be here when my grandchildren walk these beaches.

Some estimates say the garbage patch covers an area the size of Texas and that it contains millions of tons of waste. Most of what reaches Midway is plastic. Durable, light and versatile, it's one of the most useful inventions of the modern age. Just when the officer's wife was posing with her Japanese glass float, plastic was starting to become commonplace. In its many forms, it was a revolutionary substance ideally suited for the boom in consumer products of the last few decades – for everything from wrapping processed food to housing electronics to producing cheap toys. The only downside, perversely, is one of its qualities, durability – what Matt describes as tenaciousness, an ability to last decades or, probably, centuries.

As an experiment, we ask for a dozen volunteers to carry out a timed clean-up – to see how much rubbish they can collect in thirty minutes. We mark out a section of beach that seems fairly typical – in fact at first sight it looks relatively clean. Rob Magee sets up several cameras to catch different angles and, when everyone's ready, I check my watch and ask them to start. Within a few minutes, enough bottles and cigarette lighters and plastic sheeting are gathered to cover the area of a picnic rug. Soon, big plastic crates and fuel cans are added, along with netting and lengths of pipe. The collection is now rising, with plastic containers and the casings for televisions helping to create a mound, an ugly jumble of familiar objects. When the time is up, there's a heap of waste about the size of a small car. It's far more than I'd expected, a peek into the darker side of our throwaway culture.

**A toy story:** I spot this plastic figure, a couple of inches tall, amid a mound of debris on a beach. There's no way of knowing how it's reached Midway but the journey must have covered thousands of miles. *Mark Georgiou*

I take a closer look. There seem to be hundreds of tiny shampoo bottles – the sort you're given in hotels, to be used once and chucked out. There are the plastic hoops for holding together packs of cans, also used once then ripped off. And down at the bottom, half-lost in the sand, is a little toy robot, about two inches tall, wearing futuristic armour and a plumed Roman helmet. Bleached and stained, there's dirt ingrained in the scratches cut into the plastic. As I pick it up, it feels like a scene from the movie *Toy Story* – small creature, lost from home, swept to sea, found on desert island.

When I write my blog that evening, I ask Mark to post a picture of the robot toy and call on readers to let me know if any of them recognise it. Within hours, I start getting replies, as the story of Midway and its plastic bombardment catches the imagination. Many readers are moved to volunteer to help clean the island, to help fight 'the new Battle of Midway'. Others suggest schemes for using trawlers to 'fish' the rubbish from the ocean. And the toy? It's Gigantor, says one contributor, a robot from a cartoon popular in Japan and the US in the 1960s. No, says another, it's the Iron Giant from the story by Ted Hughes.

What no one can explain is its journey. Did a child let it slip from a cruise ship? Was it a free gift that came unwanted with a fast-food meal taken on a boat, the packaging and the toy itself then chucked overboard? Was it thrown into a rubbish sack which then blew into a drain, where it was ripped open, its contents washing into a river and then out to the ocean? Or, more likely, did it end up in some city's waste being shipped out to sea in stinking barges and dumped?

And then I wonder how long the little figure was afloat. It's an incredible thought, but did it make a complete circuit of the Great Gyre, bobbing past Asia, across to America and then back again? Might it have been travelling for years? Given its size, it was most likely spotted by one of the gliding, magisterial albatrosses, plucked from the waves, swallowed, and carried back to Midway where it was regurgitated into the gaping beak of a chick. A cheap bauble with the power to kill.

It's the destructive potential of ordinary objects that's so shocking – things that are standard features of modern life. We get called to a patch of grass near a jetty. Someone has spotted an albatross chick in trouble: there's a bright green plastic hook jutting from the side of its beak and the bird apparently can't get it out. Up close, wildlife specialist John Klavitter points out that the hook has been there so long that the edge of the beak is deformed. This will affect its ability to eat.

He asks me to hold the bird still. With one hand he steadies its head and with the other he gently grips the hook and pulls. John's action is very cautious – he's worried that something may be attached to the hook and damage the chick's throat as it's removed. Very gingerly, he keeps tugging and eventually the hook is out and with it, dangling from its end, a small piece of plastic netting, maybe four or five inches long.

As with my first sight of the inside of a dead albatross, I can't quite work out what I'm looking at – what is this little net attached to a hook? John puzzles over it as well, and then comes up with an answer: we've both seen lots of nets like this before.

It's the kind of thing used in supermarkets to hold a few tangerines or avocado pears or nuts, the hook allowing the assistants to hang the item in a display. Once bought, and the contents consumed, the net would have been discarded. Somehow it ended up here, stuck in an albatross chick's beak – a seemingly innocuous element of consumer culture, useful in itself and convenient, but turning dangerous.

I ask John what difference the net and its hook made to the chick.

They weren't killing it quickly, he says. But they were probably getting in the way of proper feeding.

What does that mean?

That the chick was starving slowly to death. John is emphatic about that.

**Death by plastic:** a hook is stuck in the jaws of an albatross chick on Midway Atoll in the Pacific. The island is bombarded by waste circulating in a giant 'garbage patch' fouling the ocean.                                                                    *Mark Georgiou*

I try to piece this together. A flimsy piece of net attached to a plastic hook, designed to be used just once, serves its purpose and is then thrown away. But surely something is going badly wrong if that perfectly ordinary sequence of events nearly kills a rare bird? It dawns on me that it's the language that's misleading, the phrase 'throwing away' doesn't convey what's really involved. The act of throwing means we get something away from ourselves. In the case of throwing away rubbish, this is a relief, it's even satisfying – we've got rid of something unwanted and feel cleaner as a result. But the word 'away' implies that where the rubbish is going is some abstract space of no consequence when in fact 'away' has to be a physical location. 'Away' is always another place – a dump or an ocean. The stuff has to end up somewhere. Like Midway.

Walking among the birds, I picture how each one is involved in a lottery of our making: they're all eating our waste but some will get more of it than others and die. And

I'm struck by how obviously short-sighted we're being. Not through any kind of maliciousness, but through ignorance of the consequences, the casual act of dropping something unwanted into a bin can lead to a needless death on a remote shore, and on a scale that is spoiling an entire ocean.

All my career I've worked hard to remain detached from stories –partly out of an instinctive wish to remain impartial, partly out of self-protection. I have been shocked before, but usually by some traumatic event or senseless cruelty – the wounding of two children we'd befriended in Bosnia, the dignity of a boy in Sierra Leone mutilated by a bullet that killed his mother. But here I am moved for the first time by a process, the needless destruction of the environment. The thought of the toothbrushes and the cigarette lighters circulating in their millions around the Pacific leaves me stunned at the sheer stupidity of a society in which so much is used so briefly and then junked so harmfully.

I talk to Matt about the scale of this problem.

It's going to last centuries, he says, if not millennia. And we keep adding to it every day.


A launch picks up speed as we cross the lagoon, the colours glowing, the breeze welcome. An atoll is a circular coral reef and Midway's is spectacular, a vast marine lake. In the bow wave, I see a flash of grey. It's a dolphin, keeping just ahead of us. The last time I saw a great mammal from a boat there was the explosion of a Norwegian harpoon and the sea turned red. By contrast this one is safe, protected by law, and seems to want human company. Others join it and soon they're surging forward, rising above the water and leaping into the air, twisting. These are spinning dolphins and it's impossible not to laugh at their play.

At the edge of the lagoon, we moor just inside the reef. The rollers of the open ocean are crashing onto its outer edge but it's calm where we climb onto the rock. The coral is like a bed of nails and without boots and gloves every slip or stumble would draw blood. Around us there are great lengths of net and rope snagged in the fissures, twists of plastic fibre jammed tight onto the coral spikes. I try lifting one clear but it's stuck so fast that it's almost embedded. As I look along the reef, I see more clumps of blue and yellow rope. And underwater it's the same. Rob has a camera in a waterproof housing and films a menacing swirl, the plastic waving in the current of the incoming tide. The lagoon should be a sanctuary from the ocean but instead has become treacherous.

John Klavitter explains that, all too often, dolphins, seals and turtles become entangled in the plastic and drown. Last year alone he freed four seals from ropes and nets, a small victory in a losing war. He shows us how he tries to keep the plastic at bay: there isn't much he can do except cut the ropes and haul them away. He hands me a serrated knife to join the work and I find that it saws through easily enough. The hard task is then manhandling the sodden bundles of material into the boat – they're incredibly heavy.

There's another problem as well. Sawing through the ropes is rather like slicing a crusty loaf of bread – there's never a completely clean cut. With a loaf, crumbs are scattered. With the rope, hundreds of tiny fibres are released, little hairs of plastic that catch on the wind and slip into the sea. Initially, I try to grab them but there are too many and they're blown beyond my reach too fast for me to catch. In doing one good act, by clearing plastic from the reef, I may be creating a bigger problem – the plastic you can't see may be more dangerous.

Half a world away, in a lab of the University of Plymouth in south-west England, a researcher in a white coat is peering into glass jars and metal trays filled with sand. At least, it looks like sand. Richard Thompson has collected typical samples of whatever is lying around at the high-tide mark of several local beaches and they turn out to be a mix of ingredients, some expected, others not. Together with the sand, there are fragments of seaweed and leaves and wood – all perfectly healthy and natural. But about a quarter of each sample is made up of tiny particles of plastic. Without anyone realising, the beaches have become partly artificial.

The largest of the particles are known as 'mermaid's tears', little balls of plastic the size of a grain of rice which are the raw material for many plastics industries. The grains are shipped around the world and occasionally spill out, either at ports or during the journey. Particles of this kind have been found on the shores of every continent including Antarctica – like the toy robot and the cigarette lighters on Midway, material gets caught in the currents and can travel globally.

But the mermaid's tears are still large enough to be visible to the naked eye. What concerns Richard Thompson and others is the plastic that's even smaller – the result of bags and bottles and nets gradually being broken down into ever tinier fragments. And his studies have shown how the ocean's smallest creatures do what Midway's albatrosses do – they mistake plastic for food. Sandhoppers – like fleas – have been dissected and found to have it in their bellies. In a tank in Richard's lab, I watch him scattering powdered plastic over the water – he's recorded how the barnacles growing inside will ingest the particles. This way, plastic is entering the lowest elements of the food chain.

That would be bad enough but, in an additional twist, each particle of plastic may be toxic as well. Richard explains that because plastic is produced from oil, its chemistry means that it can never mix with water. By contrast, the plastic will bond with other products derived from oil – including any contaminants, like the insecticide DDT, which are also adrift in the ocean. The effect is that any piece of plastic, particularly the billions of microscopic fragments, will attract the toxins – like magnets luring iron filings. The effect, as Richard puts it, is that you can get concentrations of contaminants several thousand times greater than in the surrounding water.

And if those poison pills are swallowed, the chances are that once in the guts of marine organisms the toxins will be released. And if those creatures are eaten by something bigger, the toxins will be passed on. Scientists call this 'bio-accumulation', contaminants becoming more concentrated as they pass higher up the food chain. What's conjured up is a nightmare image of an infinite number of plastic fragments – bits of carrier bags, fibres from the ropes I cut, tiny flakes from the toy robot – all drifting beyond our control, gathering the worst poisons, and gradually infecting everything that lives in the ocean.

On a dune, busy with albatrosses, we set up for a series of live broadcasts using Midway's satellite link to the Internet. It's a very cheap form of broadcasting but it's totally dependent on the speed of the line and Rob's tests have shown this one to be slow, mainly because it's shared by everyone on the island. He's already managed to send our video reports – every minute of video taking about half an hour to get through – but as our bulletins approach, editors keep checking whether we can in addition 'go live' as promised. Mark realises that there's no alternative but to ask the manager Barry Christenson a massive favour: asking all

Midway's Internet users to switch off at our key times to give us the largest possible bandwidth on the line.

To our relief, he agrees and at 10.55 am – 9.55 pm in London, just before the *News at Ten* – a message goes out by walkie-talkie announcing that the BBC is about to go on air. Rob is staring intently at the screen of his laptop, watching for the indications that the connection has been made, and for what feels like an age nothing happens. Mark is on a hand-held satellite phone to London waiting to confirm that the link is successfully carrying sound and vision; as the minutes pass, his pacing becomes more rapid. I'd like to pace too but I've got to stay in position in case the link comes to life and I find myself on air so instead I just watch the twitching of an albatross chick which can't pace either.

Our slot in the bulletin is fast approaching. Rob, trying to establish the connection, is looking frustrated, Mark has picked up some speed, and I'm distracted because the chick is now looking back me. The sound in my earpiece is a distant echo and I wonder if this will go down as one of several attempted broadcasts that failed – we are in the middle of the world's largest ocean after all. But suddenly Mark says they can hear me and see me. That's good but I can't hear them, and unless I can I won't know when to speak. Mark confers with Rob and with London. The sound in my earpiece is now more like the distant roar you hear when you listen to a seashell. The albatross chick is still watching me. I look at my watch. In the studio, eleven hours ahead, our moment can only be seconds away. The line is holding so it's agreed that Mark will keep listening to the bulletin over his satellite phone and will drop his arm as a signal for me to say my piece. Rob dashes from the laptop to his camera. The remote roar continues, Mark's arm drops and another live broadcast from somewhere improbable gets under way.

I've rarely known a response like it. The birds, the plastic, the poisons, the helpless island – all combine to trigger reactions at once fascinated and appalled. Not since the Gulf War of 1991 have I had so many people get in touch. Back then, amazement at the new weaponry mingled with horror at the casualties and the letters reflected some very volatile emotions about the news and about those reporting it which, in a few cases, involved rather intimate declarations about me. This time, the responses are passionate but less personal.

The director of one of the television studios comes across the line before one broadcast to tell me that her nephew wants to help clean Midway's beaches.

A radio presenter, listening to an explanation of the fragments of plastic accumulating toxins, blurts out that hearing this is really depressing.

Our website receives hundreds of comments and questions.

David from Inverness in Scotland wonders if the oil companies, whose products led to the plastic, should be made responsible. I respond that a study is under way to see if the plastic waste can yield a chemical fingerprint to identify where it was made.

Jack in North Palm Beach, Florida asks what happens to the collected plastic. Matt Brown, in an online reply, says it's shipped to Hawaii to be incinerated or buried.

Lesley from Northumberland in England wants to join the clean-up. The US Fish and Wildlife Service has had more offers than it can handle and Matt tells her that it's better to start where she lives – a beach, park or school ground. Picking up the rubbish locally, he says, will stop it from entering the marine ecosystem and reaching places like Midway.


The people on Midway have gone out of their way to help us report on the island's plight so as we leave we present them with a gift. Two years before our visit a BBC camerawoman, Rebecca Hosking, came to the island to make a documentary and she was so moved by the plastic problem that she began a campaign to ban plastic bags in her home town of Modbury in Devon. It was a movement that gathered momentum across the country with Modbury's shoppers leading the way in using cloth bags instead. While seeing Rebecca before our trip, we picked up one of the bags and Barry and Matt, receiving it, seem delighted that the Midway's battle is recognised so far away.

One of the women has a gift for me. Hearing that I have a daughter – Kitty, then aged thirteen – she presents me with a necklace of giant brightly coloured plastic beads, all of them found on Midway's beaches. It's the ultimate in eco-chic.


Our journey home takes us through Honolulu where a missed connection means we spend the night in a crowded airport hotel. At breakfast, I join a queue pressing towards a buffet table. At one end of it, there are trays and, beside them, piles of bowls, plates and cups. I pick up one of each: they're all made of plastic. I take some cereal, bread and coffee. When I find a table, I realise that I haven't collected any cutlery – I'd missed it back at the buffet where there's a box containing sets of knives, forks and spoons. They're all made of plastic too and they're also wrapped in plastic. I sit down and open a little container of milk – plastic. The tiny pot of jam – also plastic. So is the holder for the butter. As I break open all this packaging, a small mound of waste material accumulates beside me, a faint echo of the mound of rubbish our volunteers collected on Midway in that timed half-hour, a tiny sample of what's swirling out in the ocean.

I eat and tidy up. Looking around, I see that we're expected to clear up when we're finished. Near the door, on a scale you only find in America, are some huge bins. I choose one, push open the flap but find that it's jammed: it's already full. I move to another bin and slide in the items that I used for a few brief minutes: the cup, bowl, plate, knife, fork, spoon, milk container, jam pot and butter packet, plus the mass of wrapping. I take my time over the process, checking exactly what I'm getting rid of, but I sense a restlessness behind me: I turn and see that there are people impatiently waiting with even bigger loads than mine, towering heaps of waste. I wonder how it can be that we've got into a state where it's acceptable to use so many things once and then 'throw them away'.

I approach one of the staff, who's opened a bin to haul out a bulging sack of rubbish. It's a very busy morning for him but he pauses and tries to be helpful. I ask where the waste will go. He looks at me strangely – maybe with the din he hasn't heard me properly or finds my accent impenetrable. But then I realise that no one has ever asked him this question before and he's never needed to know the answer. He just shrugs. I want to ask if anything gets recycled but realise there's no point: the giant bins offer no chance for me or anyone else to sort the waste, to separate the scraps from the plastic, or the plastic from the paper.

After the shock of Midway's plastic invasion and the drama of broadcasting live from somewhere so remote, I've woken this morning feeling stale, even a bit low. Now, as I watch the waiter manhandling the rubbish sack through the packed dining hall, past the line of people waiting to load up at the all-plastic buffet, I realise I'm experiencing a novel emotion in my career as a journalist, one already familiar to less inhibited colleagues, a feeling that catches me by surprise: anger.

# 8

# A toxic toast

There's a tapping at the windows, a scratching on the door. I'm in a farmhouse at the end of an unlit track and gusts of wind are catching the vines growing up the walls. It's a blustery winter's evening, exactly the right conditions for a visit to Transylvania, the region of Romania infamous as the blood-drenched domain of the mysterious Count Dracula. Across a small courtyard there's a barn with a few cows and sheep. It's poor here and there's a history of violence so the property, like its neighbours, is guarded by a set of sturdy, ornately carved gates.

Our hosts are friendly but nervous. Geza Matefi, a stocky figure with a sad face, aged well beyond his years, pours me a glass of his home-made wine. His wife Berta, tidying the table, keeps checking if I want anything to eat. I'm hungry but decline: in this sparse kitchen, they don't seem to have much for themselves. And the wine is faintly off-putting, smelling of cider, as home-made wines often seem to, reminding me of my only attempt to make some, as a teenager using blackcurrants, the outcome undrinkable. This liquid is similarly murky and I dread having to taste it. Cameraman Rob Magee, with me again, is also given a glass and smiles politely but keeps himself busy with his lights, setting up for an interview.

We're visiting the family to hear their story, a tale of two horses. The animals had belonged to Berta's father, now dead, and had been kept at the farm. They were his great joy and a source of pride for them all, not every family in the area being able to afford one horse, let alone two.

But one day someone noticed that the animals had lost their normal liveliness and were moving slowly.

It's like they were drugged, Berta says, they became really sluggish.

A vet was called. But he couldn't understand what was wrong. The horses did not seem to have any known illness so he had no idea how to help and left.

I ask if there was any outward sign of injury.

Apparently not, but the horses continued to decline, their movements becoming more stumbling. A video filmed at the time shows the animals looking well-fed but unable to coordinate properly, their front legs jerking and the knees buckling.

And the next day they died.

At this point a hush descends over the table. Berta looks as if she might cry, Geza is slumped forward in despair and Berta's mother, head covered in a black veil, just stares at me.

The horses were not only precious but were also a symbol of status within the community.

After a pause, Berta embarks on a long explanation of how they responded, how the family decided to fight for compensation.

Compensation? I don't understand. There was no wounding, no evidence of this being the result of a malicious neighbour, no obvious trail leading to a perpetrator. Who did they expect to win compensation from?

Berta turns to Geza and they exchange a few words. I've clearly stumbled into sensitive territory. To my consternation, Geza gets up and leaves the room but he returns a few minutes later with several large boxes of documents: they've decided to explain things properly and start handing my translator a stream of letters and official reports. What emerges is that this family's sadness runs much deeper than the loss of two beloved animals. Geza and Berta feel that they themselves are victims of whatever cursed the horses, their lives blighted by a modern and invisible version of a horror story.

Transylvania is best-known as the land of the vampire, the result of a mangling of history, Victorian Gothic novels and Hollywood movies, a marketing dream now underpinned by an industry of merchandise. But there's another far less exotic reason for the region's notoriety, one that's brought me here: the impact of the heavy industries transplanted into this land of farms and valleys. Just a mile away from the Matefi farmhouse is the ugly sprawl of Copsa Mica which in the late 1980s attracted the title of 'most polluted town in Europe'. A factory had for decades produced what's known as 'carbon black', a black dye for shoe polish, a process that constantly emitted soot. Children's faces, buildings and trees all turned black. Washing left hanging on a line was filthy in minutes. There was so much soot in the air outside the factory that even the white sheep became dark. Pictures taken at the time captured the defeated eyes, rimmed in black, of desperate people who needed to live here for the work but knew that it was ruining their health. In satellite photographs, the valley stood out as a long, malevolent stain.

It was a scourge that caught the media's attention in the immediate aftermath of the overthrow of Communist rule in Romania in 1989 – it seemed to confirm one of the most brutal aspects of life under a vicious regime. The ensuing publicity triggered a series of international inquiries and soon the pressure to close the plant became overwhelming.

In the new Europe, no longer divided by the Iron Curtain, pollution this outrageous simply could not be tolerated. The clouds of black were stopped and within a few years new satellite pictures revealed a scene transformed, the valley scrubbed clean, an environmental success story. Naturally, the flow of media teams dried up.

The carbon-black factory with its belching chimneys had been overtly damaging, a clear-cut case of pollution not unlike the plastic waste drifting towards Midway. The evidence in both places was tangible and overwhelming and, as I've come to see, the most obvious environmental threats are the ones that are most likely to attract attention.

But what about threats you can't see? A closer look at Copsa Mica revealed that it always had two factories, the much-filmed one that spewed out soot and another one beside it which went unnoticed. This second plant, a sprawling tangle of buildings and pipes, was ignored because it was not releasing anything visibly unpleasant. From this factory's chimneys came puffs of white and pale grey that did nothing to change the colour of the sheep or anyone's washing, so offered little for anyone to film or care about. And it's still going.

The first sight of Copsa Mica is eerie: after following the gentle curves of a pretty valley, past quaint villages and wooded hills, we turn a final bend to confront what looks like a monstrous steam engine, a dark machine of vast towers and halls. There's none of the soot of the old days but within minutes of getting out of the car I feel the air stinging my eyes and there's a smell that's slightly sweet. After a little longer I realise that there's another sensation as well – the air actually tastes sweet, a bit like cheap chewing gum.

The town feels like a clumsy copy of the worst of the old Soviet Union. There are rows of concrete apartment blocks, the shops have pitifully little on offer, a few elderly men have horribly puffed faces. Two young mothers with babies in pushchairs have their peroxide hair piled high. A teenage boy saunters past in torn tracksuit trousers and ancient trainers. The road is potholed, the pavements are pitted and a railway scythes right through the middle of it all, a reminder that everything revolves around the industry here, that the place would be even poorer without it.

In the distance are the vast buildings of the old carbon factory, the one that made Copsa Mica notorious, its red-brick walls still black. But closer at hand, towering over the battered heart of the town itself, are the chimneys of the 'other' factory, the one still at work, the one that rarely got mentioned. It's a plant that processes metals, the ugly but essential stage of transforming ores into useful materials. And this one handles the so-called heavy metals, the most hazardous: lead, zinc and cadmium, products needed for car manufacturing and electrical machinery. Since it was set up in the 1940s, the plant has employed thousands of people and even now about 1,000 people work there.

But while the dye factory was darkening the valley, what was the metals plant doing? Initially, it proves surprisingly hard to find out. The major investigations ran out of steam once the belching of the soot had stopped. But I track down a small group of environmental scientists based at the university in the nearest city, Sibiu. Led by a youthful professor, Doru Banaduc, they've carried out a chemical survey of the landscape. We meet beside the river that runs through the town and hear about the findings.

In samples of soil around Copsa Mica they found lead concentrations not just slightly above the level recommended by the World Health Organisation but 92 times the limit. An analysis of the vegetation showed a lead content 22 times the norm. And an investigation into the digestive tracts of snails revealed lead 38 times higher than the permitted concentration – and a cadmium level even higher, running at 200 times the safe limit.

But is there any chance this could be natural, a quirk of geology?

No way, says Professor Banaduc. Measurements were made in other valleys in the region and they show nothing like this contamination, the sampling in fact confirming that every other place was well within health limits.

So what does this mean for Copsa Mica?

The professor is emphatic: the toxins are now firmly embedded in the food chain, a legacy of 60 years of pollution from the metals plant. The innocent-looking smoke rising from the chimneys contains traces of the poisons that drifted in the air and then settled downwind over the plants, animals and people.

Given what he knows about the heavy metals, I ask light-heartedly whether he would ever consider living in Copsa Mica.

Never, it's a really dangerous place. He isn't joking.

Everything you touch here, he says, everything you eat, you drink, you breathe, brings you serious health problems.

My first reaction is entirely selfish: thank God we're not staying here – our hotel is at least fifteen miles away.

I ask what's known about the human impacts.

The largest health research project, studying children aged two to twelve years old, recorded above average levels of lead and suggested that their development was being slowed as a result.

And the most recent study produced an appalling conclusion: that on average the lifespan of anyone living in Copsa Mica would be nine years shorter than the national average. Nine years – it's almost too much to be credible.

So we visit the nearest hospital to see if this is indeed plausible. Breaking off from her rounds is a doctor, Marina

Maries, who initially greets us with suspicion. She's sharply made-up with heavy eyeliner which, against her pale skin, makes her look severe, even aggressive.

She demands to know if we are going to distort the facts, like so many other journalists?

Well, no, I reply, taken aback. I assume I've entered a time warp into old Communist times and that she will assert that there's no problem with the pollution at all.

But then Marina leads us at high speed down a poorly lit corridor into one of the wards, a gloomy room with a handful of men. She marches up to one of them, a tired figure in a yellow Romania football shirt, and without much warning reaches towards his mouth with both her hands to pull back his gums.

It's a shocking sight – first because it's all happened so rapidly that I'm not clear what she's doing, and second, because the man's teeth are a mess, some missing and the rest yellow.

I have to ask my translator to slow her down so she can tell me what I'm meant to learn from this grim spectacle.

She looks at me as if I'm dim, but then explains.

The man is a senior supervisor at the metals processing factory in Copsa Mica and Marina introduces him as Andre Pirvu – he nods at the mention of his name – and he's in hospital because he's been poisoned by lead. She knows that because, among other things, if we look closely behind his upper lip at his gums we'll see a thin blue line.

Having heard all this, the patient himself pulls back his lip and we all lean forward. Frankly, seeing anything in a stained mouth in a dark ward is not easy but with a bit of help I do see a blue smudge just above his teeth – it's apparently the most overt symptom of lead poisoning.

But it occurs to me that even while brushing your teeth you might not notice the colour of the upper gums. So I ask Andre Pirvu how he knew he'd been poisoned.

The stomach pains, he says.

What are they like?

They're the worst of it, I always hate them.

What do you mean 'always'? Have you had them before?

Sure, he says. This is my fifth time in the hospital.

I'm stunned. In this crowded ward, this man is telling me that he's been repeatedly poisoned by the lead.

How on earth can you keep going back into that factory?

Well, he shrugs, the pains go away, and so does the dark line in my mouth. It's no big deal.

I'm appalled. In the doctor's office I have a chance to ask what she makes of this.

Is the patient right to say that the symptoms pass and that the lead isn't that poisonous?

Yes, she says, but she also believes that repeated poisoning must have a debilitating effect on the body, that it must undermine your overall health and in the end shorten your life.

So why does this patient play it all down?

Obvious: he's worried about offending his bosses and losing his job so of course he's going to say everything's fine.

How many cases do you get?

Last year alone: eighty.

This figure, though high, is only a snapshot and I realise I need an overall sense of the scale of the human impact. So my translator, Mihai Radu, arranges a meeting at the regional health ministry and, although Romania has now been accepted into the European Union, I sense, as with my first impression of the doctor, that I'm stepping back into the country's closed past. A large room is filled with tense officials. They admit Copsa Mica is a problem, a big one, but they pass the buck and stall and obfuscate when I press them to produce the records for the number of pollution-related health cases. Given the importance of this problem, they must have a figure, but several hours pass fruitlessly. Tea is brought, phone calls are made, photocopies are ordered of papers that prove to be irrelevant. In the end I conclude that the legacy of totalitarianism has combined with shyness, as members of the new Europe, about sharing dirty secrets, so I leave empty-handed.

Around their kitchen table, Geza and Berta are not surprised to hear this; their own story is one of a far harder fight. When their horses died, they managed to call in the national veterinary service and its researchers investigated every possible factor – how the animals were kept, what they were fed, where they were watered. Guided to the key conclusions in their report, Mihai reads out a long list of hard results, a chilling experience because this amounts to hard, official evidence, and seems to back up what the professor and his team found in the fields and streams nearby.

I make sure I note down the findings carefully:

The hay that the horses had been fed contained ten times more than the recommended limit for lead – and fifteen times the limit for cadmium.

The horses' livers had six times more lead than the norm and 70 times more cadmium.

Their kidneys had lead four times above the safety limit and cadmium 40 times above it.

Even the bones were contaminated with ten times the recommended level of lead and the same for cadmium.

I ask what happened after this report was produced.

Geza and Berta smile: they won some compensation. After a lengthy struggle, the metals factory did not accept liability but did agree to make a payment nevertheless.

But their relief was fleeting. Both of them used to work at the factory but when the plant went through a contraction Berta found herself among those laid off.

Maybe that was coincidence?

Maybe, says Geza, but he was then reassigned from his role as an electrical mechanic to join the ranks of the cleaning staff. He felt he couldn't stay – he was accused of a lack of loyalty. He's since found it hard to get another job, saying he's weakened by lead poisoning and other companies aren't willing to take him on. So they're both out of work.

I ask how they keep going. Berta explains that they simply can't afford to buy any food so they grow what they can.

**Your good health:** a glass of home-made wine stands untouched at the home of the Matefi family in Copsa Mica, Romania. I picture the pollutants that the grapes must have absorbed but don't want to appear unfriendly. *BBC*

Is that the same land, I wonder, that the poisoned hay was grown on?

Yes.

Are your chickens scratching over the same ground that the two horses used to graze on?

Yes.

Do you feed any home-grown food to your children?

Of course. But what can we do? We can't afford to do anything else. Berta's voice has dropped.

I've seen a mound of potatoes in their barn and think of the soil they were grown in.

I glance at my home-made wine. I don't need to ask the next question.

That the toxins have entered the food chain is beyond doubt. The poisoning of the horses is just one example of many we hear – horses dying, lambs born deformed, sometimes compensation paid, sometimes not.


Our next task is to approach the factory itself. Not long before our visit it was bought by a Greek company which does not exactly welcome media attention. We've been told over the phone by a spokesman that new investment is bringing the pollution down to European standards and that it's deeply unfair for the new owners to be blamed for past mistakes made during the long years of state ownership. The spokesman insists that the company will not give us an interview or allow a visit but on the morning we're due to leave there's a last-minute change of heart.

At the main gate, with the chimneys above us, we're allowed into a security hut. After twenty minutes we're guided under heavy escort to a waiting room. The security men treat us as if we are the toxic ones.

After half an hour, our visit takes an even more surreal turn. An executive bursts in. Her black hair is loose and her eyes are wide with anger. She's screaming in a mixture of Romanian and Greek, with the odd burst of English, apparently furious with some BBC radio coverage several months ago that I wasn't aware of. I lose track of how long this venting lasts. A child would have found her decibel level upsetting but as I can't understand any of her diatribe, including the English bits, I find myself either studying the contortions of her crudely applied lipstick or allowing my mind to wander off altogether. Eventually she dries up, spent, and leaves.

An hour after that, another official arrives. We wonder if he'll explode too but instead he leads us to a boardroom. Maybe at last we'll be getting our interview. But nothing here is straightforward. It turns out there are half a dozen people waiting for us on one side of a huge table – this looks like being an inquisition – and, in the corner, a man in overalls is poised with a video camera pointing in our direction to record every move. I toy with some jibe about whether they'd ever actually heard of the phrase 'media relations' but have a much better idea: I ask Rob to grab a discreet shot of the man with the camera, it'll prove very useful later.

After protracted argument we manage to record a few short questions with the production director – to their surprise, we do actually want to hear their side of the story – and he repeats the line that we'd heard on the phone: that whatever happened in the past, new filters have been installed which have brought pollution levels down to the correct European standards.

I ask to see these new filters, a request which triggers a burst of hurried consultation and a firm 'No'.

With that, we are escorted off the premises, the security men warning us that as soon as we leave the boardroom we must stop filming. Rob, of course, keeps rolling, the camera hanging by his side, and our last shots of the factory that has poisoned a valley are of black boots stomping through the guardhouse.


Back at the farm, I ask Berta how she copes.

We get used to it, she says, because we've grown up in this environment but it's like a poison for the children.

Would they like to move away?

Of course, but we don't have the money.

I picture the chimneys and the half-century of contamination and poisoned guts of the snails and say how sorry I am.

Rob has filmed every possible shot of our scene around the kitchen table and is packing up.

Our glasses of Geza's home-made wine are still untouched and it's become embarrassing.

Geza pleads with us to join him in a toast. Rob keeps himself busy with his gear but I don't have any excuse.

I think of the vines just outside, and how last summer's grapes would have been exposed to the damaging jets of invisible toxins from the factory, how the same contaminants that poisoned the horses' hay and killed them must have made it through to the glass now in my hand. Everyone is watching me, it's a test of my sincerity.

So I do the right thing and knock the wine back. It's very bitter and very rough. I say it's delicious but want to retch as I say goodbye.

In the car I remember the doctor at the hospital describing how most lead is passed out so I drink an entire bottle of water. I'll be fine but, as Geza, Berta and their children wave us off, what about them? I can't help thinking that if dangers were more visible, they'd have fled by now. It may be why global warming can be so hard to understand: the gases are unseen, you can't see their impact and no single event can be directly attributed to them. Plastic choking the ocean? Easy, people can't miss it and they want to respond, that's human nature. But carbon dioxide?

# 9

# An iceberg as big as Manhattan

I can see the brilliant white of the frozen Arctic Sea as the pilot Rodney Fishbrook yells out from the cockpit of our small Twin Otter plane that he's happy to attempt a landing. As we drop, I just hope that the experts we're with are right that the ice we're about to touch down on is actually thick enough to hold our weight. I have to trust them – we've come too far now – but as we swoop towards the rolling fields of snow I can't help thinking of the treachery of the crevasses in Antarctica and worrying that no one, however experienced in polar travel, can always be totally sure what lies beneath that deceptively picturesque layer of untouched white.

I'm not scared but I am tense – this assignment had seemed so straightforward back in London – because what we're about to do is completely new to me. Previous expeditions in the polar regions have involved landing on some ridiculously makeshift runways – perched on the cliffs in Greenland or made of rough gravel in the far North of Canada – but at least they *were* runways, and a few even had the odd light or two. Other journeys were by helicopter, which are unnervingly fragile but do have the merit of being able to land anywhere and lift off at the first sign of trouble.

All that's ahead of our plane now is an unmarked and undulating landscape, the exact opposite of an airport, and the prospect of landing where no one else has ever been.

I try to think of the nearest equivalent. Flying to the besieged city of Quito in Angola, I watched the crew of an aid plane study the latest aerial pictures of the runway, plotting the positions of the shell craters and trying to find a straight path between them. They brought the plane down on a sharp diagonal, hurtling between the holes in the concrete, dust billowing from the heaps of rubble, all of us hoping the rebel guns would be quiet that day. Only after we came to a halt did I realise how rigidly my shoulders were locked, and how my neck, arms and legs were taut, too; good experience should you ever feel the need to test your nerves, or confirm control of the sphincter.

I don't have time to dwell on this because there's a sharp lurch as the plane's skis make contact with the snow, a small blizzard blasts the windows and Rodney revs the engines so that the plane surges over the surface, assessing its strength and smoothing out a track for us to take off from later. When he stops, and the propellers are stilled, the silence is deafening. I turn around and realise that we're all grinning. We've made it, the only souls on an iceberg as big as Manhattan.

The cameraman on this assignment is Duncan Stone, who'd been trapped with me in Siberia, and the producer Mark Georgiou – who is the first to remember his manners by leading us in a round of applause for Rodney's skill in getting us here. Two scientists with us, Luke Copland of the University of Ottawa and Derek Mueller, now of Trent University, Ontario, join in but they're too familiar with polar travel to see this as an adventure so I sense that their clapping is out of politeness, not from the relief that the rest of us feel.

We're within 400 miles of the North Pole and we're now adrift on the largest single piece of ice in the Arctic, an island of ice a staggering ten miles long and three miles wide. This great block used to be attached to the northern coast of Canada, a major geographical feature called the Ayles Ice Shelf, a mass of ice fixed to the shore of Ellesmere Island for at least 3,000 years. In a sudden fracture, it then broke away with the force of a small earthquake. The result: a new feature of the Arctic map, an ice shelf that became an ice island, and we're on the first mission to study it.

First question: who should get out of the plane first? This is television after all, and the precise pattern of the filming matters. In the days before this flight, we'd discussed this amongst ourselves but never settled on an answer.

Maybe I should be the first? I favour the idea but the others aren't sure; I think they're worried I might feel obliged to come out with a Neil Armstrong reference which could easily fall flat.

Perhaps Duncan should get out first? At least he'd be in a good position to film the moment of me clambering onto the ice, presumably on the condition that I don't say anything.

Or – a more cautious option – shouldn't the pioneers be Luke and Derek? They've been researching the Arctic for years, they know this kind of terrain and could venture out to check where it's safe for us novices to walk.

This exchange goes on for a few minutes until we're stunned by a totally unexpected sound: the passenger door of the plane being wrenched open – from the outside.

While we've been wasting time planning one of our key shots, the co-pilot, who knows nothing of the tortured debates of television, has just jumped out of the cockpit, calmly plodded through the snow and done what any normal airman would do: help us out and urge us to get on with whatever we've come for.

So I step out into snow that's already well-trodden – no need to mention anything about a small step for a BBC man – and realise that there's another problem: I can't really see anything. The Arctic sky is so brilliant and the snow so dazzling that I'm unable to open my eyes. Only when I put on sunglasses can I actually look around, which creates another anguished debate unique to television.

**The Martin Bell mumble:** the war correspondent famously prepared his words by pacing and muttering to himself. I try the same technique on this ice island near the North Pole – until Duncan Stone gets bored. *Mark Georgiou*

Sunglasses are a bit like headgear – convention dictates that if a reporter is filmed wearing anything unusual on their heads it's an issue, either because the team think you look funny or because the newsroom will or because viewers will be so surprised or amused that they won't listen to anything you say. I'm not exaggerating: between them, the black woollen hat and lopsided red safety helmet I wore in Antarctica attracted more comment than almost anything else. Safety helmets have become a bit more accepted – so many factories and construction sites now demand them. But safety goggles are borderline. And hairnets, of the sort required in some laboratories, are a guaranteed source of hilarity. Especially if they're a lurid baby blue. Luckily, I don't need any headgear here because although it's minus 18 degrees Celsius there's no wind and I'm warm enough in jeans. But we all agree, reluctantly, that the shades have to stay.

As we start work, the co-pilot stands ready with a shotgun, embarrassed when Duncan moves in for a close-up – people will think I'm a redneck, he protests. But under Canadian law, anyone working in the open in the Arctic must have an armed guard in case of polar bears. A few years before, on a trip to Hudson Bay, I'd seen the extraordinary speed of the bears and the lethal power of their paws, how one of these cuddly icons of Arctic wildlife had torn apart a wooden shed. So I'm glad we've got the gun, though the idea of it being used is a nightmare: think of the gleeful publicity if, to keep a BBC crew safe, one of these much-loved but endangered animals was shot dead.

While we're getting our first footage, Luke and Derek are preparing their equipment. Using a small radar device, they start a series of measurements to gauge the thickness of the island, the radar beam invisibly penetrating the ice.

The first readings come through.

How thick is it?

Forty metres, Luke announces, picture something like a ten-storey building.

I try, but it's not easy. To understand the scale of the ice I have to imagine being in a lift in a modest office building, descending ten floors and, at the bottom, reaching the waters of the Arctic Ocean. And all the time this great natural struc-ture is drifting, water reaching into the myriad cracks and gradually prising it all apart. It's not the moon but it's alien all the same: walking on what was a named part of Canada, now edging its way from the land, an island larger than quite a few countries, destined to melt.

Has it broken off because of global warming?

I ask because it's the obvious question.

Can't say for certain, Luke replies. But there's a pattern here: the sea ice that forms and thaws with the seasons is retreating; the glaciers are shrinking; the permafrost is melting more extensively; the temperatures are reaching record levels. So the conditions are just right for the ice shelf to break off. Like with so many changes, it's hard to say definitely that something is caused by man-made global warming. But it seems to fit into a bigger picture.

It's happened before, ice shelves snapping off to drift away as ice islands. In the Cold War, the Russians and Americans used them as floating military bases, giant aircraft carriers. But this one, Luke and Derek say, comes when so much else is changing that it's more than likely another sign of the dramatically warming Arctic.

We're standing by a long line of heaped blue chunks of ice, a wall of luminous sculptures, water dripping off them in the afternoon warmth. It's where the island split and then re-formed, the first signs of its break-up.

I check my watch.

It's coming up to 10 pm in London. We're too far north to do any live television – there's no satellite that could pick us up – so I try to get through on a satphone, audio being better than nothing. I reach London but the connection only seems to hold up for about three to four minutes. If I call again too early, the line might drop off just before I go on air. If I wait, it may take me several attempts to get another connection by which time I'll be too late. I opt to go early. The first person I talk to is a technician in Television Centre – he keeps saying he can't believe he's connected to someone on an iceberg. The news presenter's voice sounds excited too as I describe the ice and the snow and the scientists' findings. But what no one beyond the island knows is how incredibly close we came to not making it.

The assignment had begun not at an airport or in the newsroom but in the office of a senior editor, Peter Horrocks. It was the start of the year and I was pitching possible stories, deliberately avoiding anything remotely polar. Don't mention the ice, I kept telling myself. I knew that I was becoming known as an 'Arctic anorak' – colleagues catching sight of me in corridors always asking why I wasn't at the North Pole again. So I'd assumed a deep winter of 'ice fatigue' had set in. I had seen a report from the Canadian Ice Service about the fracturing of the Ayles Ice Shelf, and the comparison of the ice island with Manhattan had caught my eye, but I'd written it off and did not bring it up.

So I was taken by surprise when, having run through my suggested stories, Peter asked me about it.

Sounds amazing, he said. Do you think you could get there?

I don't know – but I thought you were all bored of ice?

This is different.

How?

It's an event, it's a serious change, it's altered the Arctic map.

He was right, this wouldn't be just another report from the Arctic. But it would be difficult, my biggest worry being the weather.

You know it can be terrible up there? We might try to land and not make it.

I know it's a risk, he replied, but give it a go.

And so we went, choosing our timing very carefully. Too soon and the Arctic nights would still be long and the temperatures miserable. Too late and the summer melt would start making the snow mushy and any kind of landing impossible. That narrowed it down to April or May. As in Greenland and Siberia, we'd need clear skies. Too cloudy and the pilot wouldn't see the horizon. Too warm and fog might form. We hadn't even set off and the Arctic weather reports were becoming a constant, brooding threat.

Our journey took us first to Resolute, one of the most northerly Inuit settlements. There we boarded our chartered Twin Otter, Rodney at the controls, for the two-hour leg over the mountains of Ellesmere Island to the remote weather station at Eureka. The next day, refuelled, we took off in icy sunshine and headed north, crossing fjords choked with icebergs and mountains smoothed by glaciers. With the GPS showing us edging closer to the Pole, we knew the ice island was dead ahead. Could it really be this easy?

No. As soon as we crossed the coastline, the skies over the Arctic Ocean turned cloudy. And then dark grey. We could see great cracks running through the frozen sea but nothing distinctive. We consulted maps and checked satellite pictures. We were in the right place. But we couldn't see enough. Four days of travel from London had brought us to within sight of the island but it was just beyond reach. In a swirl of different shades of grey, we had to turn back. I'd warned editors repeatedly of the risks of just this happening. But still I felt I was to blame.

The journey then seemed to become unusually turbulent. I edged close to the stream of cold air coming from a gap in the door. It wasn't enough to help me, though. As we approached Eureka, I was back on the whaling ship all over again, nausea combining with a sense of failure, not my finest hour and one which was all the more humiliating because of an unusual strand of family history. I'd long known how my grandmother on my mother's side, Margaret Fairweather, had been a pioneering aviator, one of the first eight women recruited by the armed forces to fly planes in the Second World War. The first woman allowed to pilot a Spitfire, she was a hardy character who had to endure endless hours without heating or any sort of navigational aid, coping with the worst of weather. She'd have thought nothing of bumping through the Arctic cloud. Sadly, she died after a crash landing when her engine failed. Had she lived, and seen this grandson of hers, pale green and hunched over a bag, I don't imagine there would have been much sympathy.

Three days passed in the weather station during which we slept and fretted and pored over the latest satellite pictures. Luke's wife, Trudi Wohlleben, an Ice Service meteorologist, was doing her best to guide us from Ottawa. We watched weather systems rise and fall on her black-and-white radar images. We read reports of wind speeds and watched Rodney calculate the likely timing of great spirals of cloud. Our problem was that Rodney and his co-pilot were due to return on a fixed day, and we dreaded having to call London about whether to extend the charter.

Our last possible day was a Monday. Few of us got much sleep. We checked the evening radar picture and then Rodney and Luke were up early to scan the first morning shot. Their view? There was a window between two fronts. The sky ought to be clear over the ice island by the time we got there. It was a gamble, there was no one further north than us to offer any advice. I thought about ringing editors to explain our situation and remind them, yet again, of the vagaries of the polar weather but, wisely, Mark stopped me – what's the point? It's possibly our last shot, he said, so we may as well just take it.

And we did, and ended up walking on a piece of the planet that was disappearing, the last people to do so.


Before we take off from the iceberg, Luke leaves a tracking beacon, wedged into the snow. He wants to monitor the ice island's movement and our website will show its route too. In a grey tube, decorated with a BBC sticker, the device is a solitary reminder of our visit. Sadly, it wasn't to work for long, possibly falling over as the snow melted, but no one knows; it just stopped transmitting. The island later split into two and started to disintegrate. But our last sight of it, from a tiny camera that Duncan had taped to the strut of one of the aircraft's skis, was of this vast feature intact, an accumulation of ancient ice destined to inch into the warmer currents and sink.

I ask Luke and Derek if ice shelves can ever regrow.

Yes, if the conditions are right.

But now?

No way. It's far too warm, it's a change that's one way, irreversible.

It's a memorable line and, back at Eureka, I use it.

Mark has negotiated access to a satellite link used by a consortium of university researchers and we are the first to attempt to broadcast live television on it. So about 600 miles from the North Pole, with Duncan, like Tony in Antarctica, using his anorak to shield his laptop from the sun, we become the world's most northerly television outpost.


On the way back, we stop at Resolute to wait for our connecting flight south. The settlement's tiny grid of snow-filled streets is home to a few hundred people. A place where it's normal for washing lines to be straining not under clothes but sealskins; for babies, blinking in the cold, to be strapped to their mother's backs; for teenage boys to race snowmobiles up the steep hill behind the settlement in the brightness of the early hours; for the long winter nights to be so depressing that all alcohol is banned; for the freezer in the village school, used to store samples to be dissected in biology classes, to contain the remains not of mice or worms but of a polar bear.

We visit the school so that Luke and Derek can explain what they've found out. The rows of mainly Inuit faces listen to the descriptions of how their world is changing and watch projected images of how the ice shelves are breaking off, how the map is being altered in their own lifetimes. I join in, talking about our work and then have an idea: in all our coverage of the ice island, we've never found out what it's called in Inuktitut, the Inuit language. This prompts a flurry of debate. What type of ice is it made of? There are many different kinds. Is it sea ice or glacial ice? In fact it's a mixture of both and we get an answer: *aujuittuq qikiqtaq*.

I learn about other aspects of the language. Its constructions of words to describe modern concepts are sometimes too long to fit on a screen as subtitles. New words have had to be invented to cope with the arrival of previously unseen insects, like wasps. And the phrase 'global warming' is a new part of the lexicon as well. As one Inuit leader once told me, we're the first to feel the effects of something you caused.

There's never an elegant way to deal with a mob of journalists. Faced with a scrum to get hold of some vital new document, I succumb to the general loss of inhibition, elbows and voices raised, no qualms about barging past more timid colleagues in a naked display of natural selection. Our quest, one morning at the UNESCO building in Paris, is to get the latest report from the UN's Intergovernmental Panel on Climate Change. We've all previewed this weighty publication, five years in the making, and described it as 'long-awaited' – a pointless phrase which serves only to whip ourselves into a greater frenzy, everyone for themselves, all camaraderie abandoned.

But once the paper is in hand, and the first hurried glance is over, we forgive the tumult of the past few minutes and edge together in little clusters, needing companionship in the face of confusion, help interpreting what we're reading. What we're holding is the twenty-page summary of the first of three volumes of research into climate change, the result of a five-year study by committees of scientists of what's meant to be the most reliable work. There are countless reports on climate change but the distinguishing feature of this one is supposed to be that there's layer upon layer of filtering with the words of the summary argued over and then approved by governments from all over the world. No other scientific question is scrutinised so closely. But that's no guarantee of infallibility and three years later we'll learn of major errors – staggering inaccuracies about Himalayan glaciers and assertions based on campaign literature not published science. The IPCC's reputation would suffer. Today, though, the scientists are relieved to have survived five days of grilling. Government delegations went through their conclusions line by line before endorsing the final text. One line says that 'warming is unequivocal' and I later hear that the researchers involved fought a hard battle to keep it in.

But the biggest contest was over the central conclusion, the one that matters, the question that led me to make the long climb to the top of Mauna Loa: whether we're to blame for the warming. When we find it, the key phrase, long disputed, says that it's 'very likely' that most recent warming has been caused by man-made emissions of greenhouse gases. The authors, I'm told, wanted to use the phrase 'extremely likely' which, translated, would have meant a 98 percent likelihood of being accurate. But they had to give ground and settle for 'very likely' instead, which means a 90 percent likelihood of being right. So that day in February 2007, delegations from the Bush Administration, from oil states like Kuwait and Saudi Arabia, from all the major industrialised countries and the rapidly growing ones – all signed up to the principle that mankind is behind at least some global warming. Not for certain and not all of it – but here was the clearest official endorsement yet for the idea that we have a hand in those puffs of carbon dioxide first tracked by Charles David Keeling in Hawaii and spotted in the bubbles of Antarctica.

This was a time when climate change was soaring up the political agenda. Reaching very different audiences, Al Gore's film *An Inconvenient Truth* and Nicholas Stern's report for the UK Treasury on the economics of global warming combined with the IPCC to transform awareness of the issue. My email in-box became a barometer of change. A few years back, it was mainly scientific organisations and environmental groups who would be in touch about emissions and rising temperatures and it was rare for a company to trumpet its eco-credentials. Now, a watershed was being crossed, and all manner of people and corporations announced how they were turning green. From one year to the next it was suddenly unusual not to declare support for the environment – sometimes sincerely, sometimes not. And, as with the famine in Ethiopia or the struggle against apartheid, climate change was now a concern for the fashionable to engage with. Up to a point, it was even glamorous.

At Wembley Stadium, the massive sound system is being tested and two producers lead me to a room set aside for make-up. I'm shown to a seat beside a famous comedian. It's the day of Al Gore's Live Earth concerts and I'm due to take part in the BBC's coverage of the London event. Between dabs of foundation and powder, I say hello but the comedian only grunts in reply, staring fixedly at the mirror. Maybe that's normal for show business, I don't know. More likely he hasn't a clue who I am, or does but couldn't care, or he's lost in his own private rehearsal of climate-change jokes. We're from different worlds. He's been hired to be amusing about global warming; my job is to be a voice of BBC impartiality about it, in other words to be as level-headed and straight as I can. Various senior figures have been reminding me of the importance of the task. No pressure, a colleague jokes. I have a few lines worked out.

The presenter of the BBC's Live Earth programme is Jonathan Ross, an ebullient, cheeky figure, sober in a pin-striped suit, a man more at ease with music, film and comedy than the hard science of climate change. In a rehearsal, he'd made me very welcome. Sitting on electric-blue sofas, with the cameras and lights being adjusted, we'd chatted about the event and he'd asked me what bands or singers I liked. I hesitated, aware that he wasn't quite sure what to make of me and because he's such a high-profile arbiter of modern taste. But I opted for honesty and declared a lifelong enthusiasm for the 1970s American southern rock band Lynyrd Skynyrd. He nodded approvingly and we both recalled how the musicians had died when their plane crashed and caught fire.

When we meet on the sofas again it's for real, the programme on air and the concert starting. Razorlight have come by the BBC studio, Genesis are due on soon, Madonna will appear later. The whole room is thick with celebrities – apparently; I realise I'm not very good at spotting them. James Blunt is shorter than I'd thought and Fergie of the Black Eyed Peas prettier. When the Pussycat Dolls arrive, dressed for an orgy, the whole place is immobilised, eyes yanked like magnets and no one knowing quite what to do. In a surreal twist, they've just been briefed by a Met Office scientist, Richard Betts, the climate modeller who joined our filming in the Amazon. He's on hand to provide expertise and he's clearly bowled over – 'they're aware of far more of the science than I'd expected,' he says, blushing.

The producers check me over. There's been a lot of discussion about what Mr Impartial should wear. No tie obviously, but maybe a suit? No, too weird at a rock event, it's decided. I opt for jeans and an open shirt. Jonathan Ross offers a handshake as I sit down. I never catch his first question, it's too noisy, the music has erupted, so I say what I'd planned to anyway: that I'm a correspondent not a campaigner, that there are things the scientists know and quite a lot they don't know, that the science has never been firmer on the basic idea that our greenhouse gases are having some effect on the climate but, whatever people say, we don't know with certainty what the impact will be, let alone when. I try to keep it steady, to spell out how I understand it, to make clear my distance from Al Gore's campaign. I think I'm understood, or at least heard.

Soon my segment is over and Jonathan Ross thanks me, turns to the camera, reminds viewers that they were hearing from the BBC's environment correspondent and announces that I'm a Lynyrd Skynyrd fan. He then adds a half-mumbled, high-speed aside that I can't quite believe and which I alone pick up: that they were a great band that unfortunately made their own unique contribution to global warming. The producers, greeting me as I come off the set, say they don't know what he was talking about. They're too young.

The event – the connection with Gore, the green preaching by millionaire rock stars – comes in for a lot of criticism. To their credit, the organisers did try to minimise the carbon footprint, using generators powered by biofuel and low-energy bulbs, but stories leak out about some of the bands arriving by private jet and the damage is done. No one likes being lectured, least of all by people as extravagant as these. It's impossible not to be reminded of an episode of the cartoon *South Park* featuring a 'smug alert' in which drivers of hybrid cars are so self-satisfied that they create a pollution hazard of 'smug'.

At midnight, as we all try to leave – the audience, the campaigners, the personalities and the impartial – the roads around Wembley are gridlocked. It's a warm night but I keep the window shut because, ironically, the fumes are terrible.

While the rock stars were calling for action on climate change, the planet was altering at its own pace. The ice island had split and scientists were monitoring the seasonal melt of the frozen sea. Every summer the area covered by ice shrinks and every winter it refreezes, a perfectly natural process. But since satellites first started photographing the Arctic in the late 1970s, researchers have plotted a gradual decline which, if continued at the same rate, would see the Arctic entirely without ice in summer by the 2080s or 2090s. When I started this job in 2003, the 'end of the century' line was commonplace. However the summer of 2005 had bucked that trend, melting more than normal, and the summer of 2007 was showing a faster than average decline too.

The peak of the melt comes in mid-September. I'd got into the habit of checking the polar websites in the approach to that time but after covering the ice island I genuinely couldn't believe I'd be heading anywhere icy for years. Then two things happened. The 2007 melt was so extreme, such a record-breaker, that it shrank the ice to the extent previously forecast for the distant year 2055. And a report dropped from the European Space Agency: satellite pictures of the waterways running between the islands of the Canadian Arctic showed them completely clear of ice. This was the long-sought Northwest Passage, the elusive sea route from Europe to Asia, sought by mariners for centuries but usually blocked, and often the scene of terrible deaths from cold and scurvy. Now, for the first time, there was no ice to be seen in it – the passage was open water. This was a moment of Arctic history. And editors who'd declared themselves bored with ice asked for a studio report that night and then couldn't wait for me to get up there.

We had a stroke of luck. The challenge wasn't just to be at the Northwest Passage – not hard, just fly back to

Resolute which lies beside it. The prize was to find a ship sailing through it. Mark Georgiou immediately called Luke and Derek, our ice-island scientists in Canada. They put him in touch with a Canadian professor running a network of Arctic research. As it happened, he was in charge of an expedition by ice-breaker that was on the point of entering the Northwest Passage and, just before Mark rang, a team of three scientists had suddenly pulled out.

So, the professor said, I have three spaces free. How many do you need?

Three, Mark replied. Him, me and Rob Magee. We were on. With just two phone calls. The instructions? Bring thick snow boots with reinforced toecaps and get yourselves to Resolute.


Resolute is where we'll join the ship, at the eastern end of the Northwest Passage. By the time we get there, in early October, it's transformed from our visit in May. The snow is crusty and dirty, the peeling paint of the houses exposed, the days short and the sea grey. Along the shore the ripples look heavy with grease, the first sign of the approaching winter freeze when the sea thickens into a grainy oil and then turns solid. I've read that Robert McClure, one of the more successful Victorian explorers, always found this to be the most depressing month, the dark descending and the temperature tumbling: 'no pen can tell of the unredeemed loneliness of an October evening in this polar world.' He was right.

Founded in the 1950s to plant a Canadian flag in the High Arctic, Resolute is exceptionally lonely, and feels flimsy enough to be abandoned overnight. The streets are empty, nothing grows here, there isn't much hunting, and everything that keeps life going has to be shipped in. The one shop stocks the cheapest kind of frozen food and an array of snow shovels. Rob points out a grim joke from a guidebook: that

Resolute should rhyme with 'desolate'. He starts calling it 'Des Res'.

We've arrived a day early so we can file preview reports, explaining the record retreat of the ice this year and the significance of the opening of the Northwest Passage. We have no idea whether there'll be a workable satellite connection on board ship – no one seems to be sure – so this may be our last opportunity to broadcast till we leave the vessel at the end of the trip hundreds of miles away. So, with the Northwest Passage as a backdrop, we run through some live interviews for television programmes, all of them passing smoothly enough for us to tell the flagship *News at Ten*, with reasonable confidence, that we should be able to do a turn for them too.

Everything seems fine our end. Though the wind is picking up and the huskies are howling, the signal remains adequate. I turn and notice that our ship, the *Amundsen*, has arrived, the red and white of the Canadian Coast Guard distinct in the bay behind me. This is perfect. I can point out the ship and announce that we're about to get on board, a great line for a live broadcast. I should have remembered how I'd once thought that the first snow of the Siberian winter was a great line too. These things have consequences. I hear the presenter Huw Edwards ask me a question and I start to speak. But then there's a silence in my earpiece. They've cut the line. It's all over.

Later we hear what happened. The picture was good but the audio was not. Huw put his question to me, live on air, but some misfortune with the satellites or circuitry meant that his words were delayed reaching me. As far as I could tell, I replied promptly. But in reality 13 seconds had passed between the last words of his question and the first of my answer. In television terms, this may as well have been 13 hours, precious air time haemorrhaging as I just stood there simple-faced, apparently unwilling or unable to speak, gazing pointlessly at a puzzled audience, the studio people no doubt wincing and furious.

For a legendary nautical journey, Resolute isn't the most promising place to start. It deserves a spectacular harbour like New York or Rio or Sydney but in fact it hasn't got a harbour at all. When ships come in the summer, cargo has to be transferred to barges. The easiest way to get us on board is by helicopter, landing delicately on the *Amundsen's* slender stern as dusk falls. Once Rob's gear is unloaded, the ship is turned to the west and picks up speed. There's a timetable to keep, a fabled passage to transit.

We're shown to our cabins, handing flight cases down steep stairways, trying to avoid blocking the corridors. The *Amundsen* feels busy, lots of people on the move, crew in uniform greeting us in Québécois French, an international mix of researchers, everyone friendly but without much time to linger because it's the hour for supper and we're hurried to the captain's table. Lise Marchand rises formally to introduce herself and her officers. Three courses are served and conversation is polite, almost formal. It must be strange for them having us drop in, with our small iceberg of equipment and ambitious plans to trumpet every detail of the journey to a global audience. And for me, travelling from an Arctic village via a lost 13 seconds and a helicopter flight to a French-speaking meal, it's quite a jolt too. We agree to call it an early night.

I pick the lower bunk, Rob the upper. It dawns on me that the last time I was in the Arctic with him we ended up stuck in Greenland. It also hits me that the last time I was on a vessel in the Arctic was with the Norwegian whalers. A chill seeps into my belly. After the experience with the Vikings, I'd vowed never to do a story involving any kind of ship ever again. Especially in the Arctic. And the Northwest

Passage is not the narrow, sheltered channel that the name suggests. It runs between islands which lie dozens of miles apart, separated by wide stretches of exposed and turbulent ocean. Surely I should have remembered to avoid this kind of scenario? If not the vow then at least the misery? When I get the chance, I comment on this with incredulity in my blog: 'How does an otherwise serviceable human brain allow that level of forgetfulness? These days at sea should give me time to consider that.'

I watch for signs of swell but the ship is mercifully steady and I drift off to the throb of the engines. Or would do, if it wasn't for a loud cheeping sound every few seconds, like a bird with a single annoying call. I assume it's the alarm on some gadget of Rob's but it's coming from beyond our door. I step outside into the corridor to look: nothing. Except that the cheep is louder there. It turns out to be the sonar system, sending out a signal to map the seabed, hugely important work no doubt but, as I try to blank it out, I do seriously wonder whether the crew would mind switching it off for a bit and putting up with a few long gaps in the surveying. And then I stop myself: this is the Northwest Passage I'm on, a sea route that took four centuries to conquer and still isn't fully charted, the burial ground for countless brave souls, and each mile is taking me through waters that many only imagined.

The words littering the map of the Canadian Arctic could have been lifted from the lobby of the Royal Geographical Society: name after illustrious name given to channels and islands marking the daring, expensive and painful exploration of one of the most forbidding corners of the planet. Royalty litters the twists and turns of this rugged landscape: Prince of Wales Island, Victoria Island, King William Island. Aristocratic sponsors of this great quest are honoured too: Viscount Melville Sound, Cornwallis Island, Ellesmere Island. Commercial sponsors feature with Felix Booth, wealthy from Booth's Gin, funding an expedition that led to the naming of Boothia Peninsula, plus dozens of little inlets and headlands named after his children, nephews and nieces. One challenge in those days of venturing beyond the map was to have the right supplies and equipment; another was bringing enough names for all the new places.

It was Henry VII who first commissioned John Cabot in 1496 to find a short cut to the Indies, the start of a peculiarly British obsession with seeking a route through the Arctic to Asia. The first motive was trade: to establish an efficient route to the riches of India, avoiding the long and hazardous slog round Cape Horn and waters later controlled by the hostile Spanish and Portuguese. By the eighteenth century, the aim had changed: this was an age of discovery and blank maps, such as those of the Arctic, were a challenge to pioneers such as Hudson and Baffin. A century later, after the Napoleonic Wars, an ambitious Admiralty official, John Barrow, kept his otherwise unemployed officers busy by despatching them on charting expeditions: the Northwest Passage was a goal that was the Royal Navy's to seize.

Step by step, the blanks were shrunk, by ship from Alaska in the west and the Atlantic in the east, and also by foot overland from the Canadian mainland. But the suffering was extreme. John Franklin, on one expedition, became famous for recording that food was in such short supply that, 'the whole party ate the remains of their old shoes.' Ships were regularly trapped in the winter ice, gangs using saws to cut a path, frostbite, snow blindness and starvation routine. But worse was to come. In 1845 and by now knighted, Sir John was despatched with two well-equipped ships, the *Terror* and *Erebus*, laden with provisions to last four years, the prestige of the Empire on the line with this most determined of efforts to defeat the ice and reach the Pacific. It was to end in disaster. Search parties eventually found traces of remains, and the grim likelihood of cannibalism. Ironically these rescue expeditions, numerous and thorough, helped achieve Franklin's purpose: they succeeded in discovering how the gap on the map could be filled, proving that there was, indeed, a Northwest Passage.

But there was a final twist: the British expeditions had completed the journey on foot, which in an age of sea power didn't quite count. In the end, it was a Norwegian, Roald Amundsen, who first sailed the passage, his converted herring boat taking four difficult years to make it through, arriving in open water in 1906. And his triumph is commemorated in the vessel I'm on now. Originally called the *Franklin*, the Canadian Coast Guard refurbished her as a research vessel and thought it might be more optimistic, more positive, to refresh her with a new name.


I can't sleep. It's not the chirping of the sonar, it's my mind racing. I dip into my collection of books about the North-west Passage but I'm too restless to read so pull my clothes on and head up to the bridge. The computer screens are glowing but otherwise the place is dark, two crewmen quiet over the controls, and ahead of them what at first seems to be a vast cinema screen, the plate-glass windows showing an eerie vista of pale light cast over our path. It's like looking into an aquarium, so much to take in, too much to grasp. We're sailing fast by floodlight, the beams picking out the dark water and occasional patches of ice, white on the surface, lurid turquoise below. There's a small jolt. The ice has become thicker, the bow slicing through it with a loud hiss. It's mesmerising: the driving power of the vessel, the sensation of surfing over this immaculate terrain, the thought of who else sailed here.

When we boarded at Resolute, we were close to Beechey Island where Franklin's doomed expedition is known to have spent its first winter, and where three of his crew were buried. Now we're heading along a route he must have taken during the next thaw, west along Barrow Strait, the *Amundsen*'s engines pushing us at a speed those men can only have dreamed of. Electronic charts mark our position and route. Radar displays show scans of the ice, not just its location but also its thickness. Heavy glass keeps us insulated from the freeze outside.

A ribbon of white lies ahead. It seems thicker than the rest and with no obvious way through. The helmsman slows down, selects a weak point and adjusts his course. The bow, strengthened like a battering ram, charges ahead, rising over the ice and then bringing the ship's weight down onto it. Sergei Zimov's armoured personnel carrier, floating over the saplings, had nothing on this. I can't tear myself away. It's addictive, far better than late-night television, never being sure what'll appear next, but knowing that I really should get to bed.

I'm woken by a shake and a muffled banging. This feels different to the roll and twist of the Norwegian whaler. It's irregular and noisy, unsettling rather than nauseating, the boom of metal on ice followed by tremors running the length of the ship. Our porthole, just above the waterline, reveals a mass of icy lumps, a gnarled landscape like severed tree stumps. The rasping and clanging of one chunk passes along the hull, right by our cabin and on to the stern. The engine slows, the ship almost stopping. This must mean there's serious ice ahead. I reckon we'll be relatively steady for a while and convince myself that it's my best chance to shave. Not the best of ideas, trying to wield a blade between bumps.

From the bridge, the scene is completely new. From being in open water yesterday evening and the thin ice during the night, the view now seems more like land than sea. We've entered Viscount Melville Sound which the satellite pictures had shown as clear just a month ago. Now it's choked with ice and the radar reveals it to be thick – what's called multi-year ice because it's tough enough to have survived the thaw of several summers.

I ask everyone I meet the same question: surely the Northwest Passage is meant to be free of ice? Isn't that why we're here?

Yes, but it turns out two things have changed.

First, we've passed the peak of the summer melt so the winter freeze is starting. From the ship I can see what look like clusters of icy grains binding together in the shape of grey pancakes, bobbing on the waves, these grey discs then coagulating to form a thin sheet. Soon the sea will be locked solid.

The other development is more unusual. The melt was so extreme in August and early September that it dislodged the oldest, toughest ice from near the North Pole and freed it to drift into our path. The Northwest Passage *was* clear of ice for a while but is now on the receiving end of a traffic jam of floes, blocks of ice the size of houses or tennis courts, jostling and nudging their way south.

One of these lies directly ahead. The *Amundsen* probes a section of it and rears up, engines roaring, but does not manage to punch through. We reverse and try another point but fail again. This keeps going for hours, the researchers eager to press on into this particular channel – one of several possible routes making up the Northwest Passage – but the ice may as well be concrete. Before the ship turns, however, and heads for an easier waterway, one of the scientists, Professor Bruno Tremblay, wants to investigate.

The ship's helicopter carries him and a colleague out to one of the ice floes and Rob and I squeeze into the back, skimming over the jumble of heaving ice, landing on a clean patch of white. It's like returning to the ice island, a few souls adrift in the Arctic. What's different is that the autumn light is weaker, much of the ice is sculpted into strange towers and curls, and what we're walking on is far thinner – about five metres thick, not forty. The professor sets about drilling through it to make measurements and to provide a deep fixing for a satellite tracking beacon. As with the ice island, he wants to follow its path over the coming year to see where the currents flow. But the task takes longer than planned. The drill is hell to start – we all lend a hand – and, as the hours pass, the pilot, who's on polar bear duty with a gun, keeps checking his watch.

It's the middle of the night in London so I ring up and offer live interviews to the World Service and Radio Five Live on the satphone. The BBC operators who handle the calls work in a unit called 'traffic' and they've long since ceased to be impressed by correspondents announcing the bizarre location they're ringing from. Even this one.

You're in the Arctic again? On another iceberg? What are you talking about this time?

When I'm put on air, I try to explain the scene of the drilling and the ice-breaker and the tough ice blocking our path and how I'm floating on the famous Northwest Passage. But it's hard to explain all this after being in the cold all day and, faced with a ranting correspondent on a poor line, the presenter sounds wary rather than curious. What I try to convey is that the Arctic melt isn't a straightforward story. A natural assumption would be that a record melt would free the passage for normal shipping, that container ships and oil tankers would sail through immediately, lopping thousands of miles off the journey between Europe and Asia. That may be possible in the future, in fact it's likely. But right now I'm finding that real life is more complicated, that the melt did leave the route free of ice for a month or so but that it also broke up older ice that's actually a greater threat, and will be for years to come.

I pull out my emergency rations. Franklin and his men would have had dried meat. I've brought a small bag of chocolate raisins and hand them out; everyone's ravenous, and the scientists, exasperated by their faltering drill, are hollow-eyed with exhaustion. As the light fails, it's time to leave; the red-and-white sanctuary of the *Amundsen*, beckoning from a few miles away, already feels like home.

**Icy irony:** heavy floes in the fabled Northwest Passage. A month before, the channel was clear of ice but the record melt dislodged old ice which has drifted into our path. I choose this moment to try to shave.                                                    *Mark Georgiou*

We return to find Mark, indeed much of the ship, in a high state of excitement. While we were out on the ice, and the pilot was keeping watch with his shotgun, two polar bears actually approached the *Amundsen*. Mark filmed their advance, a mother and cub checking out this intruder, and going through the movements that make them so appealing: the mother pulling herself up to her full height, the cub practising the rhythmic beating of the ice to break through to catch seals. I'm thrilled that he's got great footage. But

I'm also taken aback. The business of being armed on the ice now makes real sense. We'd been, at most, three miles away. Maybe the bears had passed close to us without us even realising? And what if they'd turned up when we were working in different parts of the ice floe, the scientists at one end, Rob and I at the other, the pilot's gun too distant to help us?

It's a sobering reality check and prompts me to ask about safety generally. We've been through the drills of donning immersion suits and sitting in a claustrophobic lifeboat but I wonder what would really happen if the ship was holed.

I ask the captain. Who would rescue us if we hit a sharp iceberg and had to abandon ship?

Lise Marchand laughs. We are the rescue, the *Amundsen* is the only rescue ship in this region of the Arctic, that's one reason we're here.

That night in my bunk I ignore the cheep of the sonar and listen more attentively than usual, as the hull pushes through the ice, to the thuds and clangs.

We turn south into M'Clintock Channel, named after Francis McClintock, a naval officer who developed a British version of the Inuits' sledges which allowed him to roam far in the Arctic and even discover what was left of the Franklin expedition. Low cloud and sleet mean there's no view but these very waters are where he – and Franklin – must have passed, pressing into terrain that was beyond the map.

As we plough on, we come to understand the patterns of life on board. Every few hours, various instruments are lowered into the sea, most impressive being a 'rosette', a water sampling device the size of a very large bin, researchers swarming around to collect bottles filled at different depths. One major task is simply to understand the biology and chemistry of the ocean. Another device, brought by a team of British scientists from the University of Plymouth, is a scoop that sinks into the mud on the sea floor and neatly extracts it. The aim is to preserve the individual layers of the sediment because, like tree rings, they can be dated and the relative quantities of a particular oil within them reveal the state of the algae year by year. This in turn provides a history of the advance and retreat of the sea ice, because the algae do better or worse according to how much ice is available for them to grow under.

Two young women researchers take it in turns to swaddle up and visit an air sampling device above the bridge – every two hours, around the clock, whatever the weather.

I ask if they mind the broken nights, the bitter cold, the sheer hardship.

No, not at all, they reply cheerily.

This degree of motivation is impressive. Another researcher has to descend into the din and stench of the engine room twice a day to collect water samples gathered from the bottom of the hull. Rob and I join two more women scientists on an inflatable, moving far away enough from the ship to measure the water's natural turbulence. It's grinding work, lowering and hauling in a series of instruments, all in a stinging snow shower, the sea forming into pancake ice around us, a freezing mist killing Rob's main camera, a brief taste of life in an open boat exposed to the Arctic October.

As with the others, I ask them why they picked this region for their research – why not instead study more benign waters, maybe at some coral reef in the tropics?

No, they react with horror. We love it here. And they genuinely do, the whole ship focused on the extraordinary job of getting to grips with the Arctic and how it's changing. I've nothing but admiration for this level of dedication, and grit. When Mark films us climbing back on board, our faces look drained.

The next day, news reaches us that provides another insight into the scientific mind. The Nobel Peace Prize for

2007 is awarded jointly to Al Gore and the Intergovernmental Panel on Climate Change. Even in this distant community, the deliberate nature of this decision is obvious, that the Nobel Committee is using its worldwide prestige to make an overt statement that global warming is important. But when I canvas opinion, the results are surprising. Initially, the researchers are delighted that climate change should be given this profile – as they labour in the cold, they feel some reward, however indirect. But scratch a bit deeper and some are uneasy about the sharing of the prize. Al Gore is a politician and campaigner, they point out, while the IPCC is designed to be scientifically rigorous, marshalling facts and analysis but not lobbying. One of the senior scientists sums up the problem: 'anyone who thinks Gore is a bore and that global warming is a hoax will say the same about the IPCC, if they've ever heard of it.'

The newsroom asks Mark if we can file a short video report about this. With the satellite signal coming and going, we're not sure. But we record a short piece and Rob starts to send it just in case the connection holds. It does get through, the first video report sent from a moving ship sailing through the Northwest Passage. Naturally, I wonder what Franklin would have made of that: after he set off in 1845, no word was heard from him again.

King William Island is coming up on our left. I've been tracking our progress and hoping for a chance to land there because it's where the remains of Franklin's expedition were found. His ships, the *Terror* and *Erebus,* remain lost but rescue parties discovered skeletons and the belongings of crewmen who'd obviously come ashore. Sadly, though, our route takes us at least fifty miles from the island – the channel is over 100 miles wide – and the captain is under pressure to keep going. The sea is now completely open, without a trace of ice, but the light is too murky and the cloud too low for any kind of view. As we press south, I wonder at what point those generously stocked vessels became uninhabitable, exactly why 100 men chose to abandon them. Were they being crushed? Or were the crews impatient at being trapped for so long? It must have been a terrible moment choosing to risk surviving without shelter in the unremitting gloom I'm sailing through now. Even before the winter, it's best not to stay out on the deck for too long.

As the days pass, we're becoming better known. One of the cooks has spotted how I like porridge and always wants a little laugh about being Scottish. The captain smiles ruefully even before I've asked her, yet again, about the likely timings of our journey – it's the Arctic, she always replies, who can know? When there's Internet access, the researchers start to follow my blog, our constant questions and intrusion into their work given purpose.

And we're discovering how to live on board. Our first rule, learned with some difficulty, is to allow enough time to dress for the outside. Thermals are essential but the ship's too warm to wear them indoors. So we've got into a drill of heading to the cabin, undressing, and then pulling on three layers for the legs and five on top, plus the heavy boots. Gloves and spares are in our jacket pockets already. Rob grabs the spares bag and camera and I take the tripod. By this time we're sweating and all that matters is rushing for the door. Lingering in the warmth is a nightmare, particularly if, before embarking on this process, you forgot to pee.


Now we enter Victoria Strait, one of the missing links of the Northwest Passage. Franklin had been heading in the right direction and, if he'd only got a bit further, he might have breached the worst of the ice and made it through. There are hundreds of miles still to run to the Beaufort Sea and

Alaska but soon we cross onto a part of the map that had been charted by explorers coming not from the east, like us, but from the west. It was in this region that some of the last white spaces could be filled in. In our centrally heated, well-fed way, we've cracked it too.

In those days, the fascination was with achieving closure on the geography. For the scientists now, the drive is to understand how the water, ice and biology interact. And for the Canadian Government, funding the expedition, there's another purpose still: ensuring that the world gets the message that these waters are Canadian, that the Northwest Passage, should it ever become navigable, is a Canadian waterway. It's a sensitive point. The United States and many European countries argue that the land is Canadian, no question, but the channels are so wide that the shipping lanes through them must be considered international.

It's a paradox that few Canadians have ever been anywhere near their vast Arctic territories but a little foreign flag-waving triggers a powerfully nationalist reaction. The year before, when the Danes planted their colours on tiny Hans Island which lies between Greenland (which is owned by Denmark) and Canada, Ottawa immediately despatched ministers in snow boots. And when Russia planted a flag (made of rust-proof titanium) on the seabed at the North Pole, the Canadians dismissed this as childish behaviour from the Middle Ages but then talked of ordering ice capable warships. Having the *Amundsen* steam through the Northwest Passage is another way of staking out ownership and, because we're on hand to film it, we're pawns in this geo-strategic game.

We're now so far west that we've crossed two time zones since setting off. Reaching Coronation Gulf, the wind drops, the waters are almost blue and there are treeless hills in the distance. We've been on board for a week and we're now looking for a lift to the nearest settlement so that we can edit and file our main reports. Not far away is the village of Kugluktuk, formerly Coppermine, and it's agreed that we'll be flown there. On our last evening, we're invited again to the captain's table, the atmosphere far jollier than the first night, the officers relieved that they're on schedule, the scientists mostly satisfied with their research, and us bowled over with the experience.

It's time to say thank you. Before we left London, Mark had visited the Royal Geographical Society and bought colour photocopies of three nineteenth-century maps showing the faltering attempts to find the passage. We used them in our filming and he now has the great idea of giving them away as farewell presents. To a packed lounge, I describe how much we've enjoyed our time on board and then offer our gifts, one for Captain Lise Marchand, one for the chief scientist Jean-Eric Tremblay and one for the *Amundsen*. The maps are beautiful in their own right, our precise location adding poignancy.

In our last hour, I visit the ship's gift shop and find myself spending emotionally rather than rationally: T-shirts I'll never wear, a coffee mug, a pen. And then I have a better idea and rush to the Captain's office with three of my Northwest Passage books. I ask a final favour: that she sign them, confirming that these books have actually made the journey. She agrees and does better by pulling out her large official stamp: 'Amundsen, Commandant'. I give one each to Rob and Mark and keep one for myself.

As we lift off the deck, my eyes are prickling. The ship has been our home for one of the world's last great journeys, the retreat of the ice allowing me to sail where so many died trying, one week at sea achieving a goal that defeated the Admiralty's finest for hundreds of years. And now the map those mariners strived so hard to complete is changing, not only on a timescale relevant to my children but also to me. The Arctic is set to look very different in a few decades. The ice cap, which has been a permanent feature of the planet throughout human history, is on its way to becoming a seasonal one, vanishing every summer, possibly within my lifetime.

In my first email from the shore, I send a line to the chief scientist thanking him. I must be in a more emotional state than I realise because his reply, which comes almost immediately, makes me well up: 'Today,' he writes, 'it feels like we parted with some of our own.'

# 10

# Where anyone fears to tread

Under a sweltering sky I edge towards the door of a tiny airport building, straining for the respite of some shade, when I sense the stern gaze of a woman customs officer. Long years of encountering difficult officials have instilled in me a kind of post-checkpoint stress disorder, an automatic assumption that I'm destined for the most difficult possible outcome, hours of obstinacy aggravated by memories of crossing into East Berlin or arriving almost anywhere in the old Soviet Union. Eyes down, determined to be calm, I make it out of the sun, one of a line of passengers, passports shiny with sweat, gasping for air under a slow fan, queueing for entry into Tuvalu.

Where? It's a question I've become used to while preparing for this assignment, Tuvalu being one of the world's tiniest and least well-known countries, a cluster of impossibly small islands in the vastness of the Pacific. If Midway was a dot on the map of the ocean, this place is more of a collection of flecks, a few slivers of coral, a country seemingly only just wide enough for the runway our ancient propeller plane has landed on. A lawyer, Philip Ells, summed up his two years here with the title of his book: *Where The Bloody Hell Is Tuvalu?*

And even in the age of Empire, when Tuvalu was part of a British protectorate known as the Gilbert & Ellice Islands, a young official, Arthur Grimble, found that his superiors were not entirely sure of the islands' location. In his memoirs, *A Pattern of Islands,* Grimble describes an august Colonial Office secretary, a man in charge of despatching young administrators across the globe, going through the humiliation of having to hunt through an atlas to find them: 'Let us go on a voyage of discovery together. Where ... precisely ... are the Gilbert & Ellice Islands? If you believe me, I have often been curious to know.'

These days, if anyone has heard of Tuvalu, it tends to be because it's described as one of the first countries likely to be lost to the effects of global warming. If the Arctic map is being redrawn by the melting ice, Tuvalu's may be reshaped more terminally by a rising sea. That's what we've come to investigate. But I'm faced with an immediate hurdle: the customs woman is still staring at me, neat blue uniform stretched over a stocky frame, silver badge catching the light, eyes questioning rather than suspicious, and I can't understand why. Usually, if customs are going to be difficult, it's the cameraman, loaded with expensive gear, who takes the flak. But Tony Fallshaw is up ahead of me, already with his papers out, explaining what's in his boxes, and Mark Georgiou is with him, so why can I possibly be of interest? In this nation of less than 12,000 people, with only a handful of visitors on the twice-weekly flight from Fiji, surely there's something more important for this official to do?

And then I get it: the customs officer's face is transforming from granite to grin, a huge laugh erupting, a roar that fills the crowded room and turns every head as she points to me. 'Did I see you on TV? In the ice? All dressed up for the cold?'

It turns out that she and the rest of Tuvalu can get the BBC by satellite and she'd watched our journey through the unimaginably chillier Northwest Passage a few months before. The last time she saw my face it was pale blue from an icy wind. Now it's got the unhealthy blotching of someone wrenched from a British winter into the greenhouse of the tropics and it's clearly hilarious: a reporter from the Pole turning up in a land that never sees snow.

I've made her day and, as she stamps my form and waves me through, she's still chuckling. Of all the sights I'd expected, laughter in the customs shed wasn't one of them. Welcome to Tuvalu.

From the air, Tuvalu is stunningly beautiful – but, by the standards of what normally constitutes a country, it's faintly ridiculous. The shallows fringing these slender scraps of land are a rainbow of intense colours: cobalt, aquamarine, purple, so lurid they almost look artificial, reminiscent of the chemical hues of the Aral Sea. And along their spines are bursts of vivid green, but only where there's enough soil for plants to take hold. The problem is, there isn't very much.

Of Tuvalu's nine islands, eight are inhabited, and the largest, Funafuti, is only about seven miles long and, at its widest, about half a mile wide. At its narrowest, it looks like it can just handle the width of a single road. Forming a gentle crescent with a bulge in the middle, Funafuti was selected as the only possible site for the US Navy to build a landing strip during the Second World War. Even then, the naval engineers had to excavate thousands of tons of coral and dump it on a beach to extend the island, to form a straight stretch of rock sufficiently long to handle planes. Without it, Tuvalu's only connection would be about ten days' sailing to New Zealand.

As we descend I see metal-roofed homes clustered amid the palms, one main road, a handful of larger buildings perched near one of the shorelines. First impression:

incredible vulnerability. The ocean looks so sweeping, so massive, while this little community seems so low-lying and precarious. Much of it stands only two metres above sea level. A few areas reach three metres in elevation and so-called Mount Funafuti, though marked on the map as the highest point, is just over four-and-a-half metres tall. High tides regularly see water lapping over the edges.

As we bump onto the wartime tarmac, I recall a repetitive series of nightmares from a broken sleep the night before in which a single towering dark wave wipes us all away. I don't often remember dreams and assume this one was triggered by the shattering confusion of several days of constant travel, a diet of airline meals and the erasing of an entire Wednesday caused by crossing the International Date Line. In our exhaustion, the exact times here and in London are the subject of regular argument but we are confident of one thing: that we have arrived just two days before what the Tuvaluans call a 'King Tide', the highest of the year.

As a micro-nation, Tuvalu has had to be inventive. With a population the size of a large village, it struggles to make its voice heard on the global stage. Being a member of the United Nations helps because it gives Tuvalu a vote on international issues – and that's something which attracts the interest of other powers, with self-evident benefits. The largest building is an ugly modern structure housing ministries – paid for by Taiwan, a country which feels isolated and is always eager for a friendly nod in international meetings. A crop research centre, producing badly needed fresh vegetables, lies beside the runway – it's also funded by Taiwan. The power station, just installed, was provided by Japan, whose diplomats are constantly wooing countries that may support them on an unpopular issue: whaling. A smart naval patrol boat is anchored in the harbour – donated by Australia. And even the dawn of the Internet age has proved useful: Tuvalu was allocated a domain name of '.tv' which has sold well to television companies.

But, for all this, Tuvalu remains poor and isolated. Despite earning money from a fortuitous web address, it's very rare that you can get a connection. We suddenly understand why our repeated emails to ministers and officials went unanswered: the line was too slow or intermittent for them to even open them. I try to check my emails at an Internet café but get nowhere. I persuade an official to sneak me into the government's own IT department but the screens are cut off there too.

The heat doesn't help. It's so suffocating that even the islanders talk about it – but very few places have any air conditioning or even fans; most people raise the bamboo curtains at the sides of their houses to catch some breeze, or just sweat a lot, nothing happening quickly, lethargy becoming a virtue. It's usually too hot for any formal clothing, many men opting for a *sulu,* a sarong, instead of trousers; jackets are a rare sight and ties too constricting even to contemplate.

The few cars are hand-me-downs from distant cities, exhausts smoking, lopsided with ruined suspension. Mark hires us one for the week: a battered yellow cab with a cracked windscreen, a squeak so piercing that it sounds like gouging metal, and handles so decrepit that only one of the doors can be opened from the outside. The others manoeuvre me into doing the driving which turns out to be a trial. I never get the hang of the creaking gearbox, keep stalling and once caused what could have been Tuvalu's first traffic jam.

So the South Pacific image may be one of exotic lagoons and swaying palms but the reality is tawdry, more fragile. Our first evening, staying in the only hotel, we sit down to dinner. A young boy asks if we'd like sushi. Sure, we say, not quite sure what to expect, but he brings a plate of exceptionally fresh tuna sashimi. So far so good. Then, we ask, is there a main course? No problem: tuna steaks with rice. Also good. But that's all there is, every meal, every day, tuna raw or cooked, apart from when it's too stormy for the fishermen to go out and the freezer has to be opened. The problem is that apart from the Taiwan-funded vegetables, very little is cultivated here so much of the food has to be shipped in, encouraging a processed diet that's already reflected in rising levels of obesity.

Our first stop is the Tuvalu Met Office. Like all the key institutions, it's close to the runway, a shabby, single-storey building heaped with equipment and papers. We visit to find out what the latest research is saying about the sea level because, as so often, it's easy to assume that Tuvalu will drown without knowing the facts. The answer isn't straight-forward. For a start, no one thought it worth taking mea-surements until fairly recently and, when they did, the first tidal gauge was soon found to have been sinking slowly. But we're shown the most recent records which track the sea level for the past 15 years. The results are not dramatic – there's no evidence of an immediate threat, the country won't go under tomorrow – but readings of the high tides do show a modest but steady trend: that the highest have been getting higher.

The science of sea level rise is more complicated than I had thought. As the sinking of Tuvalu's first gauge showed, researchers first have to account for the land subsiding. Then there are patterns in the ocean currents that can affect the sea's height at different points. But the conclusion of the UN's Intergovernmental Panel on Climate Change is that the average ocean temperature is warming and, as it does, the water's volume increases, meaning that it takes up more space – a basic physical principle known as thermal expansion. As a result, the sea level has been rising at a rate of about 1.8 mm per year since 1870, accelerating to 3.1 mm per year since 1993. By the end of the century, according to the IPCC, the sea level could be between 18-59 cm higher. For a diminutive and unprotected country like Tuvalu, this is serious.

However that forecast does not take account of the melting of any ice from Greenland or Antarctica, the IPCC judging that the volumes and rates of the melt were too uncertain to include. But factor in what Koni Steffen has been finding out about the Greenland ice sheet – how its slide towards the sea is accelerating in the longer summers – and it's not unreasonable to think that the rise in sea level may be higher than the IPCC forecasts. Koni himself estimates a likely rise of one metre by the end of the century. What matters is the effect of that on the most dangerous moments when the seas are at their highest, during a storm which also coincides with a King Tide, like the one now just 24 hours away.

We've arranged an interview with one of Tuvalu's leading spokesmen, a man who was the country's first ambassador to the United Nations and is now the senior official running its Foreign Ministry. Though minute, Tuvalu has the full panoply of government, with a cabinet, ministers and civil servants. The only difference in this Lilliputian state is that with such a small population to draw from, a ministry may consist of a single office with half a dozen people, as does the Foreign Ministry which I find along a corridor in the Taiwan-donated government building.

I knock and enter an incongruous scene. There are the desks and computers you'd expect in any modern office, and the earnest faces of any government department, but in a unique twist everyone is wearing bright tropical shirts. It's the first time I've encountered bureaucrats who look like they're dressed for a barbecue. It's a lively and charming sight. The boss himself, Enele Sopoaga, is in a dark blue number adorned with a pattern of huge blooms. He asks me to wait a minute while he reaches for something behind his desk. Is he looking for more traditional diplomatic garb, a jacket or tie perhaps? Or a more sober shirt? No, he produces a generously filled garland of pink and yellow flowers and hooks it round his neck. He notices me staring.

It's our culture, he explains. This is how I want the world to see us, we're proud of it.

His argument is simple: that Tuvalu's existence as a nation is threatened by actions far beyond its shores, that its problems stem from the effects of climate change. Those who caused the warming must take responsibility for it and offer assistance to those suffering from it.

The polluter-pays principle must apply – you must help us, please, he appeals.

I ask how long he thinks the nation of Tuvalu will survive on these islands.

Fifty years – no longer.

What then?

This is our home, we have nowhere else to go.

Enele's case is that if rich countries like Holland and Dubai can control the sea – with massive dykes or the construction of entirely new islands – then Tuvalu has the right to claim support to do the same and to stay put. I don't like to say that I can't see that happening, investments running into billions to save just 12,000 people. The alternative is to give up and flee. Already around thirty Tuvaluans emigrate every year to New Zealand – which accepts them as economic migrants, not climate refugees – and that trickle could conceivably become a flood. But that would mark the end of the nation, a once-proud people dissipated.

Interview over, Enele suggests we visit him again that evening, not at his office but at a community hall. You can film some dancing, he says, a tiny hint of a smile on his lips.

The moon is bright and I picture it tugging at the sea, tomorrow being the day of the King Tide. Tonight though, in a muddy lane shaded by dense trees, our feeble headlights pick a path to an open-sided building already busy with several dozen people. I manage to catch a wheel in an unseen rut, rev the engine furiously to free it and generally guarantee that everyone notices our arrival. Enele introduces us and explains that this is a rehearsal for a dance competition. The group runs through a spirited performance, the women and a few men swaying, hands raised, fingers and wrists delicately twisting, two musicians banging out the rhythms on improvised drums.

Enele keeps looking my way and I know what'll happen: he'll invite me to join in and insist that I wear a flower necklace. I decline – I can see that with Tony still filming and Mark poised with his camera, it's far too risky for me. If hats on television are laughable, flowers are career-threatening. But the pressure is relentless and reluctantly I rise to my feet and try to mimic the others, clumsily following the steps. At least Enele seems to have forgotten the flowers. But then he appears with something far more outrageous, a creation so far beyond the usual conventions that I feel myself crashing out of any known comfort zone. He's carrying a circular garland to be worn on my head. I have no choice, on it goes, a herbaceous border to encircle the cranium. Never mind the black woollen hats of the Poles or the sunglasses of the ice island, this is off the scale of television headgear shame.

Drunk with disorientation, dancing just hours before the rising sea will reach its new peak, I convince myself to enjoy the moment, to raise my arms and sway, catching the Tuvaluans grinning at each other, avoiding the smirks of Tony and Mark in the shadows. When my companions spin round, I do the same. When they start to clap in keeping with the drums, I join in too. It's fun and maybe, just maybe, I'm not doing too badly.

**The ultimate in headgear shame:** in a community hall on Tuvalu, I try to ignore the garland of flowers and join in a dance rehearsal. In the heat I misguidedly think I'm not embarrassing myself too much. *Mark Georgiou*

The song accelerates and I can sense the excitement. What I don't sense is when the song will end and, without warning, and far sooner and far more abruptly than I expect, everything suddenly stops. The metal-roofed hall falls totally silent and the dancers freeze. But my exuberant hands have acquired momentum and I fail to prevent a solitary but very distinctive clap from echoing into the dark. The place erupts, the rows of Pacific faces break into gales of laughter, flowers are shaken loose, tears are wiped away and even Enele, who has the future of his nation to worry about, is shaking helplessly.

By mid afternoon, the wind has turned the lagoon into froth and the first wave breaks over the main road, foam washing leaves, bark and plastic towards the nearest homes. It's normally the road's busiest time but the stream of motorcycles and bikes halts to avoid being hit by the next surge. A fisherman strains to lift his canoe off the shore and tie it into a tree. A mother and her children lash extra ropes over the plastic sheeting covering their hut. It's an hour before the peak of the King Tide and the flood is intimidating but by no means terminal: a few small groups gather to watch but the children are laughing at the spectacle. If this is to be the first country to be wiped off the map, people are pausing rather than panicking.

Tony films the scene and we move on. The road, though right beside the coast, is actually slightly raised and we've been told that some of the more vulnerable areas lie inland. So we drive down a lane towards the runway, a route we know well, but find it barely recognisable. In the space of an hour, during the tide's rise, great pools have formed. An area of open ground in front of a church has become a small lake. As we pass, mourners are arriving for a funeral. The King Tide won't delay it but I watch the priest, cassock raised, having to tiptoe through the muddy water. Minutes later three women turn up, turned out in immaculate white, their hair adorned with flowers, white shoes clutched to their sides. They lift their clothes above the knee and tread warily to avoid the deepest mud, a determined dignity, a vision of elegance amid a sea of brown.

Earlier in the day we'd met a family living at one end of the runway. The mother, Teimana Avanitele, has told us that they're so often flooded that their small plot of land becomes unworkable. A jovial, plump figure, she was eager for us to capture what happens so Tony has set up a time-lapse camera. As we reach her now, the house is still dry but her yard is already water-logged. As we watch its level rise, an unusual feature of Tuvalu's vulnerability becomes apparent. Unlike a normal flood, this water isn't flowing in from somewhere else – it's not breaking the banks of a river or spilling from the waves crashing onto beaches. Instead it's flowing *up* from underground. It's not an easy image to grasp at first. But seawater is being pushed by the King Tide into the island's coral foundations, through its infinite gaps and passageways, and up into the soil where it now lies. It occurs to me that Tuvalu, built on a porous rock, is literally holed below the waterline.

And we can see it happening: in the lowest dips in the ground, tiny streams of bubbles rise from little holes in the coral and reveal where the Pacific is penetrating the land. I'm reminded of the bubbles of methane in Siberia: those were larger and slower, while these are smaller but more insistent; but both are signs of potential trouble. According to the timer on the camera, the flood welled up in about 30 minutes, like a sudden leak filling the hold of a sinking ship.

Teimana's children don't seem remotely concerned; in fact they're splashing through the water. But Teimana herself leads me to the side of her house where she's trying to cultivate vegetables. The plants are submerged. The flood will clear in a matter of hours, she tells me, but the salt will remain and it's having a cumulative impact on her soil. It's already hard to grow anything, apparently, the earth is so poisoned.

It makes me feel scared, she says, eyes wide. What will happen to us in ten years' time?

She has another worry too: hygiene. Most of the houses are not equipped with mains sewerage; waste is allowed to subside into pits in the ground. In normal times, this is manageable and the place can be kept relatively clean. But when the waters rise through the rock they sometimes have the effect of flushing up what's meant to be kept down. The pools now forming on the ground are not exactly pure. Every flood runs the risk of spreading infection and disease and fouling the drinking water. I'd been warned about this; and I'm glad I've brought rubber boots.

It's Mark who points out that what's happening to Tuvalu isn't sudden, it's nothing like a tsunami. By contrast we're witnessing a slow process, the gradual encroachment of salt into soil, the creeping sabotage of sustainable life. Long before the seas are high enough to drown these islands, the streams of tiny bubbles may well have made them uninhabitable.

The King Tide reaches its peak just after dusk and the lagoon is now frenzied, rough waves pounding on the concrete sea wall running beside the hotel. I'm getting ready for a live broadcast on the *Today* programme. The dishes of our satellite phones are pointing almost vertically, aiming for the spacecraft orbiting the equator that will connect us with London. Gusts are hammering at the windows and I wonder if the noise will be distracting; radio producers like some 'atmosphere' in the background but not too much. But then I become aware of another, more surprising sound. It's not the whirring of the ceiling fan or the whistling of a hot draught through a gap in the door; instead it's the roar of animated voices shouting over music. I pull open the window for a look: below me is a throng enjoying a party. It's the celebration of a wedding. The benches are packed with people drinking beer and everyone is sporting a garland of flowers. Occasional bursts of spray rise over the sea wall and cries of alarm go up but only because the dresses are getting splashed. No one flinches, let alone leaves.

What's striking is that the party doesn't miss a beat. The tide may be spilling into their island home but why let that spoil things? An obvious comparison comes to mind:

the band playing as the *Titanic* sank. But that's unfair. The ship went down rapidly and irreversibly; Tuvalu's demise may take decades and could possibly be avoided. But if it comes, the television crews on hand to film the last people leaving will see something heartening and unexpected: the determined good humour of the Tuvaluans, whatever the circumstances.

One afternoon, during a vicious downpour, I watch a brother and sister dance and giggle in the storm. A girl riding pillion on a motorbike, struggling to hold a large and very heavy tuna, moves as if to wave at me but laughs and shoots me a smile instead. A small crowd in the hotel bar, watching our report on BBC World, cheers at the people they recognise, even though the report itself was not exactly optimistic about their future. A group of children, barefoot and growing up in a land that they may have to abandon, shout with delight when Mark shows them a documentary by David Attenborough which features Tuvalu. Teimana, despite being surrounded by flood water, leads us into her kitchen for tea and makes us all laugh. Everything acquires a lighter side – from my being the only person on the island with wellington boots to the hilarity of Tony, a great cook, wanting to know Teimana's recipe for pork using 'toddy', a syrup she makes from her palm tree. And at the airport, the woman customs officer still finds me funny and my last sight of the Tuvaluans, as I walk to the plane, is of her grinning.

Our coverage provokes some fierce debate back home. My eldest son Jack thinks that no one could possibly be interested in the fate of such a remote and miniscule country, let alone that anyone would feel moved to respond. The rationale of your report, he argues, is that we should do something about Tuvalu – contribute to its safety or switch off the lights or something – when few people will care. No one's going to feel sorry for anyone living on a tropical beach, he says. My response is laboured: I stress my impartiality, that it's not my role to do any more than cover what's happening – and if a member state of the UN risks becoming uninhabitable then it's reasonable to report that to a wider audience. Jack's not convinced: the numbers are too small and the scenery too exotic to provoke even the slightest concern.

His younger brother Harry takes a different, no less critical, view. He feels sorry for the Tuvaluans and thinks it is interesting to hear about them but he worries that I might unwittingly have had a hand in accelerating their end. If their days are numbered, he asks, because of a rise in sea level caused by greenhouse gases, then hasn't my journey there made things worse for them? Three flights to cross twelve time zones and then three flights back home – hasn't my carbon footprint served to hasten the very process ruining their country? And most telling is Harry's own mental picture of our departure: they'll all have waved you off, he says, but be unable to leave Tuvalu themselves, instead having to stay, watching the trails of your exhaust while waiting for the next big wave.

But the boys' criticisms are just a snapshot of opinions provoked – and hackles raised. Most vocal are those who claim that I've let myself be hoodwinked by a massive hoax. Others accuse me of being an activist in a great green conspiracy. And there's hostility from the other side too, committed environmentalists arguing that we in the mainstream media are burying the 'truth' about global warming and are allowing ourselves to be censored by the lobbyists of the big multinationals.

Reporting on a protest outside a coal-fired power station, one demonstrator, a woman in her twenties with spiky blonde hair, turns on me with an extraordinary allegation:

that I'm 'obeying establishment orders' by not telling the public about the dangers of climate change. I'm so taken aback by this I don't have the wit to respond as I should, by explaining that my in-box is more regularly filled with critics claiming the opposite, that I'm obeying orders to ramp up public alarm about global warming. A similar theme emerges during a panel discussion, when a senior figure in a conservation organisation aims a vehement complaint at me: that the media should recognise that we're on course for five degrees of warming this century, that the human species is at risk of extinction and that we should ditch almost all other news to report nightly on this planetary emergency. I start to picture how I'd raise that idea with editors but give up.

The problem, as I'm discovering, is partly to do with unrealistic expectations of the news media and partly with the nature of the subject. To my mind an 'emergency' is something immediate – a fire or bomb or flood, and newsrooms know how to respond. The predictions for the impacts of climate change are far slower and longer-term – sea levels, for example, may rise by a certain amount by the end of the century, not tonight or next week or even next year. Tuvalu showed how we're dealing with a process lasting decades rather than being a one-off event, and editors will always favour the latter. They'll also be attracted to anything new. 'Ice fatigue' set in because of the apparent repetition of the images and story. 'Flooding fatigue' runs the same risk. So when the idea came up of reporting on the impact of rising seas on Bangladesh, some editors and producers shrugged dismissively, as if to say that we already know that this low-lying country is bound to go under, that it's a global warming cliché – haven't we been hearing that for years, what's different now?

The first step is the hardest. Tony has gone ahead with the camera and I've got to follow, climbing off the boat too, knowing that when I stand on the muddy bank I'll sink so deep that my boots will flood. Tony's already in up to his calves. I'm not squeamish, in fact I'm easily tempted to swim almost anywhere. But the waters I'm looking at now began in the Himalayas, forming the River Ganges, flowing through the teeming cities of northern India, before crossing into densely crowded Bangladesh and ending up here beside Gabura Island in the tidal flats where the rivers eventually meet the Bay of Bengal. It may be holy but this is water that has also served a variety of purposes for hundreds of millions of people upstream – praying in it, washing in it, throwing their rubbish into it, scattering the ashes of their dead onto it, and, of course, using it as a giant open sewer.

As I say, the first step is the hardest and I recoil as my boots slide into the ooze. First it's the water that reaches my feet, pleasantly cool on a burning monsoon day, but then the squelch of mud gets inside too. I've tied the laces very tightly but that's no protection: this mud is like a chocolate milkshake, viscous but fluid. I try to think of it as pure and unsullied, no different from wading on an English riverbank during a summer picnic, but that doesn't work because I also imagine the mud as a natural Petri dish, a highly efficient incubator, not only warm but also repeatedly enriched, a flourishing Eden for innumerable bacteria and diseases.

The facts don't help. In addition to India upstream, there are 156 million people in Bangladesh alone – it's the world's eighth most populous nation, and one of the poorest – and most of them lack proper sanitation. And in this remote corner, at the southern tip of Satkhira, one of the least developed provinces, there are thousands of people crammed onto islands of mud that only just break the surface of the water.

It's Tuvalu on a vastly larger and poorer scale and I'm standing at the wrong end of it, downstream. There's a bottle of hand sanitiser in my pocket but it's only useful as a talisman of hygiene – a good-luck charm – because, being knee-deep in the murk, it's already far too late to do anything about my feet.

Luckily I'm quickly distracted. The scene we've climbed into is like something from ancient times, a great multitude of labourers toiling in shorts and shirts, passing lumps of mud from one to another to be pushed into a long embankment. They laugh at the sight of Tony, slipping under the weight of the camera, and then again when I stagger behind with the tripod, along with Mark gingerly carrying two more cameras – one that's waterproof and another for stills. Our arrival amuses everyone but doesn't halt the rhythm of the human chains, a splash as the first man extracts mud from underwater, grunts as the heavy load is delivered up the line, and a splat as it's thrown into the wall. Overseers bellow instructions, directing the positioning of the mud and urging the men to hurry because the tide is on the turn.

There are no tools, there's no protective clothing, everyone is working barefoot and barehanded. No one stops for a rest or to drink or eat; in fact there's no sign of any supplies at all for a working shift that lasts five hours, in a climate as hot and humid as a sauna. Apart from the designs on some of the shirts – from European football clubs or long-forgotten corporate promotional events – there's nothing modern about this operation, nothing mechanical, nothing electronic. The workers' transport is a fleet of wooden canoes, tethered nearby. So standing among these men, the air thick with flicks of mud and splashes of water, it occurs to me that this can't be that different from the gargantuan projects of the Egyptian pharaohs, using swarms of people to build the pyramids, or the Romans setting huge gangs to work constructing roads. It's a throwback to a pre-industrial age, a glimpse of life before machines.

The word 'apocalyptic' comes to mind, too, images of Noah rushing to build his Ark before the Biblical flood. The sea wall is part of a network of defences. But a cyclone in May 2009 whipped up a surge – a massive upwelling of water – that overwhelmed nearly 1,000 miles of these embankments. The outer defences protecting Gabura Island, home to at least 20,000 people, were breached in four places and the inner defences were then damaged too. The gaps in the walls have exposed the island's villages to a twice-daily ordeal: when the tide comes in, there's nothing to stop it pouring into people's homes and fields. The marketplace becomes a lake, the plots of rice and the pools of the shrimp-farms just vanish, and people tuck their possessions into makeshift shelves in the roofs of their huts. Many flee to a narrow camp, crowded and desperate, strung out along the top of the largest remaining embankment. Normal life has to stop and it won't resume until the walls are fixed.

The work I'm witnessing, though involving some 200 workers, is only the start of a very long and hazardous job. The repairs can only take place at low tide and the only material available to restore the embankments is mud. If it can be hauled up from the lowest areas, it's more like clay and therefore more useful; I see one group of men literally diving underwater to bring up armfuls of this precious stuff. But there's no budget for earth-moving equipment or barges or teams of engineers deploying sheets of steel and concrete. Faced with a task like this, the Dutch would have floodlights and massive pumps and acres of plastic sheeting. All that can be afforded here is the local manpower, each labourer paid five kilos of rice per day, though with all the paddy fields flooded, food is in short supply and no one seems to complain about the rate.

In fact, the atmosphere is one of quiet dignity and good-will. I had worried that we might be resented, quite justifiably, as visitors from the rich world turning up as spectators to this plight. Our comparative wealth might be aggravating too: we're carrying technology that these men have never seen before. Tony's camera is probably worth more than the entire island's income for a year, my useless hand sanitiser worth a month's average wages. But as we gingerly try to manoeuvre ourselves in the mud, boots sinking, water rising past our knees and thighs to our waists, we encounter nothing but politeness, the only restraint being a puzzled uncertainty about what we're here for.

At one point, when we record a piece to camera, Tony gets me to stand amongst the thickest part of the workforce while he keeps back to show the scale of the operation. We're a hundreds yards apart but I'm wearing a radio mic so Tony can still hear me. He gives me a wave and I start to speak, describing the importance of this embankment and the work going on, voice boosted by adrenalin and the din around me. At first the men closest to me stop in surprise, startled at how I'm apparently shouting to myself. A few of them watch me, presumably wondering if this bizarre stranger, who's chosen willingly to get dirty in the mud and is now speaking in an unfamiliar tongue to no one in particular, needs some help. When I use the word 'Bangladesh', some of them murmur approval and grin at me. I smile back and point at Tony and his distant camera but my gestures make no sense; I only hope that people regard me as harmless rather than dangerous.

We become even more of a spectacle when Tony asks me to move slightly to improve the shot and I realise that I can't shift at all because my right boot is stuck, clamped in the mire. This produces a lot of laughs until I sound genuinely alarmed and two of the men reach out to help. It's now that I realise the power of dignity in adversity, as with the white-clad mourners in Tuvalu who were determined to remain clean to honour their dead. When I try to grab the hands of my helpers they flinch, they won't have it: their hands are too dirty, they signal, too muddy for me to touch, and they turn to offer me their upper arms instead – they're cleaner. And minutes later, when Tony himself tries to change position and sinks up to his chest, three workers rally round immediately, cheerfully plucking him to safety, the muddiest hands again kept at a discreet distance, their arms gallantly linked under his.

All the time we've been filming, the tide has been rising and soon the work has to stop – there's no point hauling mud that will soon be washed away. The men gather in their canoes to head home but they pause before setting off, curious to watch our progress back to our boat, slithering and unsteady. One of those in charge calls out and a huge cheer goes up, a rousing send-off. I'm not entirely sure if it's out of relief that we didn't get ourselves into more trouble or out of gratitude that we proved so entertaining. Either way, I feel we should say thank you so we offer three cheers in return, spirited and heartfelt, but they're puny in comparison to the massed roar, and everyone laughs again.

The embankments, when repaired, will buy Bangladesh some time. The question is, how much? Listen to some environmentalists and the whole country could go under in a matter of days – which obviously can't be right. The truth is that no one can know for certain. But out of the limelight, in a sidestreet in the capital Dhaka, teams of hydrologists, geographers, statisticians and computer modellers working for the institute CEGIS are trying to narrow down the uncertainties. The offices are dim with poor lighting, most do not have air conditioning, the computers are a generation old. But it's here that the most accurate forecasting is attempted.

One of the directors, Ahmadul Hassan, a kindly professorial type, runs through his latest prediction. Everything quantifiable has been factored in: the precise contours of

**Sinking feeling:** Tony Fallshaw and I sense our boots subsiding into the Bangladeshi mud as we film repair-gangs fixing a sea wall with their bare hands. Our presence is greeted as a source of hilarity. *Mark Georgiou*

Bangladesh's terrain (even the flat areas aren't exactly flat), the seasonal flows of the great rivers, the patterns of the monsoon, the likely rise of the sea level at current rates (5 mm per year, he tells me), the locations of the densest populations. And as the years of the century unfold beside a bright-green map of the country, more and more pixels turn blue, a few along the coast and then more inland until by the year 2100 a great swathe of the southwest of Bangladesh has changed colour. It's a visual description of an utter calamity which, it turns out, is not as obvious as it looks.

Several features are surprising, Dr Hassan says. The topography means that most flooding will occur not where you'd expect, on the coast; instead there's a natural 'lip' of land beside the sea so the inundation will be worse inland. The flooding will be seasonal – it won't be permanent but instead will last four to five months when the rains are heaviest. Third, that's still a potential disaster because although people won't drown they will have to move, their livelihoods ruined, because the flood water will be saline. Fourth, this region of Bangladesh is one of its most important rice baskets – much of the rice is grown in just these areas and at just the times when the flooding will be worst.

So it's not a simple story of flooding. It's potentially cataclysmic but for more complicated reasons.

Assuming you're right, I ask, and the sea rises as you forecast and the flooding occurs in these rice-rich regions as your map suggests, how many people will be affected?

Dr Hassan hardly pauses, he has the answer ready: about twenty million.

Twenty million?

Yes, all these people will be unable to stay in these places. They'll have to leave.

The numbers are staggering, the scale so enormous. Twenty million is a third of the population of Britain. It's so large that the entire nation of Tuvalu would pass unnoticed. Can it really be the case, as we sit here in this stuffy office, overlooking the crowded streets of Dhaka, that this animated version of the destruction of Bangladesh is actually accurate?

Dr Hassan takes me through it again. The shape of the land is well established. The eleven coastal monitoring stations have recorded an average sea level rise of 5 mm per year over the past thirty years with an increasing trend in the most recent. The frequency and severity of cyclones has been increasing. All of that is confirmed. So, what next? Well, once again it's down to computer models. They yield a variety of results but all show an increasing likelihood of sea level rise the faster emissions of greenhouse gases rise.

How sure can you be about this?

Dr Hassan smiles: no one can be sure.

He's a modest, reasonable man, not a scaremonger. He's a hydrologist by training and I imagine how, in another age, he might have had a more genial job studying Bangladesh's water supply or its rivers, not the task of studying its fate.

What's your reaction when you see these forecasts, see the green areas on the map turning blue?

I'm frightened, he admits. But then he smiles. It's impossible to be scared all the time. Like other climate modellers, he has a life of contradictions, spending the day peering into an apparently terrible future, and then going home through the traffic like everybody else.

It's almost too painful to watch. Sukhjan Khatun, a grandmother, is walking, step by careful step, along a makeshift bridge that consists of a single length of bamboo. It's no wider than a tightrope and bends under her weight. With the high tide on Gabura Island an hour away, and her village flooded, this is the only connection between her hut and her daughter's next door. With one arm she's holding a baby grandson and with her free hand she clutches at an upright pole to steady herself. But to move forward she has to let it go in order to be able to take a step and reach the next one. Her sense of balance is all that keeps her from falling into water that is too deep to stand in, too dirty for safety. Her journey couldn't look more precarious. But Sukhjan remains composed, head high and full-length sari somehow still clean. Even her feet seem to have avoided the mud, pale toes curling around the bamboo for support.

The breaching of the defences has made a poor life far tougher. The twice-daily ritual of the flood means that the ground-level part of her home is regularly submerged so she and her husband, Abdul Aziz, a fisherman, have had to create a sleeping area on a little platform just under the roof. It's got about as much room as a very small one-man tent. There's some meagre bedding, a few containers for food and, safely away from the water, a tiny black-and-white television powered by battery.

It's like a hell, she tells me. It's too difficult to live.

We're standing beside her hut while her son readies a canoe. In a few minutes the family will climb aboard and

**Life on a tightrope:** Sukhjan Khatun carries her grandson across a single bamboo pole suspended above the flood water of Gabura Island in southern Bangladesh. Every high tide, the sea breaches the coastal defences.                    *BBC*

travel for two miles through the submerged trees and houses of their village to a camp on the highest of the embankments, refugees in their own land. They have a tent there where they'll stay for the few hours of the high tide. It's safer for the children. But abandoning their homes, even for a short while, carries its own risks: it means no one is around to prevent the flood from causing more damage and there's no chance of even attempting to salvage what's left of the shrimp farms and paddy fields.

In the past, Sukhjan says, we never had salty water coming so close to us. Now we've lost everything and have nowhere to go.

I'm not sure how to raise my next question, based on what Ahmadul Hassan told me of his computer forecasts in Dhaka. It could sound ghoulish, but I go ahead anyway. What do you make, I ask, of the scientists in Bangladesh who say that the sea is likely to get even higher, maybe a whole metre above its level now? Just looking at the flimsiness of Sukhjan's hut and the fragile little bamboo bridge, even a rise in sea level of far less than a metre would be horrific.

I've heard the water will rise, she replies, but I don't know how or why. I am scared, I don't think I'll live then, I won't survive the situation.

At the camp, the tide is now at its height. The top of the embankment is so narrow, only a few metres across, that it can only handle two lines of tents, perched on its edges, strung out for several miles in what must be one of the longest and thinnest camps in the world. A short shower turns the muddy path treacherous and the air is thick with the smells you'd expect in any gathering this dense, this impoverished. I watch Oxfam workers handing out plastic sheets, bamboo poles and rope to construct shelters. A few new wells have been dug but most of the water supply is polluted and, when a small crowd forms around us, parents bring me their babies and infants to show how their skin is broken and infected, how the children can't help scratching after being exposed for so long to dirty water.

It's a miserable scene. One young mother, Asma, is clearly frustrated. Before talking to us, she wants to make herself decent by washing the mud from her feet. She clambers down to the water's edge and does clean them but is then faced with having to walk back through the mud again, her face tense and angry. She articulates what so many specialists have long warned about: that the people of countries like Bangladesh may have no choice but to move, a mass migration of millions.

I think it's not possible to live in this country any longer, she says, her voice soft but insistent. We have to move to other countries. We can't live here.

The lift to the minister's office is out of order so we make our way up several dark flights of stairs. In the outer office, an assistant sits behind a large desk with three old-fashioned telephones. It's late afternoon during Ramadan and, exhausted by the thirst and hunger of fasting, everyone is sleepy. We're offered tea but decline: none of us could face drinking it in front of others who can't. We try to keep the conversation going but we're all faltering, straining to keep awake for our interview with a politician with a job title that most countries don't bother with: Minister for Disaster Management. Bangladesh, stricken by floods, storms and even drought, clearly needs one.

A bookish, gentle man, Dr Muhammed Abdur Razzaque uses his moment on camera to make an appeal. Bangladesh, he says, does not want to be repeatedly begging for international aid. The country has recently come close to self-sufficiency in food production and is proud of it. But the destructiveness of Cyclone Aila in 2009 has convinced the government to make a one-off appeal to help minimise its vulnerability: $5 billion over five years, he says, would secure Bangladesh's sea defences, by building bigger embankments and making the country more resilient to the expected increase in sea level and storminess.

We have to have new designs for embankments, he declares, and we have to raise their height. We want sea defences like in Holland.

I ask where he hopes this money will come from.

The developed countries, he says. As part of a new treaty on climate change.

As we meet, we're a few months from the long-awaited conference in Copenhagen where a new global agreement is meant to be reached. The treaty is supposed to see emissions reduced and to provide help for the poorest countries to achieve two things: to develop using greener technologies and to adapt to the new pressures of a changing climate. Dr Razzaque looks to Copenhagen with hope, as a chance to protect Bangladesh and prepare it for the storms to come.

The industrialised world caused most of the emissions, he says, so should take responsibility now.

The minister's request is civilised, reasonable. He's not angry. But it reflects a groundswell of opinion in the developing world, an increasingly coordinated demand not merely for assistance but for compensation. A few weeks before, at a round of climate negotiations in Bonn in August 2009, an Indian diplomat had accused me, as someone from the former colonial power, of being behind 'three centuries of oppression'. First, he said, Britain denied India the chance to industrialise (insisting that Indian cotton was processed in English mills) and now, in the name of climate change, it's denying India both the chance to develop as the rich countries have done while also failing to offer assistance to prevent the damage that will result. Your attitude is an outrage, he concluded. Dr Razzaque, in Bangladesh, is too polite to put it like that but probably feels the same way.

I think of the snail's pace of negotiations I've witnessed so far, diplomats losing themselves in a netherworld of acronyms. I also remember the frantic work of the human chains on Gabura Island, their elemental struggle of bare hands and raw mud against the rising sea. I try to put the two images together. They're meant to connect. But I can't see how.

# 11

# How doomed are we today?

When I touch the rungs of the ladder above me, I have a very male moment, whipping my hands away because the metal is shockingly warm. I immediately think of the times in our kitchen when Jess, calmly and pityingly, handles pots so hot that they make me yelp and reach for the oven gloves. I could do with her help – or some gloves – right now. I'm near the top of a vast new tower near the town of Sanlucar La Mayor in southern Spain, a futuristic monolith dominating the rolling farmland, and the temperature has been rising the higher I get.

This great structure is the centrepiece of a new kind of power station, one that harnesses the heat of the sun, a process known as 'concentrating solar power'. A landmark in the countryside west of Seville, it stands as a spectacular symbol of the potential of renewable energy. It works by focusing the sun's rays in one direction, fields of hundreds of huge mirrors – each the size of a giant billboard – reflecting the light in a massed set of scorching beams up to a giant boiler near the top of the tower.

Climbing inside, I find there are no windows, no views, no chance to get my bearings, the walls spartan, the lighting minimal. This monument to a green future is entirely grey and at first it reminds me of the kind of stark concrete battlefields featured in computer games. But when our escort explains that we're now the equivalent of forty floors up, about the height of a decent skyscraper, it's so disorientating that we could easily be forty floors below the ground instead. In fact the pallid emergency lighting and austere, brutalist architecture are similar to the dark innards of the US Air Force's underground defence centre inside Cheyenne Mountain in Colorado, both locations designed by people who've watched too many Bond films or, more likely, too much Austin Powers.

The lift that has carried us here goes no further. Hence the ladder with the hot rungs. Cameraman Duncan Stone and I, determined to reach the summit, have no choice but to try to endure the heat, drawing on our feminine sides or at least manfully stifling the whimpers. But the rungs aren't our only problem. The ladder is enclosed in a set of circular safety barriers so that it's impossible to fall off backwards. That's reassuring. But the barriers also mean it's impossible for Duncan and his camera to fit inside at the same time. And there's no question of taking the tripod: I'd unilaterally decided to abandon it long ago.

The only option is to detach the lens from the camera to make the load more manageable. Duncan slings the camera's strap over his head and, with the now-smaller body of the camera suspended at his chest, successfully squeezes inside the safety barriers and onto the ladder. That leaves me to carry the lens, the lesser of the two parts, but still heavy and made awkward by not having a strap. I can't possibly climb the ladder while holding the lens because that would leave me only one free hand. We hunt for some rope so I can sling the lens around my neck but in this sci-fi barrenness there's nothing suitable around. I need a real-life version of those fictional scenes where people replace broken fan-belts with tights. In fact tights would genuinely be useful right now and, in this land of the daintily dressed matador, with a group of Spaniards for an escort, I speculate briefly on whether finding some amongst them is totally inconceivable.

And then a more likely idea flashes to mind, a throwback to my earliest days as a father when, out walking on winter afternoons, our eldest son was small enough to be sheltered inside my coat. I wonder if the lens might be carried in the same way. So I open my shirt and find that I can settle the contraption inside. Then, safely buttoned-up and belt tightened, I start my ascent. The bulge of my shirt swings a little with each step so I feel less like a new father and more like I'm mechanically pregnant, keeping a careful watch over my precious, swaying load. But the task is very welcome: it occupies me enough to ignore the burning sensation in my hands. And this helps, because we realise it isn't just one long ladder we have to climb, but four.

From the distance, the tower doesn't seem real, the concrete bathed in an aura, the very molecules of the air apparently glowing with pale gold. If the beams are aimed correctly, with the mirrors being adjusted to follow the path of the sun, the boiler can be heated to a temperature of 400 degrees Celsius. Water, passing through it, is turned into steam which is channelled at high pressure into turbines which then generate electricity.

The technology was pioneered in the United States in the 1970s so isn't exactly new. But in places with plenty of sunshine – southern Spain, Nevada, Algeria – it's suddenly attracting more interest. One idea gathering support is for vast tracts of North Africa to be given over to solar power stations with the electricity piped north to Europe through undersea cables. The system is certainly eye-catching: the gleam of the mirrors, the simplicity of the concept, the ability to generate power without greenhouse gases. When I first saw a photograph of this installation in Spain, I realised it had television potential too, and that it might also be a cause for some optimism, a shining example of one possible answer to an environmental problem. That would be no bad thing.

I plan the visit at a time when the 'Mr Doom' jokes are spiralling out of control at the BBC, the result of the cumulative effect of being the man reporting on the bubbling of the permafrost and the trashing of the Amazon and the melting of the ice sheets. The cry of 'the end is nigh' from colleagues in the corridors has long become routine. One favourite of mine is the question: 'So, David, tell me, just how doomed are we?' It puts me in a curious position, as someone who's usually cheery, to be cast as a town crier bellowing out unwelcome declarations of approaching Armageddon, a bearer of sandwich boards announcing global death and destruction. Jack, cutting in a way that only one's own children can be, suggests that I might deserve an award for 'services to alarmism'. And Kitty, then aged fourteen, hearing of an approaching assignment, says disdainfully that, 'I suppose it's something really gloomy again'. Craig Oliver, then editor of the *News at Ten*, asks if I can't occasionally offer stories that 'might show a way out'.

So the trip to Spain is partly an attempt to turn a corner in the coverage by exploring solutions – and there are plenty of ideas around: forests of wind turbines out at sea, strange devices to capture the power of the tides and waves, cars running on electricity. And the solar power station is certainly visually stunning, even uplifting. The problem however, having sat through conferences on the topic, is that exciting new forms of power generation are not always the most effective or the cheapest ways to reduce carbon emissions. Often the task is more easily achieved simply by saving energy rather than coming up with clever techniques for making it. If walls are clad in thick insulation, heating costs go down. If old boilers are replaced by newer ones, less gas is needed. If roofs are properly fitted with thick padding, the bills are reduced. But television, rightly or wrongly, relies on images to hold the audience's interest and, after one report on energy efficiency in the home, an editor confessed his boredom with the mundane nature of the pictures and begged me not to show any more video, for a long time at least, of workmen hunched in an attic unrolling loft insulation.

**Boiling point:** at the very top of a solar tower near Seville, the reflected rays of a thousand mirrors arc towards us. It's such an exhilarating sight that Duncan Stone has to tell me to stop shouting into the microphone.                                        *BBC*

The final ladder is the hardest but brings us to our summit, out into the dazzling sunshine and clear air of a narrow roof at the very top of the tower. The view is immense and stirring: on one side, the farms and villages of Andalusia, on the other, a blaze of white, the fields alight with a thousand diamond glints from the rows of highly polished mirrors. The beams are being aimed at the boiler just below us, so it's possible to look towards them without being blinded, though not for long. Being so close to the focus of such raw power, with the arcs of light reaching towards us, is enthralling. So much so that when we start to record a piece to camera Duncan yanks off his headphones. His ears are hurting, I've been deafening him, and he warns me to talk into the microphone rather than shout at it.

But will it work? We're filming in the perfect conditions of a cloudless day and the power generated is still fairly puny, about one-hundredth of the amount produced by a big old-fashioned fossil-fuel station burning coal or gas. And the costs are heavily subsidised. Company officials admit that, however alluring, this particular system may not in the end prove to be a runner. As in any industrial revolution, there are winners and losers, designs may look promising but later fail, duller ones thriving instead. Left to the audience, the answer would be obvious. The web version of the solar tower story receives a record number of hits, readers apparently gripped by this luminous vision standing as a beacon of hope. It tells me that there's an appetite for coverage that explores solutions, an interest in seeing how the world responds.

Montreal, Nairobi, Bali, Poznan, Copenhagen – the roll-call of the UN's global warming meetings for the past five years, an event now as regular as the seasons or the great migrations of the natural world, the tribes of negotiators engaged in a business-class trek from city to city, trailed and harassed by campaigners and lobbyists. It's like the annual run of massed sardines surging past South Africa or the herds of wildebeest crossing the dust of the Serengeti, predators stalking and snapping in their wake, whole ecosystems of delegates advancing or retreating. This is the UN's 'framework convention' on climate change, a series of conferences, painfully slow and ridiculously complicated, but offering the only formal mechanism for the world to act together on global warming.

In Montreal, in December 2005, I had my first, sleepless taste of this process. Though familiar with the agonisingly nuanced debates that afflict NATO and the European Union, I was a novice in this new arena. Long hours waiting for agreement on tank numbers or all-night vigils during rows about fish quotas were nothing compared to the constipation of the UN climate talks. I spent the last night of this first conference dozing in our edit room while the Russian delegates, worried by one particular clause, were trying to contact Vladimir Putin on a plane somewhere over the distant Urals, his phone apparently not working. Cameraman Ron Skeans chose to retreat for shelter beneath his desk, producer Nora Dennehy created a makeshift bed from two office chairs while I stretched out on the floor, the draft negotiating text for a pillow.

When the words of the closing communiqué were finally agreed, just before 6am, we were woken by cheers and barged past security into the hall to interview the then British environment secretary, Margaret Beckett. Her eyes were watering, tears welling with relief that the sleep deprivation was at last over and with joy that, against the odds, the world had managed to agree on something – not the goal of actually cutting greenhouse gas emissions but of merely continuing to talk about it. Filing immediately for the lunchtime news in London, minutes away from being on air, I struggled to find the right balance between explaining how, in relative terms, much had been achieved, while trying to make plain how little difference it would make.

Tears were to become a theme. In December 2007, the UN conference in Bali was even more fraught. Holding the talks on this famous holiday island made everyone ill at ease. Those worried about their carbon footprints felt guilty being there and I dreaded every phone call to London because each conversation was prefaced by an obligatory barracking. The words varied slightly but followed one theme:

While we're freezing our arses off in a British winter, I expect you're lolling with a margarita under a palm tree, aren't you?

For the record, I'd reply, I've only seen one beach because we went to film it, I haven't had anything decent to drink, and I'm up most nights because the *News at Six* is on air at 2am and the *News at Ten* at 6am.

But it never lessened the resentment.

The negotiators faced an even harder struggle. On the last day, queueing for coffee after two nights of broken sleep, I bumped into the chairman of the talks, Yvo de Boer, a charming Dutchman. I'd always known Yvo to be happy to spare me time, his earthy wit knifing through the diplomatic verbiage. This morning however he looked pale, his features rigid. Uncharacteristically, he offered only the briefest greeting and he didn't want coffee. Something was wrong.

A few hours later, a colleague and I got a clue, encountering one of President Bush's special envoys to the talks. A tall, gaunt figure with a face like Uncle Sam and armed with a big walking stick, he was powering himself down a hallway to the American delegation office.

How's it going? My colleague called out.

It ain't over yet, came the harsh reply.

Minutes afterwards, Britain's man at the talks, the environment secretary Hilary Benn, always one to stop, was actually sprinting past us, faced flushed and tie flapping. Cameraman Joe Phua grabbed a shot of this minister on the run. I called after him but to no avail. In these last frantic hours, the crowds of media, activists and officials surged and twisted through the halls in restless and unhappy shoals, red-eyed, fractious and confused, no different to dense packs of reef fish unsure where to feed or whether to flee.

The single most important objective of the talks was to keep alive the hope of a new treaty on climate change. But it was looking vulnerable, one of many disputes being over a footnote, literally. In this particular struggle, the prize was deciding how to refer to the report of the Intergovernmental Panel on Climate Change. This was the study, released to a media scrum in Paris earlier that year, which concluded that it's very likely most recent warming has been man-made. The Europeans wanted the IPCC's recommendations explicitly restated; the Americans would tolerate only a glancing mention – and eventually won, a single digit appearing in print as a reference to a footnote about the IPCC and as a badge of victory in this weirdest of wars. People often ask me what happens in these negotiations and, when I tell this story, no one quite believes me.

Later, the American team was booed (for objecting to another element of the text), an incredibly rare sound for any international forum. Chinese diplomats, meanwhile, never noted for being outspoken, launched a loud complaint about the scheduling of a committee meeting. By this stage I was in the press centre. Perversely, it was easier to follow this unhappy event on a video link relayed to our edit room, a partitioned cubicle in a marquee with feeble air conditioning. It's a secret of the trade that however close you are geographically to diplomatic negotiations, the best view often comes from watching the internal television. The official cameras captured the anger of the Chinese more effectively than I could have seen from the press gallery.

One camera zoomed in on the haggard face of Yvo on the podium. Because it was the last day of the talks, he'd shown politeness to his Indonesian hosts by dressing in one of the colourful batik shirts they'd given all the VIPs. But, like watching a train crash in slow motion, the mood was becoming fractious, even hostile, the collapse of the talks was a real possibility and suddenly the bright material stretched over Yvo's shoulders was shaking. The man trying to keep the world talking about climate change was so upset that he had to leave the chamber.

Only after raucous scenes, including a tactical retreat by the American team, was an agreement of sorts reached. Yvo had recovered, the White House thought the US negotiators had conceded too much, Hilary Benn told me he was delighted, and environmental campaigners unleashed a torrent of press releases condemning the conclusion as a sell-out. The tables of our little cubicle were soon overflowing with hurriedly printed pages of protest, a small forest felled in the cause of angry denunciation.

As in Montreal, the agreement would not itself cut greenhouse gases. Far from it. Bali had created a 'road map' that would in theory lead towards a successor to the Kyoto Protocol and that, in theory, would yield cuts in emissions. I've always been uneasy about road maps. I recall reporting on the one for the Middle East. I'm sure there was talk of one in Northern Ireland too. But the words 'road' and 'map' suggest momentum and purpose while in the choking Asian heat, with tempers flaring, there wasn't much sign of either, as the courteous Balinese, disconcerted by the tension, watched the noisy hordes resume their migration, this time a two-year journey that would end in Copenhagen in December 2009 and the distant prospect of a new treaty.

While the negotiators stuttered and snarled, the vocabulary of climate change was percolating into unexpected areas. Rear Admiral Gene Brooks, commander of the US Coast Guard in Alaska, is not your stereotypical green, indeed more of a red-blooded carnivore, but one unexpectedly troubled by global warming. Ebullient, outspoken, bearish, he's about as far from an environmental campaigner or climate modeller as you could get. Well-cast as the man in charge of thousands of miles of coastline, his forces guard America's maritime border with Russia and its mineral wealth. We meet at the admiral's base on Kodiak Island where he commands an arsenal of firepower that would delight quite a few countries. Ships line the quayside, aircraft manoeuvre over the tarmac and a helicopter hurtling above us lets rip with its machine gun, the rattle of gunpowder echoing off the cliffs. The helicopter's side door is open and we can see the flashes of the weapon's muzzle, part of an exercise to rehearse the defence of oil rigs, a display of polar machismo.

It's the peak of the Arctic melt season – September 2008 – and the retreat of the ice is the second greatest since satellite records began. The admiral is deploying a Coast Guard patrol plane to Alaska's Arctic coast and he's invited Duncan Stone, Mark Georgiou and I to join him on the flight. The plane is a massive C-130 of the sort I haven't flown since getting lifts into the war zones of Angola and the Gulf. There are just eight seats inside the huge hold, fixed beside pallets of supplies. We're given headsets because otherwise it's too noisy to talk. I look at our flight plan and see we'll pass America's highest mountain, Mount McKinley; its most depressing place-name, Deadhorse; and its Arctic oil fields at Prudhoe Bay. We're due to land at the coastal town of Barrow, named after the Royal Navy official John Barrow whose determination had led to the opening up of the Arctic in the first place.

For the aircrew, this is an unfamiliar route. Until recently, they haven't had to head this way.

I ask the pilot if he can let me know when we cross the Arctic Circle.

He looks puzzled. Where's that exactly?

I can't decide if I feel proud or a bore to know the answer: 66 degrees North, the latitude beyond which midsummer sees 24 hours of daylight and midwinter 24 hours of dark.

The pilot didn't know that. Until now he hasn't needed to.

The Arctic is new to the US Coast Guard. When the sea was mostly frozen, there were no intruders, hardly any ships, in fact very little activity at all. No reason to brave the cold.

But that's changed and Admiral Brooks has a remarkably straightforward perspective.

My job, he bellows over the intercom, is to patrol the waters around the United States and there's now a lot of water where there used to be ice, simple as that. I don't care how it's happening or why it's happening, he continues, but what I can tell you is that the ice is going and we've got to move in.

Admiral Brooks says he was stunned by the record thaw of 2007. That cleared the ice from the North West Passage which I had then sailed through, created new hopes for Arctic shipping, triggered a scramble of flag-planting and raised tensions. The melt a year later is almost as severe.

If there's water, we have to be there, the admiral declares. No fussing about the arguments over the causes of the warming or the intricacies of climate forecasts. Less ice means more Coast Guard, period. So for the past few months, he's sent pioneering units of patrol boats and aircraft up to the newly freed Arctic coast. It's what Admiral Brooks calls a new maritime frontier. If cruise ships come through, we have to be ready. If oil and gas reserves are exploited, we have to be on hand.

And what about your borders? Every nation with shores on the Arctic Ocean – Denmark, Norway, Russia, Canada and the United States – is involved in at least one dispute over the precise lines on the map. At this point, we've crossed the coastline and are flying low over mile after mile of open water. The aircrew have opened the massive loading ramp at the rear of the plane and fitted Duncan and I with sturdy safety belts so we can walk towards the very edge and film the grey seas that the admiral now feels obliged to guard.

As long as the region was locked in ice, the border disagreements didn't matter, they were deep frozen. Now thawed, they're relevant and volatile.

Admiral Brooks is clear on the dangers and wants the BBC to know it: with undetermined boundaries and great wealth, he says, the potential is there for conflict or competition. There's always a risk of conflict where you do not have established, delineated, agreed-upon borders. He keeps stressing the point.

Until now, I'd seen the changing Arctic more in terms of the impact on polar bears or the potential for new trade routes or the threat of rising sea levels. Here was an entirely new take on global warming: far from the climate conferences and the green demonstrations and the controversies over carbon footprints, the retreating ice is a cause for geopolitical concern and it's caught the attention of people with guns. How different this brief looked just a few years back: too soft, I'd worried, for a former defence correspondent.

The admiral isn't alone in being alerted to climate change. An extraordinary range of people and organisations wakes up to it. One of the medical community's most august bodies, the Royal College of Physicians, asks me to chair a conference on the possible health impacts of warming. When I'm called to the stage, I see that arranged behind a long table are a few ordinary seats and, occupying the central position, an extravagantly grandiose throne. Which one should the chairman pick? As it happens, I'm just back from Tuvalu, exhausted by jet lag and bruised from a succession of tortuous flights in economy. The throne beckons.

And from my regal position, I hear speaker after speaker raise concerns about diseases, prevalent in warmer regions, which may soon be reaching our shores. But one contribution stills the room more effectively than any other. A fund manager, specialising in environmental technologies, announces a new company policy: that no one will take a flight to meet colleagues for internal business and that any flight to meet clients has to be vetted by a climate committee. To any regular traveller, this is stunning. And for the high-carbon chairman, on his mighty throne, it's a little awkward, too.

Similar questions surface in the self-consciously cool world of music. The British Phonographic Industry – the association representing the recording studios and record labels – is aware that its mainly young customers expect a green response. Research throws up some surprises: the biggest elements of the industry's carbon footprint are from audiences travelling to live events and from the manufacture of plastic CD cases. At a BPI meeting, it's hard to gauge people's reactions to this: we're in a darkened auditorium and everyone seems to be dressed exclusively, and fashionably, in black.

More mundane is a symposium of European packaging industries. I hear how some big-name companies are simultaneously cutting emissions and costs: Colgate Palmolive by using thinner plastic for its toothpaste tubes; Ikea by packing its tea lights in lighter containers; and the newspaper distribution firm Menzies by planning its deliveries more efficiently. And this isn't through altruism. As one senior figure from the telecoms giant BT puts it to a conference, her firm's low-carbon initiatives are designed to 'save money or make money'.

In a briefing by the oil giant Exxon, lambasted by environmentalists for funding climate-sceptic think tanks, executives come out with something astounding. When I ask about the central finding of the IPCC, that it's very likely that most recent warming is man-made, they categorically state that they agree with it. A contractor for the oil industry, himself unsure of the evidence for human-induced climate change, is struck by the Saudis demanding an increase in the tolerance of his equipment to high temperatures: the desert is getting hotter so the usual upper limit of 40 degrees Celsius in the shade has to be increased to a new maximum of 52 degrees. As a stockbroker invites me to an evening discussion on climate change, there's a note of surprise in his voice: his clients, he says, are genuinely interested in exploring what to do. An official in charge of maintaining the defences that prevent low-lying Norfolk from flooding shares with me an anxiety: whether the next generation of pumps will be adequate.

In the space of a year or two, the corporate world seems to have undergone a transformation: it used to be unusual to have a green strategy, now it's unthinkable not to have one, or at least not to be seen to have one. Companies that look green are no longer distinctive. Talk of climate dangers, renewable energy, the need for emissions to peak sooner rather than later – all this enters the mainstream, no longer the preserve of campaigners but featuring in press releases from the Confederation of British Industry, the big insurance firms and all the major political parties.

At a major City law firm, a debate on the Obama presidency's climate policies has drawn investment bankers, accountants and financial traders. The questions come thick and fast – the prospects for a new treaty, the likely attitude of the Senate, the responses of other countries. If I close my eyes the audience could easily be environmentalists, green voices raising exactly the same points. I also puzzle over something that no one raises: criticism of the basic science. I assume there must be a silent minority, or even a majority, who doubt it. I know that amongst the public there are plenty who do because they complain to me. Surely this bastion of the financial establishment would be a safe place to raise objections? Maybe they feel too shy to challenge the prevailing political trend. Or think there's no point. Or – radical thought – they reckon that the evidence does suggest mankind is affecting the climate.

In Wolvercote, on the edge of Oxford, a green evening fills the village hall to capacity. The talk is of leading a low-carbon movement, with one question dominating: what can we, as individuals, do to make a difference? I make sure everyone knows I came by bike.

Some bales have burst open and their contents are heaped on the floor of a poorly lit warehouse: newspapers several months old, unwashed plastic milk containers stinking of cheese, sodden pizza boxes ringed with mould, cans greasy with unused soup. Gingerly, I pick my way through this mess. We're recording a piece to camera and the cameraman tells me to crouch down really close to one particularly noxious pile to improve the shot. I try to breathe through my mouth. This is the least appealing part of my job but I'm under some pressure back home. My kids say I'm acquiring a reputation for focusing too much on the plight of sun-kissed tropical islands. And, according to Kitty, most people's idea of the environment involves the issue she was once in charge of in her class: recycling.

The smell in the warehouse could be a lot worse but it's a freezing day in January 2009, on the edge of Durham, and luckily there's no heating. This is the underbelly of green ambition, recycling's dark side. Around me is the familiar material thrown out by householders, not into rubbish bins, but into those new features of our homes, the blue and green boxes, the orange and red bags. Normally the 'recyclables', as the industry calls them, are sold on to middlemen who in turn sell them to the industries – glass, paper, plastic and metal – which use them instead of more expensive raw materials. But when the recession struck in 2008, the market shrank, China's appetite stalled entirely and the result is what I'm stepping through now: a rotting accumulation of what nobody, for the moment, wants.

It's a sight that provokes a stiff public reaction. On the doorsteps of a Durham suburb, people angrily ask me why they should bother sorting their rubbish if it ends up in a warehouse or dumped in landfill. One protester questions whether any recycled material is ever reused. Rubbish hits a nerve: the prospect of paying more, the new rules about it, the lack of explanation about why we can't just chuck everything into a big hole in the ground like we used to. And conversations about waste quickly broaden to other objections to a green agenda. Recycling serves as a lightning rod for angry questions about the apparent absence of global warming for the past few summers or plans for higher taxes on flights and cars. If there's one trigger for an anti-green backlash, this is it.

As it happens, the market recovers and the 'recyclables' flow again. What I'd witnessed in the warehouse was a blip and there are industries that genuinely use the stuff. But the reasons for recycling obviously aren't getting through to people: that landfill is so wasteful and contaminating that the EU has collectively decided it should be limited; that natural resources are finite so it makes sense to reuse whatever we can; and that methane seeping from the dumps is such a potent warming gas that we should try to avoid creating too much more of it.

At a large industrial site near Leicester, I'm shown a process that may make more sense to the public: waste that can't be recycled is used to make power. I'm given ear defenders, a hard hat and a safety briefing but what I really need is something to block my nostrils – perhaps a 'nosegay', one of those small perfumed bags popular in the Middle

Ages to mask the unrestrained stench of the streets. When a fireproof door opens, I'm ushered inside a gloomy, deafening hall where the smell is so intense, the air so penetrating, that I genuinely can't tell whether I'll retch first or faint. Shallow breathing doesn't help, the stink is so powerful, surging in waves from an enormous rotating drum. But the machine isn't only malodorous. It's also clattering with a din so loud it could be breaking loose. All kinds of waste are being channelled into it to be pulverised by ball bearings the size of grapefruits. What emerges from this nightmarish contraption is a stream of fragments, little scraps of food, mangled pieces of sodden cardboard, twists of used kitchen roll, stuff no one could sell for recycling. Even in the dim light I can see that cameraman Tony Smith's face is pale, while producer Natalie Morton's is taut with disgust. They both look as revolted as I feel. We keep the filming to an absolute minimum. What's happening couldn't be more ecologically friendly but, as we make it outside and gasp for fresh air, I wonder how many self-appointed green gurus could endure it.

The steaming, pulverised waste is fed into a series of tanks. Fortunately they're all sealed tight. Inside, the material is digested – bacteria getting to work in exactly the same way as they do in the thawing soils of the Siberian permafrost. The result is that methane emerges. Unlike the bubbles rising from the lakes of the Russian Arctic, this gas is trapped and piped into a storage tank. From there it's drawn as fuel for a generator which yields a small amount of electricity. This is only a pilot plant but the principle is established: that rubbish can make power. The tedious, resented household task of sorting waste may come to have a more demonstrable value. It's an idea that's catching on. But the process itself? The clashing, reeking hell of that chamber? It's not what most people would picture for a green-tinged future.

Another hot ladder, this time warmed not by the sun but by coal. As in the solar power station in Spain, whoever designed the lift failed to make it reach the top floor. I'm climbing to the roof of the main hall of Kingsnorth power station in Kent, the epicentre of British protests against the dirtiest of fossil fuels. Below me is the field where a climate camp was set up to highlight the impact of burning coal on the atmosphere. And towering above me is the main chimney, a shimmer of exhaust emanating from its top, scaled by Greenpeace demonstrators who were arrested but then acquitted on all charges after a jury heard evidence about coal's effect on the climate. Wisps of steam emerge from vents and the roof itself is hot from the giant boilers down below.

If I look over a railing to one side, I see a moonscape of black, a vast mound of coal, earth-movers like toys guiding it towards the conveyors that lead to the furnaces. In the distance a ship has docked at the quay and a fresh cargo of coal is being unloaded, the most recent deliveries coming from as far away as Russia and Colombia. I'm about to ask about the wisdom of shipping one-off fuels from the bowels of one country across an ocean to another. But I'm cut short by what sounds like a rocket. At the other end of the hall, a jet of steam is bursting from a vent, a column of intense mist. Our escorts hurry to explain that one of the boilers has just been serviced, that it's not properly tuned, that there's no danger. Above the noise, it's hard to follow it all. What I'm thinking about isn't the risk of the whole place blowing up, it's that the technology is decades old and wastes so much heat and energy. The steam, the warm building, the hot ladder – all are signs that some of the coal lugged here from distant lands was burned in vain, and released greenhouse gases without any benefit.

Standing on this monumental structure, I'm struck by our reliance on coal. It's what powered the Industrial Revolution and it remains integral to modern economies two centuries later, producing a quarter of our electricity, half of America's, most of China's and nearly all of Poland's. I've been reaching for light switches all my life without even thinking about how the electricity is going to reach me; most of us don't. It's the power equivalent of urban children thinking milk comes from cartons or plastic bottles. I don't want to exaggerate but, having seen what can be involved in mining coal, I like to think that I'm fractionally less wasteful. In West Virginia, instead of incurring the cost of tunnelling down to the seams, the tops of the mountains are simply removed to expose them, hundreds of peaks dynamited off the map. On a flight with the environmental charity SouthWings, I'm shown the battered remains of the Appalachians, tracts of forest cleared away to reveal bare rock, the contours over dozens of miles blasted into new, unnatural shapes.

At Poland's largest coal mine at Belchatow, the landscape is also being rearranged. I drive so deep into an open-cast pit that I'm below sea level; excavators the length of small streets gouge constantly at the soft brown seams, conveyor belts, miles long, ferrying the broken lumps to a power station belching on the skyline. I make my visit while the Polish government is hosting a round of UN climate negotiations. No one seems to spot the irony. In fact, the staff at the mine are proud.

This is how we keep the lights on, one official tells me. What else are we going to do?

One theoretical option for what they could do is suggested on a billboard outside Charleston in West Virginia. It's emblazoned with the words 'clean coal', a bold assertion, as if saying 'coal is clean' will make it so. Concern about climate change is forcing the coal industry to make a green case for itself and one idea is to trap carbon dioxide in power station chimneys and bury the gas underground. This would indeed make coal 'clean' but no systems exist for doing this yet, except on an experimental scale. The billboard is merely an aspiration.

Several hours' drive to the north, one of America's largest power companies is keen to show me how it's taking carbon capture seriously. It's December 2008, just after the election of Barack Obama, and in a snowy corner of a wood, what looks like a fire hydrant is pumping carbon dioxide into the ground. A network of monitors is checking that it stays down there, an experiment to see if the gas can be kept out of the atmosphere.

I point out to the executive with me that it doesn't look like much. I'm polite but we have driven a very long way to see what appears to be a relatively puny investment given the might and wealth of the fossil fuel industry in America. At this rate, I suggest, the idea of applying this green technology across the whole power sector, of making coal 'clean', will be decades away.

The executive agrees. We're only just starting, we don't even know if it can be made to work, he says.

In his campaign, Barack Obama had promised to clamp down on greenhouse gases, suggesting that he'd create conditions under which it wouldn't be worthwhile building a new coal-fired power station.

Standing in the snow, I ask the power man what he thinks of this.

We'll see, he says, sounding remarkably relaxed. The country needs coal, in fact the whole world needs coal, Mr Obama will come to understand that.

As the afternoon light fades and I look at this one small carbon pump, it occurs to me that the timings don't match, that plans for a green future clash with how the modern world actually functions. Coal is a major source of power and will remain so. Carbon capture could make it cleaner. But no one is yet running a fully scaled-up version. That will take at least another five years. And it'll then be years more to see the systems fitted on a scale that might make a difference. That takes us into the late 2020s or 2030s. And the scientists say emissions should start falling by 2015 or 2020 to avoid the worst effects of climate change later this century.

Am I optimistic or pessimistic? An earnest woman, rising to her feet at a seminar, wants to know. The UN climate conference in Copenhagen is two months away and campaigners and politicians talk of the event as if it could be a watershed for humankind, a gathering of unprecedented importance for shaping the world's destiny. But the negotiations are faltering in the face of the recession, national pressures, vested interests and political opposition. I tell her that I feel as if I'm witnessing a contest between the lure of the new against the reliability of the old, between imagination and inertia. Sometimes it feels as if we're on the cusp of a low-carbon revolution, that the tide of investment could be turning, that if Warren Buffett invests $250 million in China's largest electric car maker then something must be up. But quite often, I say, the opposite looks more realistic, just judging from my own experience. I was thrilled at the wheel of a rocket-speed

Tesla battery-powered sports car – the ultimate in green chic – but I was also relieved that on a long filming trip across the Arizona desert our hire car had a conventional petrol engine with plenty of muscle. Ahead of a cousin's wedding in France, I had read about the new fast trains linking Britain to the rest of Europe but chose the quicker and cheaper 99p seats on a budget airline instead. I fit our house with low-energy light bulbs but, sitting at my desk in the winter, I miss the warmth given off by the old ones.

And the contrast between these two worldviews – one we know, one we may need – is most stark in the United States. Each perspective even has its own rhythms and colours. In Texas, I watch the rise and fall of the 'nodding donkeys' and listen to the hum and squeak as they pump black oil from nearly a mile below. Each move draws another pulse of the lifeblood of modern society, another delivery of the raw material that allowed me to fly across the Atlantic and then drive out here from Houston. The first 'gusher' burst from the Texas rock, not far away from here, a century ago and it's hard to conceive of a day when I haven't benefited from the oil boom that followed. And chatting to the oil men, sensing their quiet confidence, it occurs to me that when every day brings easy riches, when new discoveries promise wealth for children and grandchildren, there's absolutely no reason to change anything.

What about the risk of fossil fuels to climate change? I ask.

What about it? 'Tad' Mayfield speaks for the independent oil producers of Texas. He's thoughtful and modest, not the Stetson-wearing gung-ho figure I'd expected.

I've read a lot of the science about this, Tad says, and I'm not convinced. You can see the sun beating on my face right now – that's a pretty big climate driver. Carbon dioxide? Well, there are just such minute quantities in the atmosphere, what difference can they make?

Tad's not hostile to renewable energy or rude about environmental campaigners; he's just calmly, decisively, content to keep things going as they are. His is a third-generation business; a friend of Tad's, talking with us, says his has lasted five generations. As we talk, a crew on a drilling rig is preparing a new well. There's plenty down there, they tell me. And for a moment, as I listen to them, and catch the sweet smell of the first crude to be brought up, I see this is a way of life that will surely continue. We need the oil and they're happy to sell it.

I put to Tad and his friend the findings of the Intergovernmental Panel of Climate Change. But my words sound laboured, I lose my bearings and I start to wonder if all those scenes I've witnessed of scientists toiling in bizarre locations to gather data ever really happened.

And then I leave the oil men and arrive in California to hear a different rhythm and see a different colour. Off Highway 8, which runs along the border with Mexico and past the huge farms of Imperial Valley, comes the splash of paddle wheels. In a dusty compound run by a company called Biolight Harvesting, the wheels are stirring the bright green waters of vast ponds which are laid out in the shape of racetracks. The beat of the wheels is steady, the flow of the waters gentle and the green is from algae, dense formations of microscopic plants blossoming under the desert sun. I drop my hand into a pond and scoop up what looks like luminous emerald paint. It's a potential source of renewable oil, green rather than black.

For years, this research centre has been a backwater, quietly hunting for ways to cultivate algae and then extract the tiny amounts of fat which the organisms produce. The fat can be processed into fuel and in molecular terms it's no different to Texas crude. And since the algae absorb carbon dioxide when they grow, they may offer a low-carbon, home-grown future. So this little centre, sandwiched between industrial-scale fields of maize and fruit, now finds itself at the heart of a renewable energy frenzy. The centre's manager, Jim DeMattia, tells me that in the past year he's hosted visits from the Pentagon's advanced projects office, the space agency NASA, the car maker Toyota, oil people from Brazil and China. Executives from Exxon studied the paddle wheels before announcing a $600 million algae venture with the genetics pioneer Craig Venter. And all are asking the same question: is it possible to mass-produce oil from pond scum?

Amid the faint reek of a stagnant pool, Jim explains why this green revolution is feasible. The algae do not need clean water but can grow in the run-off from crops. Their cultivation is not sophisticated and could be handled by farmers. And huge funds are now being directed to solving the practicalities of a fledgling industry with its own new lexicon: 'harvesting oil' and 'bio-refining'. Listening to this, it's easy to be enthused. In a way never possible with 'old' oil, 'green' oil seems cool.

At Sapphire Energy, an algae fuel firm on the Californian coast at La Jolla, the lobby holds a stack of surfboards. Most of the employees are young and, when a good swell comes in, a few abandon their bubbling flasks of green to hit the waves. But amid the T-shirts, spiky hair and piercings there's a powerful sense of motivation. These highly qualified twenty-somethings help us to film but are also eager to turn back to their test-tubes and microscopes. The firm has already produced enough algae fuel to help fly a passenger jet and to power a car across the US to Washington to lobby for a new climate-change law.

Talking to Sapphire's smiling chief executive, Jason Pyle, it occurs to me that he represents the exact opposite of the Texan oilman Tad Mayfield. Both are polite and well-intentioned, anxious to be cooperative with the filming, self-consciously checking the collars of their open shirts. But Jason is convinced by the science of global warming, believes we cannot keep burning fossil fuels and is determined to green America's oil supply. By contrast, Tad supports continuity, knows that black oil works and is confident that it has no downside. Jason has generous backing from the mighty Wellcome Trust – and his competitors are attracting serious money too – but he's on an uncertain path: algae fuel may prove to be too expensive or difficult. Tad, meanwhile, earns money with every stroke of his pumps and is sure his children will as well. Two men, two outlooks, America at a crossroads. The world's most inventive economy is on the brink of a momentous choice: between Jason, eager for change, and Tad who doesn't see the need to risk it.

I've swallowed a seasickness pill, convinced myself I'll be all right but can't help fingering the packet just in case. It's now one month to go to Copenhagen and on a raw November day I'm on a filming trip off the Orkney Islands in the far north of Scotland. These turbulent waters are the test bed for machines that could exploit a potentially radical new source of energy: the pure, natural strength of the waves and the tides. The seas off Britain are said to hold the equivalent of a dozen power stations' worth of energy. The big question: can it be harnessed? And like any green businesses, the companies involved in this work are on tenterhooks, awaiting the outcome of the climate conference. For them, it'll be a test of whether the world is serious about tackling global warming. Expectations for the event are rising dramatically as Barack Obama, Wen Jiabao, Gordon Brown and other leaders announce that they'll attend. But whole industries, like the one I'm visiting now, need to know if they'll achieve anything.

Our boat ploughs through a notoriously fast-flowing strait known as the Fall of Warness, a forbidding name better suited to Lord of the Rings than to pioneer eco-engineering. It's rough out here, memories of the North Cape flood back and a cold spray shoots up from the bow. I keep my gaze on the horizon and cheer myself with the thought that at least there are no Norwegians on board. More useful, the sight ahead is strange enough to be distracting: a giant fan poised above the waves. About six metres or twenty feet across, it's like an enormous propeller, the misplaced part of some vast ship. It's a tide turbine, like a wind turbine except that its blades are spun by the currents. The fan has been raised so we can film it. When in operation, the device is lowered into the path of the water that surges from the North Atlantic to the North Sea and back every day at nearly ten miles an hour. Its makers, OpenHydro, envisage hundreds of the devices on the seabed, their spinning blades generating power that's cabled ashore, an attractively simple notion which does actually work. The problem is, it's too early to know if it can succeed on a grand scale.

The same question confronts many companies in this field including the one behind the so-called 'oyster'. Developed by Aquamarine Power, this is as apparently simple as the tide turbine. Reaching it involves another pill and another boat, this one bucking wildly in the swell. Producer Dominic Hurst and I have to lock arms around cameraman Paul Francis as he films our twisting, rolling approach to a site known as Billia Croo and what looks like a giant yellow flap rearing above the surf. Hinged on the seabed, the flap is about twice the size of a double-decker bus and is flicked back and forth by each passing wave. Every time this great metal wall is moved, it sends a pulse of water at high pressure to a generating station onshore. Fifteen hundred 'oysters' would produce the power of a typical fossil-fuel plant.

Once again, as with the algae producers in the United States, I sense that an industrial revolution is within sight. There's faith in these technologies and the companies are attracting highly qualified people. In this hostile environment, I'm particularly struck that the operations managers of the tide turbine and the oyster are both women: Sue Barr, a former civil servant, and Frances Tierney, an engineer. Extremely articulate advocates of their systems and determined to overcome the practicalities of carbon-free electricity, they see marine energy as a no-brainer: for the sake of the next generation, why wouldn't you tap a resource that gives you power without greenhouse gases?

We talk as their sector wins unprecedented government backing, both from London and from Edinburgh. But – and it is a significant 'but' – what's unknown is whether this brave new enterprise can ever deliver power in the volume and at a cost that will make a difference. And that partly depends on seeing a clear global signal: that the world is genuinely prepared to move away from fossil fuels.

Three weeks to Copenhagen and I've just done exactly what everyone advised me not to do: run in the feeble air of the Andes. I'm in Bolivia in the slum city of El Alto, a sprawl of one million of Latin America's poorest people living beside the capital, La Paz, at a dizzying 4,000 metres, more than 13,000 feet. I'm breathless. All I've done is follow Tony Fallshaw with the tripod. We're filming a group of children making their daily journey to a communal tap to collect water. Tony has shot them setting off from home but has now sprinted ahead to capture their arrival at the tap. Instinct and duty dictate that I hurry after him. This must be what a marathon or extreme obesity feel like, lightheaded and obsessed with finding somewhere to lie down. Looking back at Dominic Hurst, arriving with the radio gear, I wonder whether any of us will need the cylinder of oxygen he's brought in our car. Maybe the special

**Running dry:** the cracked mud of one of the largest reservoirs serving El Alto, as the glaciers retreat on the mountains behind me. At 4300 metres (14,000 feet), we are all suffering from the thin air.                                                  *Dominic Hurst*

Bolivian pills we've taken will see us through: they contain a decent dose of coca powder, apparently.

We've come to Bolivia because its government is clamouring for help from the UN conference. Temperatures in the Andes have risen faster than the global average and the glaciers that provide much of the country's water are shrinking rapidly. The Bolivian case is like the one I heard in Bangladesh: that since the industrialised world caused the warming by filling the air with greenhouse gas, it should not only pay compensation and offer massive support but should also drastically cut its emissions. Unlike Bangladesh, the threat here is from having too little water rather than too much. Even now the inhabitants of El Alto struggle to find enough, like the children we're filming now.

I'm not surprised by the breathlessness – I'm no good at altitude. Nor am I that surprised by two of the famous sights of this region: the Aymara women in their distinctive bowler hats and the bulging cheeks of the men as they chew balls of coca leaves. What *is* startling is the tap we're beside: it's protected by a padlock. It's the only one for a community of eighty families, about 400 people, so it needs to be controlled. It also has to be guarded. That's because it was set up illegally and draws water from another neighbourhood's supply. The keeper of the key, the local leader Marcario Muraga, admits that disputes over water often escalate into fights. If conditions are drier in future, how much worse will things get?

Marcario's children have their containers ready. The eldest, Christian, undoes the padlock and reaches for the tap. It's a tense moment, twisting the handle, because often no water comes at all. Today the tap does run, but it sputters weakly. Christian can't prevent quite a lot of the water spilling past the necks of the containers and forming a little pool in the dust at his feet, a precious commodity wasted.

In a dried river bed nearby, a noxious stream trickles through mounds of rubbish. The smell is one of raw sewage. Tony films a few shots and then calls out to us. Using his zoom, he's spotted an astonishing scene: three women are actually standing in the water. We hurry closer. The women are hunched in the stream and are plunging their hands into the poisonous brown flow. They're washing old plastic bags, a slum version of recycling. I ask why they're doing this here. We have no choice, comes the reply, there's no other water we can use. This is how they make ends meet: collecting bags, cleaning them and then selling them. I wonder if their customers know where the bags are washed. More worrying, there's a girl aged about three sitting nearby and I think of her inhaling the fumes.

Above the river-bed, in the distance, I can see the peaks of the Andes and a few of the glaciers that are such a cause for concern. Common sense would say that melting would be helpful, freeing more water. But sudden thaws produce surges of water – which are often wasted – and after a while the flow is reduced. Ideally the melting would be steady and fresh snow would replenish the ice; problems start when those two processes are out of balance. The most graphic example is the fate of the glacier on the mountain of Chacaltaya. Until recently it had enough ice to host a ski resort, a popular destination for the wealthy of La Paz, just half-an-hour's drive away. We venture up to see what's happened. The road twists through hairpin bends, the tyres spin on wet stones, until we arrive in the gaspingly thin and freezing air of 5,300 metres, more than 17,000 feet. Of the ski resort, all that's left is a faded Swiss-style chalet. And the glacier? It's shrunk to a tiny patch of white amid vast sweeps of dark bare rock.

The fear is that Chacaltaya is a portent of a great melt to come, that many of Bolivia's glaciers could vanish within decades. I ask the governor of La Paz region, Pablo Ramos, what can be done. An earnest, elderly figure, he talks me through the options: dig more wells, build more reservoirs. But he knows that may not be enough. With some embarrassment, he then outlines much more drastic thinking: that if not enough water can be brought into the city, then people will have to move out of it or even *be* moved out. It's a cataclysmic idea, a major city running so dry that people have to be shifted elsewhere. The governor doesn't blame all of this on climate change. And the scenario may be years away. But the fact that it's even being thought about is disturbing. And for the Bolivian government, it's yet another reason to look with hope to Copenhagen.

# 12

# Hopenhagen and beyond

The posters at the airport proclaim our arrival in 'Hopenhagen'. Denmark has planned for this global event for two years and the street art and the ice sculptures all scream hope – hope for a deal, hope that the hype will yield something tangible. I wonder how pleased the marketing people must be to have come up with 'Hopenhagen', one short pun embodying a city's dream for world leaders to chart a new course in mankind's relationship with the planet. Banners hang from office buildings with cheering images of the globe, the word 'green' is applied as liberally as paint and delegates are offered free transport, invitations to eco-parties and even discounts in the red-light district. A Baltic freeze may be whistling through the streets but this crucible of goodwill is where a more sustainable future will be forged.

Pity no one told the security people at the conference venue, a dreary collection of halls known as the Bella Centre, standing in a half-built suburb. The economist Lord Stern has described this gathering as one of the most important since the Second World War but it doesn't feel much like that arriving outside it. Taxis can only come to within two hundred metres of the entrance so Duncan Stone and I decide to carry his gear in two runs. I tell the taxi driver that we'll take the first load and be back in a couple of minutes.

But the crush for accreditation is so intense that the queue doesn't move for an hour. Only one desk is open for the media. Undaunted, we agree to take it in turns to head back to get the rest of the gear – a good plan until the guards stop us from leaving. Why? For security. We're trapped in a climatic catch-22, unable to get in or get out. And every minute the taxi's meter is running. I ask a policeman if he can pass a message by radio to his colleagues out on the main road; maybe they can explain to our driver what's happening. He refuses.

Another hour passes. Usually climate conferences are a nightmare only once you're inside, not while trying to enter them as well. In the end it takes three hours to get our badges and collect the last of the gear. As it turns out, we're lucky. People arriving later were to be stuck for far longer: the head of Oxfam queued for six hours, Gordon Brown's special climate adviser for seven, and one Chinese negotiator tried to get in for three days. Not an auspicious start.

Inside, it's not much better, like the worst kind of over-crowded campsite in high summer, a Glastonbury with suits instead of music. Fifteen thousand people have filled a centre that can't cope. Queues form for everything: forty-five minutes for a hot dog, an hour for a meal. More importantly, the Danish government is struggling to host the talks themselves. The process is so huge and complicated: 192 countries (or 193 depending on who you talk to), a labyrinthine agenda, multiple versions of draft texts, endemic confusion, an increasingly fractious atmosphere.

A bid to fashion an informal deal with a more manageable group of about forty countries backfires: those not included become resentful. The African delegates boycott some of the early sessions in protest at the way they're handled. Though the biggest economies have all made offers on greenhouse gases that get close to what's needed, no one's budging any further. And the exchanges between negotiators from the two most significant countries, China and America, descend from pointed to barbed.

Campaigners from the environmental groups and charities add to the pressure. Unlike in any other international negotiations, they're allowed inside, however noisy their stunts. In polar-bear suits or dressed as trees, clutching placards and chanting slogans, they surge through the throngs of officials and diplomats. Oxfam have brought a Bangladeshi refugee all the way from Gabura Island. I'd met Shorbanu Khatun in the miserable conditions of her camp three months before. Back then she was lashing plastic sheeting to her shelter and snapping at her four children to keep the mud off their clothes. Here she cuts an elegant figure, head high, sari immaculate, patiently explaining her cause. I ask her what she makes of it all. It feels good to share my experience with all the big people, she says. They are telling me they will do something for us and I believe they will do.

It's heartening to see her so poised and determined. But I can't bear to tell her that the talks are getting nowhere. Scheduled to last for two weeks, the big guns – ministers and leaders – are due only for the last few days. Maybe they can salvage something. And all the time, gathered in a side street in the centre of Copenhagen, is a group with its own hope: that the whole thing will fail.


A hurriedly written sign marked 'climate conference' points to a doorbell. One floor up, in a turn-of-the-century apartment building, a suite of panelled rooms with elegantly painted ceilings is the venue for a far smaller rival event.

This is a meeting of climate sceptics, people who see themselves as dissidents, proud to be rallying opposition to the mistaken cause of global warming. Our arrival provokes some contradictory greetings. Very glad you're here, says one man. About time too, says another, I thought the BBC was banned from criticising climate change.

We turn up while several dozen people are listening to a lecture. A scientist is explaining his theory that the sun is the only significant cause of any variation of the climate. I've stepped into a parallel universe. Here, carbon dioxide is a good thing – plants like it. Mainstream scientists are corrupted – too scared to challenge the orthodoxy. And governments will use any excuse to raise taxes – in the name of saving the planet. The UN conference is seen as a misguided process that will cripple growth for no good reason.

Like any community, this one encompasses a range of opinions. There are researchers like the man speaking now – small in number, by any count – who flatly dispute the notion that man-made greenhouse gases are adding to any warming at all. A far greater number hold a more nuanced view: that our emissions are increasing and are having an effect on the climate but one that's too limited to be worth spending any money on. In other words, the basic physics may be right but the dangers have been wilfully exaggerated. And a further group suspect that the whole notion of global warming is ideological: that it's a socialist pretext for curbs on capitalism.

Though on the fringes of power, this movement recently received fresh ammunition. A few weeks before the summit, a decade's worth of private emails from the University of East Anglia was made public – hacked or leaked, no one is sure. The emails involved the university's Climatic Research Unit – a key body working on the global temperature record – and flashed onto sceptic websites as proof that data was being manipulated.

In one message in 1999, the director, Professor Phil Jones, wrote of preparing a graph using a 'trick' and 'hiding the decline' in temperatures recorded by one particular set of figures. He later tried to explain what he'd meant. 'Trick' was just a colloquial term for a 'clever technique'. 'Hiding the decline' was a statistical device. One batch of data from tree rings had for decades provided a reliable temperature record. But in the most recent years the tree rings showed there'd been cooling while instruments showed warming. So, the explanation went, better to hide any tree-ring data that was obviously wrong and paste over it the more accurate instrumental figures.

Logical? Conceivably. Justifiable? Not really. And the choice of words? Damaging. Other emails raised more fundamental questions. They revealed how Phil Jones urged colleagues to delete messages about the latest IPCC report – to which they had been important contributors – rather than release them under Freedom of Information requests. Under relentless pressure from sceptics challenging his working methods, he had clearly felt resentful. But openness is a guiding principle of science so the very idea of deleting mail was shocking. I remember meeting Phil Jones. A shy man, he'd struck me as cautious rather than cavalier. He'd described winning a battle to keep one key phrase in the final text of the IPCC report: that warming is 'unequivocal'. Back then, he could never have imagined the battle he is in now.

According to the sceptics in Copenhagen, the revelations are the smoking gun of a massive cover-up. In the United States, senators opposed to new laws on climate change have used the emails to challenge the reliability of all temperature data. But there's one key question: is this making any difference up the road on the edge of Copenhagen at the UN conference?

There's a jostling pack of cameramen, too dense to penetrate; Duncan and I are too late for a good position. Any minute now, we're about to see the biggest star so far in

Copenhagen: Arnie Schwarzenegger, action-movie hero and Governor of California. With the negotiations in stalemate, all 3,000 of us in the media are restless for a new angle and Arnie may provide one. I want to know what he thinks about climate sceptics – he's a Republican and many of his party are emboldened by the leaked emails. But we're struggling to get close. I feel like one of those unlucky lion cubs filmed in wildlife documentaries, the unfortunate who can't force his way through the frenzy to reach the meat.

I then notice that an official cameraman from Danish television has a prime location on a platform. I try to climb on but he rebuffs me firmly. I linger nearby. Suddenly there's a commotion: Arnie is coming, his shoulders and chest so huge that it looks like he's wearing body armour beneath his suit. Everyone strains for a view. Including the Danish cameraman. He's obliged to get to work and as his head bends down over his camera's eyepiece I hop up beside him.

Arnie gives the first question to a reporter close at hand.

Everything hinges on timing. If I launch my question while he's still speaking, he'll ignore me. Too late and someone else will jump in. I sense that he's about to wrap and let fire. Governor, over here, BBC. He turns his massive frame my way, arms hanging like sturdy branches.

What do you say to those in the United States who don't believe global warming is man-made?

The question seems to throw him at first.

Well ... you know ... I think ... the key thing is that we continue campaigning, continue communicating.

But then he gets into his stride.

Global warming is a huge obstacle and if we don't spend the money now it'll cost us five times as much later.

I put a similar question to another famous right-wing politician, one never to pass up an opportunity to bash fashionable causes: Boris Johnson, Mayor of London. Fresh from the bracing cold outside, his blond mop of hair is wilder than usual, his cheeks redder. I ask what he makes of the state of climate science, and in particular of his fellow Conservatives like Lord Lawson who say the jury is still out on man-made warming.

The jury is definitely back, Boris declares, and the evidence is overwhelming. And even if it isn't, he says, it makes excellent sense to use energy more efficiently and cut our bills. And in the conference itself, as delegate after delegate is given the chance to speak, only one even mentions the emails or raises any questions about the reliability of the evidence.

It's the man from Saudi Arabia. No surprise: the oil state that doesn't want an end to oil.

It's the final, febrile day and there's anarchy in the air, the buzz of the unknown. A senior British negotiator tells me 'it's all in the balance.' A top UN official says the talks are 'in crisis'. The main session is delayed for two hours. A draft agreement drawn up by the Danes overnight is rejected. Barack Obama gives a lacklustre speech and Premier Wen Jiabao of China offers nothing new, their rhetoric recycled.

The most important leaders are whisked from room to room beyond our view. But those from lesser countries have to run the gauntlet of the massed cameras. Duncan and I lie in wait, spot the president of the Maldives and join the white-water of media and security surging around him.

I ask how it's going.

I think we'll have an understanding in the next few hours, he replies, before being swept away.

But by mid afternoon, nothing has been achieved.

I get an email from a well-placed friend: it's a leak of a draft text. With no targets and few hard numbers, it looks incredibly weak.

In the early evening, I'm called to a briefing with Gordon Brown. Rooms are in such short supply that the only one

**In the thick of it:** on the final day of the Copenhagen conference, I accost President Mohamed Nasheed of the Maldives as he runs the gauntlet of massed cameras. He expects a deal soon – rather too soon, as it turned out.     *BBC*

available to Her Majesty's Government is an empty shop in an arcade attached to the conference centre. We're led along an echoing corridor of silent clothes stores. In one of the windows, the mannequins stand naked.

Brown's face is pale, drawn. There are real difficulties, he says, on cutting greenhouse gases and on verifying China's promises to limit emissions. For the first time, he raises the possibility of failure: alternative 'proposals' are being considered in case the talks collapse.

There are rumours of Nicolas Sarkozy heading for the airport, of others pulling out too. Wen Jiabao apparently spent most of the afternoon in his hotel. But just before 7 pm local time we hear he's meeting Barack Obama. I go live into the *News at Six*, alongside other broadcasters lined up near me – American, German, Dutch and British – and report that hopes are fading.

But the evening isn't over. An hour later I encounter a spectacle borrowed from the natural world: an entire species in panic, hundreds of journalists racing through the hall, drawn inexorably in one direction.

Obama, Obama, is the murmur on everyone's lips, he's going to give a news conference. Is this the promised breakthrough?

I pause – the endgame can't be this simple. But then I feel the pull. I'm an iron filing no different to the rest and can't resist hurtling towards the magnet of the story.

We elbow and push to the press conference room but no one can move, the place is jammed. A UN official fights his way to the podium and announces what no one wants to hear: nothing is planned, there'll be no Obama.

But what he doesn't know – and we only find out later – is that Obama is giving a press conference but not here and not to us. Instead he's speaking to the White House press corps in some secluded room.

The first sign of this comes at about 9.45 pm as the wire services flash the few short, capitalised words of breaking news: *MEANINGFUL AGREEMENT REACHED – US OFFICIAL*. It turns out Obama has been meeting not just Wen of China but also the leaders of a few of the world's other new powers – Manmohan Singh of India, Luiz Lula of Brazil, Jacob Zuma of South Africa. They've reached what the Americans claim is an 'important first step'. I know from other summits how first steps are always code for a fudge, that they're the diplomacy of the lowest common denominator.

In this case that means no mention of the firm figures that so many say are essential: targets and dates for cutting greenhouse gases.

I call a few contacts: American, UN and British. No one answers. Then I get a text from one of the closest aides to Ed Miliband, Britain's Climate Change Secretary:

'No deal imminent'.

What? The Americans are saying one thing, the Brits another and it's almost time for the *News at Ten*. Is this the long-awaited deal? Or White House spin masking failure? As I fit my earpiece and hear the studio countdown in London, it occurs to me that the British text hints at two things: that whatever the Americans are saying, the task isn't sorted yet and that the Brits, despite pushing so hard on climate change, are not in the innermost loop.

An agreement is emerging among key countries, I report, but there's also a long way to go to convince the rest.

I'm due to make another live appearance at the end of the programme in about twenty minutes but, wired in, I can't move from my position. Clutching my BlackBerry, I exchange hurried emails with colleagues.

Roger Harrabin says the Bolivians are furious that a deal's been stitched up without them: 'anti-democratic, anti-transparent'.

At 11.13 pm Richard Black reports that he's seen the final text: it's not legally binding, there's no timetable, only an aspiration to limit the rise in global temperatures to 2 degrees Celsius. Seconds later Mark Georgiou says Sarkozy describes the deal as 'not perfect'.

Back on air, presenter Fiona Bruce asks me if the conference has ended in success or failure. A fair question, journalism requires instant judgement. But live television allows no time for reflection and I'm hesitant to write the whole thing off.

It's clearly not a success. But nor is it a total failure. So I stall. The talks haven't ended yet, I explain.

On the positive side, the deal requires countries to publish their plans for limiting greenhouse gases. It sets up a fund worth $30 billion over three years for the poorest countries. Also, nobody actually walked out. But the accord is not legally binding so falls massively short of what was hoped for. And the wording is vague on when global emissions should peak: 'as soon as possible', it says, not the hard deadline of 2020 set by scientists.

For that reason, I conclude, there'll be 'a lot of unease' about whether the event will deliver what it was meant to: cuts in greenhouse gases deep enough to avoid the worst effects of global warming.

Minutes later I regret not using stronger language. A senior British official tells me there'll be a 'bloodbath' when this American-brokered text hits the conference floor.

He's right.

Many delegates have come to negotiate a treaty that might help the survival of their countries and the objections last all night and most of the next day. A hand goes up from Tuvalu. This delegate has travelled from the other side of the world for this. I think back to the waves of the King Tide breaking over his island's main road, the bubbles of seawater pushing up through the coral into Teimana's vegetable plot, how rising seas could make life impossible in a matter of decades.

With bitterness in his voice, the Tuvaluan negotiator describes how he sees the deal: it looks like we're being offered thirty pieces of silver to betray our people and our future.

His is the most eloquent intervention, a mix of anger and sadness. Others are more vitriolic. But most are resigned and by the next afternoon nearly all countries reluctantly accept the accord. As Mark Georgiou loads a batch of gear into a taxi, he offers a lift to a delegate shivering in the queue behind him. It's the environment minister of the Maldives.

We were offered something or nothing, he says, and if that's the only choice then 'something' is better.


I'm one of the last broadcasters left. The crowds have vanished and the din is replaced by the gentle clatter of catering trolleys and the chatter of cleaners sweeping away heaps of coffee cups. A few disconsolate figures seem too tired to leave. A senior Met Office scientist is openly disappointed. And a prominent Bangladeshi adviser says a golden opportunity was lost; with the leaders long since gone, he doubts whether this subject will ever attract so much attention again.

It's time for my last slot. Night has fallen and the ice on the glass roof looks grey. I remember how in this same centre earlier in the year I'd heard some really radical ideas for tackling global warming if negotiations were to fail. The talk then was of seemingly wild schemes to 'geo-engineer' the climate: ships that would spray seawater into the air to encourage reflective clouds to form; artificial trees to soak up carbon dioxide; aircraft to scatter sulphur into the high atmosphere to mimic the cooling effect of volcanoes. Shunned for years as too wacky or too dangerous to contemplate, these ideas are now moving closer to the mainstream of scientific research and given what happened – or didn't – just now in Copenhagen I assume we'll hear more of them.

Only a few dozen of us media people are still around. It reminds me how most of my reporting has been from places too remote, too obscure, to bump into other journalists. I clip a microphone to my jacket and think of fitting them to thick anoraks in the Arctic, open shirts in the Amazon, a wet-suit in the Pacific. My mind must be wandering because it takes me a second or two to realise the studio director in London is calling out to check that I can hear.

Three minutes to air, he says.

The man operating the camera is from an agency and I haven't met him before. While we wait, we chat about Christmas, then about the conference.

Didn't do a lot, he suggests.

I agree.

We both pause to listen to the story before mine: it's about Eurostar trains being paralysed by freezing conditions either side of the Channel Tunnel.

Not much global warming there, says the cameraman.

I'm tired but explain how weather and climate are different: how there'll always be weather, hot or cold, heatwaves or deep freezes, ever-changing and sometimes vicious, while climate is the kind of weather you get over a thirty-year period, the length of a typical generation, and that's what they were talking about here.

He nods and then asks: what's next?

I'm not sure. But then I look across the hall and see the stand set up by the organisers of the next big climate conference: Cancun, Mexico, December 2010. What might that produce?

I glance at the Belgian TV correspondent standing in the live position next to mine and wonder who'll be called to speak first. But then my earpiece carries the voice of the presenter in London starting her throw to me: let's cross live to Copenhagen, she's saying, for the latest.

The latest is that the prospects for reaching a treaty are more distant than ever. Months after the event, I meet some of the negotiators and officials at a seminar in London and it's like gatecrashing a session of bereavement counselling. In the lunch break, the throng around the buffet brings me close to faces that are still etched with crushed expectations. Strained and seemingly exhausted, they load up with rice and spiced chicken, and endure the discomfort of trying to eat while standing in a crowd, papers squeezed under an arm, one hand clutching a plate, the other holding a fork and a glass, desperate glances confirming that there's nowhere to put anything down. For years these people were the self-confident vanguard of a globally important agenda, a revolution in how we relate to our planet, a subject that commanded the attention of presidents and rock stars. Now they look like the victims of a disaster, enfeebled by Post Copenhagen Stress Syndrome.

Initially, with a journalist among them, there's some brave talk about restoring momentum, of Obama finding a new way to act without Congress, of clever devices for breathing new life into the Kyoto Protocol. But in private, once the plates are cleared, a surprising number recognise a less optimistic reality: that the process is stalled, possibly terminally. When I approach one official, involved in planning the UN conference in Cancun, he pulls me away to a corner. He's in a pivotal position, right at the heart of the diplomacy, and wants to tell me something. His voice is so low it's almost a murmur.

Don't quote me, he says.

OK. Under the rules of the seminar, I'm not allowed to identify him. I lean closer.

The international will, he whispers, simply doesn't exist. The chances are really bad.

I'm straining to follow him. You mean, the chances are really bad for a treaty at Cancun? That was always one scenario in the wake of Copenhagen, that the next conference would fare better.

No, no. He screws up his face in irritation. Obviously I've missed the point.

There probably won't be a treaty at all, he says.

What? You mean, not for several years? I ask because a theory doing the rounds is that Obama may be willing to give climate change another push after the next presidential elections in 2012.

No, the diplomat says. I've misunderstood him once again. There won't be a treaty. Never.

Never? This is big news. If this man can't see it happening, the prognosis must be bad, that a previously unimaginable scenario might unfold: that the years of effort, the talking and flying, the meetings and papers, come to nothing. Why? Some of the reasons are obvious: President Obama has failed to win domestic support, China won't budge, and the other big polluters don't see why they should jump if the others don't. And lurking in the background may be a wariness of public opinion which, in Britain and America, has become more sceptical. Unusually cold winters make global warming seem less plausible and questions about the integrity of climate research may have sown further confusion.

The UEA emails were only part of an unprecedented challenge to science. Within six weeks of Copenhagen, criticisms of the UEA had extended to the international body meant to marshal the best research, the UN's Intergovernmental Panel on Climate Change. I recall the packed press conference that launched its most recent report in Paris in February 2007 where words like 'landmark' and 'definitive' littered many of the stories filed that day, including mine. Now this supposed bedrock of global-warming science is revealed to contain flaws.

In one passage, a clumsily written paragraph asserts that the glaciers of the Himalayas could disappear by the year 2035. The claim is wholly implausible. The huge ice streams in the world's highest mountains could never melt that quickly. Some glaciers are showing signs of retreat – as I saw in the Andes where those at lower altitudes are especially vulnerable. But no serious forecast could possibly specify a particular year by which all of them will vanish. And worst of all: the line was taken not from any proper scientific literature but from a report by the campaign group WWF which in turn had quoted a magazine interview. And that had, in fact, suggested the year 2350, not 2035, as an approximate date for the loss of the glaciers, so not only was the use of the reference wrong, it was wrongly quoted as well.

This causes widespread dismay. Like many, I'd always imagined the IPCC reports to be diligent distillations of the most reliable science – drawing only on research that's peer-reviewed and published and then filtered through several layers of expert scrutiny. It is, after all, meant to be robust enough to act as the basis for international policy. But the mention of the year 2035 must have passed under the noses of at least half a dozen reviewers and still remained uncorrected. For the IPCC, this is a self-inflicted wound and many are now asking: what else is wrong with the work?

'Himalayagate' triggers a frenzied search for other mistakes. What emerges is not so much a long list of errors as the exposure of the fact that some conclusions about climate impacts are referenced to publications by campaigners rather than scientists. This is what's described as 'grey' literature and is not normally regarded as reliable science. All this fuels the suspicion that the report's findings are loaded in favour of alarmism.

Suddenly on the back foot, leading scientists strain to remind people of the basic tenets: that more greenhouse gas almost certainly means more warming, that the rise in carbon dioxide I witnessed on Mauna Loa is still happening, that fieldwork and satellite studies from the Arctic to the Amazon are yielding overwhelming evidence of the potential dangers, that the overall thrust of the IPCC is still valid. But for news editors, weary of environmental claims or increasingly cynical of them, this provides a rich seam of new angles and a fresh take on a flagging story.

Given the seriousness of the allegations, inquiry panels are set up to investigate the UEA emails and the work of the IPCC. Sceptics watch like hawks. The panellists are meant to be impartial and are scrutinised for signs of 'warmism', a new, derogatory term for anyone who believes in man-made climate change – I'm accused of it quite a lot. The member of one panel, the editor of the journal *Nature*, is forced to resign almost immediately. The bloggers unearthed a radio interview in which he had played down the importance of the UEA emails. It's as if climate science is on trial.

The verdicts, when they come, bring few surprises. Phil Jones and his unit at UEA should have been more open with their working methods. And he should have managed his data more effectively so that others could check it. But – the crucial point – he did not manipulate the science, his work on the global temperature record is reliable. And the IPCC? It too should have been more transparent and more careful. But its fundamental conclusions about man-made warming? They're still intact, the key points of climate science remain credible. The reaction is predictable. For sceptics, this is a whitewash, the establishment closing ranks to cover up biased science and so maintain the rationale for moving away from fossil fuels. For the government and the academic world, it's a clean bill of health, closure on an unhappy saga.

Except that the doubts linger, the blogs become angrier and opinions more polarised. For many people, chilled by snowstorms and dismayed by rising energy bills, talk of warming must be hard to grasp, if not downright dangerous, especially in the United States.

The Mayor of the town of Sweetwater in Texas knows that all too well. Don't mention the climate, Greg Wortham warns me. He isn't joking. Sweetwater is literally Middle America, lying halfway between the Atlantic and Pacific coasts and proud of being where the first metalled highway crossing the continent was completed. Now it has another claim to fame. Thousands of tall, white wind turbines crowd the mesas, the high plateaux that stretch from the town for dozens of miles. The turbines are so numerous they stand like thickets, row upon row of giant arms spinning in the ceaseless West Texas winds. Squint and the white shapes could be sailing ships, hundreds of them, jostling in a bay. Sweetwater has become an environmentalist's dream, home to the largest wind farms in the world, a vision of green energy on an industrial scale. Except that it's got nothing to do with saving the planet. Wind is big here because there's serious money to be made.

Greg takes us out of town to explain how things work. The people of West Texas, he says, are incredibly adaptable. First this was cattle country. Next, cotton dominated. And beside a field of cotton, he points out the brilliant white clusters, like balls of wool, soon ready for picking. Cotton is still an important activity here but in a corner of the field, there's also a nodding donkey, a great lump of iron pumping out oil from deep underground. So oil joined cattle and cotton as a source of income. Now wind energy is a fourth activity and on the far edge of the field stand three huge towers, their blades carving the air with a steady rhythm.

This landowner right here, Greg says, earns about $10,000 a year for allowing each of these turbines to be built. That's on top of what he gets for leasing out the mineral rights and the farming rights. Wind is just another resource. The surge in construction and the flow of revenues have transformed an otherwise declining corner of the country and several new schools have been built with the proceeds. I visit one, a gleaming set of buildings with a bright-green football field and – obviously – its own wind turbine.

We stop for a lunch at Greg's favourite diner, scruffy but friendly, everyone sharing tables. At this place, run by the same family for half a century, there's no choice, they simply bring out oversized dishes of meatloaf and beans, potatoes and gravy. Sitting next to me are a couple on a journey between places I haven't heard of, or maybe it's that I can't fathom their accent; in any event, we all laugh at mine.

As a vast platter of steaks arrives, I ask Greg about global warming. The UN conference in Cancun is just a fortnight away and we're sitting in the midst of an incredible explosion of green energy. Does anyone make the link? Is anyone interested?

He shakes his head. Carbon footprint, green, climate change, he says, are issues that are so charged in the US that they're best avoided. They distract from the fact that wind energy can bring money and security. And the topic is divisive. People who might otherwise be in favour of wind energy turn against it, purely because it's associated with a political agenda they don't like. So, as he told me before, don't mention the climate.

Developments in Washington confirm his view. A proposed bill on climate change died in the Senate during the summer. And then in the midterm Congressional elections, the Republicans won control of the House of Representatives with many new arrivals opposed to any kind of action. For some, particularly those supported by the Tea Party, global warming studies are what Sarah Palin describes as 'a bunch of snake oil science'. For her and others, the topic is a product of left-wing ideology, red disguised as green and designed to hobble industry. The c-word has become a liability.

Given the scale of this shift, I visit one of the great legends of Texas to hear his take. T. Boone Pickens is a highly unusual figure in that he's a larger-than life oilman who's also quite green: both a billionaire Republican donor and one of the largest investors in wind power. A model of a turbine stands in his lavish suite of offices, and the panelled walls are adorned with paintings of cattle drives and oil pioneers, hardy folk with sunburned faces topped with Stetsons tramping through the mud around wooden drilling rigs. Photographs capture handshakes and poses with presidents and prime ministers, including Reagan and both Bushes. There's even one with the Queen. Pickens is himself a kind of Texas royalty.

In his boardroom, where we meet, a bank of screens flashes with market data. His handshake is like iron and his opening line combative: What's this all about?

I explain that I'm interested in what an oilman who also backs renewable energy makes of the idea that our greenhouse gases are accelerating warming.

I do think, he says, that we have hurried some things along, maybe they wouldn't have happened, maybe they would.

And what about attitudes in the US?

Well, they tell me the ice cap is deteriorating and the polar bear is in trouble. I believe that to be true. But you don't get everyone to worry about a polar bear or the ice cap – their deal is more at home, it's around the table, it's with their families.

I'm left with the feeling that with people like Pickens, America may well see a lot more renewable energy projects. But it won't be because of climate change – his motivation is to reduce the country's dependence on foreign oil. All in all, an international treaty looks less likely than ever.

An editor, faced with a declining budget, asks if the Cancun conference will produce the agreement that eluded Copenhagen.

No, I respond.

So, he wonders, will the whole process come to a crashing, spectacular halt?

No. However badly it goes, the negotiators are professionals so they'll find a fudge to keep it going.

In other words, the process will stumble on without forging a new treaty or blowing up in total failure?

Right.

So it won't be big news and you don't really need to go.

Fine.

The result is that I file my reports not from Mexico but from London. In the event, the talks go a bit better than expected, producing a few modest steps. The plan for a massive aid programme for the poorest countries comes a little closer and each country's voluntary promises for emissions cuts are formalised in a legal UN text. It's not exactly groundbreaking but with the eventual outcome so uncertain, this does count as progress.

Until Copenhagen, the narrative on climate change had seemed fairly straightforward. The science would presumably become stronger, the negotiations over greenhouse gases would intensify, and the world would eventually have a framework for tackling the problem. Instead, the research has tended to provide confirmation of existing findings rather than spectacular new advances and the talks are stumbling, so much so that I was wondering whether to look in other directions for stories.

And then something wholly unexpected happened. A drilling rig exploded in the Gulf of Mexico and the environmental story of the moment switched from climate to oil.

# 13

# To the bottom of an oily sea

A quarter-dollar spins in a silvery flash. Hunched like gamblers around a table, we're on a ship steaming into a summer night in the Gulf of Mexico: two teams of broadcasters, the BBC and the American network CNN, making an effort to be polite to each other but in reality jockeying for position. As the room lurches in the swell from a distant storm, I joke about dreading seasickness and how I'm fighting the drowsiness of travel pills. There is laughter but it's brittle and fails to mask the unspoken agenda of rivalry.

In these same waters in an earlier age, a coin toss might have settled the ownership of pirated jewels or the fate of a prisoner. But this is the era of television and our prize isn't measured by wealth or force. Instead we're competing for what we treasure as gold: the chance to get somewhere really special, to film some potentially stunning video. The problem is that we both want access to a place so cramped that only one team will be able to work at a time. And because the filming can only take place if the sea is relatively calm, the crew that wins the right to go first may well get what they need, after which the weather could worsen and deny the second team an opportunity, forcing them home empty-handed, a form of journalistic purgatory.

The scene for this contest is an American research ship, the *Seward Johnson*, which is on an expedition to study the coral reefs. The captain and senior scientists have joined our gathering. The outcome of the toss matters to them, too – plans need to be made for the next day's operations. And they seem curious about us, even wary. Film crews have been on board before but always to make documentaries, a civilised process conducted at a measured pace over a period of weeks or even months. This is the first visit by news people, a more frenetic breed, impatient for instant results during a single weekend, and it's obvious that we have brought an unfamiliar edginess to the vessel.

Since the CNN correspondent is a woman, I've done the courteous thing of offering her the chance to pick heads or tails. Heads, she chooses, flashing perfect teeth and swinging a mass of blonde hair. I am briefly flattered into feeling gallant – until I look past her and notice the poker face of the CNN producer. American television people have a reputation for humourless as well as ruthless determination and this one's gaze is so steely that I assume she's wishing the BBC could be banished ashore in a small rowing boat or maybe dumped on an island. It's a perfectly reasonable assumption because, if I'm honest, I'm dreaming about exactly the same fate for them: that my prospects would be immeasurably brighter if CNN could somehow be dispatched from the scene, humanely, of course, and with generous supplies, but without delay. Filming is always easier without having to jostle with another crew. But on this assignment, we have no choice: we are guests on board and the story of the ship's mission is too newsworthy to miss.

The reefs being investigated are to the west of Florida and host some of America's most valuable fishing grounds. As it happens, they lie in the path of an oceanic stream, the Loop Current, which circulates in the Gulf of Mexico. Normally the flow serves the benign purpose of bringing nutrients to the lowest links of the food chain. But this is July 2010 and the current may now be transporting something very unwelcome, even deadly. Rather like the North Pacific Gyre that bombards Midway Atoll with plastic waste, the Loop Current could also be ferrying a kind of pollution, less tangible but no less threatening: clouds of microscopic droplets of oil.

The route of the current varies but at this time it's approaching Florida from the direction of Louisiana and an undersea valley that runs from the Louisiana shore, the Mississippi Canyon. The slopes of the canyon, stretching from the turquoise shallows of the continental shelf to the pitch-black abyss of the ocean, are known to hold vast reservoirs of oil and the giant oil companies have been risking ever deeper operations to get at it. One of the wells, nearly a mile down, is known as Macondo 252. Drilled by BP as part of its search for new fields, it had successfully struck oil, which at the time was regarded as good news. As an exploratory well – dug not to produce oil but to verify if the stuff is down there – it was in the process of being closed up and, on April 20, 2010, cement was being injected into the drill-hole.

The rig managing this operation up at the surface was one of the world's largest, the Deepwater Horizon. The men on board were waiting for signs that the cement was hardening. Instead, a burst of methane surged up from the wellhead, engulfed the rig and then, inevitably, ignited. Eleven men died in the inferno. And the flow from the well was left unchecked. This became a 'wild well', one that's uncontrolled, and it was the oil industry's first to erupt in waters too deep to be reached by divers. BP was caught unprepared. It had the technology to extract oil from extreme depths but no means of coping when its systems failed. The result was that crude gushed from the seabed for almost three months.

Most of the oil floated to the surface and formed into slicks – usually consisting of black syrup that fouled beaches or of thick brown mousse that ensnared pelicans and turtles. This was the visible impact of the spill and the images of empty resorts and struggling wildlife flashed around the world. But much of the oil stayed out of sight, down in the unlit depths. Ejected from the seabed at very high pressure, it was 'atomised' or broken up into tiny particles which were so small that they did not rise as oil usually does in water. Instead the droplets drifted in ghostly clouds, sometimes on a massive scale – one plume was found to be at least fifteen miles long. While the surface slicks were tangible and could sometimes be contained, the undersea oil, like an unseen gas, was potentially more pernicious. Harder to track and impossible to control, it was likely to be caught in the currents that could deliver it to the most vulnerable forms of marine life, including the precious corals off Florida.

Hence the task of the *Seward Johnson*, ploughing through a starless night, her course set for a spot in the ocean that might be reached by the droplets. The mission is twofold: to check the reefs for damage and, if they're clean, to assess their health to better judge how they might suffer if oil were to arrive later. It's an eighteen-hour journey and the throb of the engines, the smell of diesel and the pallid light of the canteen take me straight back to my time on board another vessel, the *Amundsen*, sailing through the Northwest Passage. Sharing the memories is cameraman Rob Magee. He's as bemused as I am by the similarities and contrasts. As before, he takes the upper bunk in our cabin. To that extent, it's like old times. Except that there's air conditioning rather than heating; crewmen in sandals not snow boots; accents that are American instead of French-Canadian; and steaks and fried chicken instead of soups and casseroles.

Both ships are built for ocean-going science and we recognise some of the same equipment used in the Arctic:

scoops for the seabed, sampling devices for the water, robotic cameras to peer into the gloom, rows of microscopes to study algae and plankton. But beyond that the *Seward Johnson* has an additional, remarkable facility for venturing into the underwater world. A machine famous in marine science for opening up new realms, it now offers a unique chance to explore the impact of the oil: a miniature submarine. The very possibility that we might descend in it has caused extraordinary excitement among editors. I've repeatedly played down the prospects, in case it doesn't happen. And what they don't know is that our chances may rest on the throw of a quarter.

Lashed to the deck, the submarine does not inspire confidence. It is definitely not some sleek marine predator. It is more of a gangling, ugly, misshapen species of prey, the sort of unhappy creature that lives briefly, manoeuvres clumsily and has to hurry to mate before being eaten. Though designed and operated by the Harbor Branch Oceanographic Institute of Florida Atlantic University, a renowned research centre, the craft has an unsettling, rather home-made look about it: a huge bulbous head, a swarm of intestinal tubing, and a tangle of tanks and pipes bound together apparently at random.

Its inelegant name, *Johnson-Sea-Link II*, does not reassure either, the multiple hyphens seemingly as precarious as the bolts holding the machine together. Named for Seward Johnson, the ocean-loving philanthropist who founded the institute, and Edwin Albert Link, a maverick inventor who built two submersibles of this design, this one dates from an uncomfortably long time ago: 1975. Older than most passenger planes flying today, and certainly more ancient than many cars on the road now, this contraption has been diving as deep as 900 metres, about 3,000 feet, for an extraordinary thirty-five years. I wonder whether the joints and seals can take so much strain and whether in this case it's wise to be ageist. I think back to other venerable craft. The decrepit helicopters in Tajikistan, offered for a trip into Afghanistan? Too risky, a flight too far. But the ancient biplane that flew me over the Aral Sea, and the 1960s Gulfstream that managed the five-hour haul to Midway? Though old, they felt sturdy.

And the little submarine has proved itself over the decades too. With room for four – a pilot, a technician and two passengers – it has performed thousands of dives. In the 1970s it was the first craft to explore the wreck of the USS *Monitor*, an ironclad from the American Civil War. And in the 1980s, in the aftermath of the crash of the space shuttle, *Challenger*, it found the wreckage of the booster rocket whose faulty seal had led to the disaster. More recently it has ventured into undersea valleys and discovered new reefs. That bulbous head is a blessing: it's a sphere made of clear acrylic, five inches thick, and for the scientists sitting inside this giant bubble it offers an unparalleled view of the deep.

I learn all this from two people who've travelled on the submarine more than most: one of the more colourful and likeable couples in science, chief pilot Don Liberatore and the expedition's head scientist, Shirley Pomponi. With ready smiles, a faintly theatrical manner and a hint of ribaldry, Don and Shirley put on quite a show, interrupting each other's stories, adding embellishments, reminiscing about their undersea adventures. While Don exudes supreme competence when talking about the submarine and Shirley, a professor in marine science, is a specialist in corals, they wear their expertise lightly and it's fun being with them. In their first briefing, they begin with a formal tone and maintain a professional distance, for a while. But it turns out to be Don's birthday and they're both in a jolly mood so, after a few minutes, Shirley can't resist some teasing and soon they both declare to us strangers that they are indeed married. The briefing ends with a very public hug. Of all the science events I've covered, this is by far the most loving and enthusiastic. So much so that I half-forget why we're at sea in the first place.

The explosion at BP's well had not seemed too serious at first. Yes, eleven men were killed and a rig was lost but industrial accidents on that scale don't usually merit international attention. And the first official accounts had suggested that no oil was leaking out from the wellhead. No spill, no story, I recall thinking, particularly since the BBC newsroom was anyway preoccupied with the frenzied final weeks of the General Election campaign. It took another ten days for views to change. The blown-out well was indeed gushing oil, it turned out. And we learned that BP had no immediate way of shutting it off. The spill was not under control and this quickly turned into a crisis.

One of my first calls was to the BP Press Office in London. How much is leaking?

No more than 1,000 barrels a day. The voice at the other end is surprisingly upbeat, no hint of the beleaguered, battered atmosphere to come.

I don't admit it but I have no idea what 1,000 barrels means. I later learn that you multiply a barrel by 42 to get the number of gallons, so this would be 42,000 gallons. What I don't know at the time – and no one could know for certain – is that the real volume of the leak is 60 times larger, at about 60,000 barrels a day. A private BP briefing note, drawn up at the time and only revealed later, speculated that the leak could be as large as 100,000 barrels a day. Maybe, at the time of my call, the press officer didn't know that. In any event, in that first conversation, I suggest that 1,000 barrels still sounds rather a lot.

Not at all, I'm told. The press officer manages to make my question sound slightly hurtful. The leak is only about the equivalent of about four truckloads, the kind of tankers that refill petrol stations. Four of them leaking every day not so bad given the size of the ocean, is it?

At this rate, I'm assured, it'll take 2,000 days to leak as much oil as when the tanker, the *Exxon Valdez*, burst open off the coast of Alaska. And the facts and assertions flow on: the oil is a light crude so most of it is floating and it's less than the thickness of a human hair. We've skimmed off a record amount already and the wind is blowing the slick away from the coast. We're mounting the largest single response in history including designing a dome to sit over the leak and trap the oil. And we'll drill a relief well as soon as we can.

It's classic corporate spin: confident, polite and with just enough technology to sound convincing. The message is clear: we'll deal with it, and fast, don't worry.

So what do more independent experts think? I ring around. One professor tells me the location of the spill is both good and bad. Good because the warm waters of the Gulf of Mexico allow bacteria to flourish, and many of them feed on oil. Bad because the Gulf is home to many vital eco-systems and the longer the spill goes on, the greater the risk of damage.

How long could it go on?

Maybe ninety days.

Ninety? That's a surprise. Back in late April that sounds implausibly distant. But dealing with a blowout under nearly a mile of water proves harder than anyone in the oil industry anticipated. And the estimate turns out to be uncannily accurate. The leak won't be shut off until July.

Another specialist thinks the media, especially in the US, have become hysterical. Oil is biodegradable, he says, and much of it will evaporate – that proves true. And the pressure behind the leak will soon subside, he believes, long before the spill reaches the size of the *Exxon Valdez* – that turns out to be wrong, by a massive margin.

A third scientist points out that the biggest factor will be the public reaction. Natural forces could erode most of the spill within a year, he tells me, but by then consumers may have made their minds up, and continue to shun Gulf of Mexico seafood and resorts long after the oil has vanished. That too is prescient.

So initially there's confusion about the scale of the problem and its likely impact. One editor has heard the line about the oil being biodegradable and is convinced that the reaction is overblown. I choose to avoid the word 'disaster', at least in these early weeks, on the grounds that it may become a disaster but isn't one yet.

By contrast, the American networks, descending on the Louisiana shore, compete to use the language of apocalypse. The fishing port of Venice, the settlement closest to the site of the spill fifty miles offshore, becomes the media epicentre. Down-at-heel and remote, this little collection of prefab homes and trailers, perched on a boggy finger of land in the Mississippi Delta, is now transformed by satellite trucks and live positions. The local shrimp fishermen, who've lost their livelihoods, stand around disconsolately, waiting to be hired or compensated by BP, and they've long since tired of being interviewed by journalists. The only place serving food – where the choice seems to be fried or deep-fried – is overwhelmed by loud voices calling news desks in New York or Atlanta. A store does a brisk trade in cold drinks and local maps; no one asks for fishing tackle or live bait.

The spill has been elevated to the status of a war. That's evident from the sight of famous presenters gracing Venice to anchor the news. The grubby quayside has never been so well-lit or seen so much hairspray. And there's a shift in vocabulary. Events are unfolding not in ordinary days but in 'Days' with a capital D. 'Days' are pronounced differently and have special meaning. Favoured during a long-running story, 'Days' provide an escalating sense of crisis, as in: 'Day 19 and BP suffered another blow ...'. When I arrive in Venice ahead of a broadcast, I listen to one high-volume correspondent boasting to his viewers of being the first to film pelicans struggling in the slick: 'Day 38 and we have shocking new evidence ...'. I wonder when the counting started: the day of the explosion or the Day the networks noticed?

A fisherman takes us out to the marshes. We cross the main stream of the Mississippi, picking a path between huge cargo ships, and enter a channel known as Pass a L'Outre, the final access to the Gulf. This area was the first to be hit by the slicks. At first, nothing seems wrong. But as we edge closer to the reeds I see that the lower parts of their stems are stained black. The oil has reached into the deepest thickets. Since the reed beds act as nurseries for young shrimp and fish, this is potentially devastating. And it's in these dense, sheltered pockets of vegetation that the natural processes of cleaning – wind, waves and sunshine – are slowest, so the oil will linger.

We draw up alongside a length of plastic orange boom, meant to protect the reeds. In the past few weeks, miles of these floating barriers have been deployed. But, in this one patch, the boom was installed too late: the oil had already penetrated the marches. I wonder if it will stop any more oil getting in. From my vantage point, on the ocean side of the barrier, a sheen lies around our boat so presumably the boom is working. But the conditions are slightly choppy and I notice little waves pushing oil not just onto the barrier but over it as well. It's not a total defence. No wonder the US Coast Guard's commanders describe the spill as an insidious enemy; it's pervasive and relentless.

Further west, at the beach resort of Grand Isle, the sands have been cleaned ahead of a visit by President Obama. Squads of labourers in white protective suits have done a very effective job and it looks like a modest victory. I'm about to report on this in a live slot for the *News at Six*, but I don't get very far because the wind picks up, disturbs the satellite dish and breaks the link with London. A vicious squall approaches so we run for cover and just make it before the rain descends in buckets. We've lost our broadcast but within an hour the clouds have cleared and we return to the beach to get ready for the next bulletin. The sand looks unchanged – until producer Rozalia Hristova wanders down to the surf and notices that the storm has driven fresh loads of oil ashore, great patches of heavy brown treacle. Cleaned once, the entire length of the beach is soiled again. It's a pattern that will be repeated, the oil turning up in bursts and on particular stretches of coastline. This isn't one massive disaster but a series of minor ones – episodic and local, but unpleasant and damaging.

Rozalia scoops a dollop of oil onto a piece of paper for me to show on air; it looks exactly like chocolate sauce and it's just as runny.

Several hours later, President Obama makes it to the beach. Not that I ever see him – only a small pool of White House reporters is allowed to get close. Instead we are ordered aside to allow his vast motorcade to pass by, a fleet of SUVs and Jeeps, flanked by outriders, a dazzling display of might which, briefly, makes me feel sorry for him. Despite being surrounded by all that strength, the most powerful leader in the world is unable to answer his youngest daughter's wish 'to plug the hole' – he's on the rack because an oil giant can't stop a leak on the seabed.

If he could see through the darkened glass of his car, Mr Obama might have noticed the lawn of one of the beach-houses: it's filled with wooden crosses mourning all that the spill has killed: tourism, shrimp, oysters, tuna, turtles. The display is meant to villify BP and its boss Tony Hayward. But the leak has left the president vulnerable too, accused of failing to stand up to a foreign company. As a result he and his officials have been forced to behave more aggressively, resorting to the language of the Wild West and the street – 'riding herd' on BP or 'keeping a boot to BP's throat'. But the bullying talk and high-profile interventions have created a new problem. The White House has banned all offshore drilling for six months and closed the fishing grounds for safety and these decisions are criticised as an overreaction that's causing more damage than the oil itself.

From the air, it's tempting to wonder what the fuss is about. I'm in an oil-industry helicopter on a flight to the site of the spill and the tracts of marshland below me seem healthily green. I can make out the delicate filaments of boom along the shore – spindly but running for miles – and clusters of boats sweeping for oil. In the distance, above a chain of islets, a helicopter is dropping huge sandbags to try to close the gaps. It looks like a model of competence. The BP press office would be delighted. That probably means I'm sitting too comfortably – views always seem rosier from business class. The helicopter is normally used to ferry workers to the rigs and, fitted out like a modern jet, it's pleasantly clean and quiet. I've only encountered plusher seats in a helicopter in what was then East Germany. Just before unification, the admiral in charge of the German People's Navy flew me in his personal machine, the two of us lounging in grandiose armchairs while his officials had to cram onto a bench; an airborne Animal Farm – four seats good, two seats better. In that broken nation, the impression was thoroughly misleading, as it is now over a sunny Gulf of Mexico.

As we head offshore, the oil becomes visible. There isn't a single mass of it ruining a vast swath of ocean. Instead there's a horde of different kinds of slicks. There are lake-sized stains of black, and curious lumps of brown that look like boulders. A US Coast Guard information sheet offers rather poetic detail: 'grey sheen' looks silvery, 'rainbow sheen' is colourful, and 'metallic sheen' reflects the colour of the sky. The helicopter's crew chief, Randy Pearman, tells me how to distinguish between slicks and shadows – they can look very similar. But where there's oil, the sea is unnaturally smooth and the waves flatter and more rounded.

And you'll smell it when we get close, Randy says.

He's right. About a mile from the ground zero of this crisis – the spot on the surface directly above the leak – a faint smell of petrol wafts into the cabin and the sea has become an unremitting carpet of black. The sight is sinister but it's by no means cataclysmic. Compared to the hellish scene of Kuwait in 1991, when the retreating Iraqi army set alight not one oil well but hundreds, the scene is relatively innocent. Back then, with the skies choked with malevolent fog, it felt like permanent night and the sands were black with crude. Texans in Stetsons and jeans were brought in to tackle the fires and I interviewed them about the machines they had improvised to allow them to get close to the well-heads – one was a giant crane shielded with sheets of corrugated iron and constantly sprayed to keep cool. Now we're circling the equivalent operation in the Gulf of Mexico in 2010. An armada of some twenty vessels and rigs, one of the greatest concentrations of oil-industry muscle, has been assembled. The challenge in Kuwait was the sheer number of wild wells. Here it's just one well – but a well that is beyond the reach of human hand a mile below on the seabed.

At the heart of the huddle is an enormous ship called the *Discoverer Enterprise*, distinctive with a huge tower, and pivotal to BP's efforts. Far below it, a 'top cap', like an upside-down funnel, has just been fitted over the leak and the device is managing to trap some of the oil – perhaps as much as a quarter of it – and this is being channelled up to the *Discoverer Enterprise*. The oil rises together with methane and the two are separated on board, the gas immediately siphoned off. The sight of a massive flare blasting from the side of the ship is the first real proof that BP is at last getting to grips with the leak – the gas is being burned and, if that is happening, it must be that oil is being captured as well. This is an emergency measure and only partially successful; it's taken six weeks to get this far.

Beside the giant jet of fire are clouds of mist. This is water and chemical dispersant being sprayed onto the sea to break up all the oil that's afloat on the surface. Safety rules would never normally allow oil and naked flame so close together but these are desperate times. The methane has to be burned off – there's no means of storing it on board – and the gas has to be dealt with if this system of capturing oil from the seabed is to work. As a stopgap, it's highly risky. In fact, just before we visit, the operation is shut down because of a lightning strike. But the future of one of the world's largest multinationals is on the line – the share price is plummeting, the law suits are mounting and the bills are running into billions – and at the moment there's no better option.

Positioned nearby in the inner circle of vessels are two rigs. These are what long-term hopes are riding on. The crews on board are drilling into the seabed to try to intercept the leaking well from below. They've made good progress but the distances involved are staggering: the drills need to reach not just through a mile of ocean but also nearly three miles of rock. That's why it'll be another couple of months before the interception can be completed and the leak sealed. Despite BP's immense wealth and technical prowess, there are physical limits to the speed of any drilling, which is why the company is flailing around for other ideas.

In BP's offices in Houston, in a hurriedly established 'crisis center', engineers brainstorm over charts and screens. For many weeks, this frantic work went on in private but eventually a few of us journalists are allowed inside. We step into a grim atmosphere. The latest attempt – a strategy called 'top kill' – has just failed and faces are long. Oil types are usually self-confident, and occasionally swaggering, working in a highly profitable industry selling to a booming market. But these people, nerves stretched, are humbled. A lot had been riding on the 'top kill' – blasting drilling fluids down the well to force back the oil – and it had been expected to work. So were about half a dozen other methods. The first, known as 'top hat', was a giant container placed over the leak but it was immediately blocked with lumps of frozen methane. A 'junk shot' of hair clippings and old golf balls, meant to jam inside the pipes at the wellhead, achieved nothing either. Time after time, a plan would be announced only for it to falter.

Told to keep my voice down to a whisper, I'm ushered into 'The Tank', a darkened room where the undersea operations are managed. Faces lit by the blue glow of twelve huge television screens, rows of experts are watching live video feeds from the seabed. As I walk in, one screen is showing a close-up of the volcano of oil. Another gives a wider view, the torrent turned a golden-brown by being lit from behind. These images are being filmed by a small army of remotely operated vehicles, controlled by technicians on board the ships at the scene but guided from this room in Houston. Every action, every attempt to shut off the flow, has to be planned and then carried out by one of these machines, a mile down at sea. I watch a mechanical claw extend, the wrist twisting, as if in slow motion. We could be watching robots at work on another planet. With the task so distant and so dark and so unfamiliar, the BP men are obviously frustrated. On camera, they talk about how upset they are, but they also manage to convey a gritty optimism.

I ask the operations director, Kent Wells, how he felt when he realised that their best hope so far, the top kill, had not worked.

If something doesn't work, he says, that's just a test of leadership, you push straight on to find something else.

The pilot of the helicopter flying us over the spill is blunter. Jim Borger has flown for the oil industry for decades and says what the oil men won't admit.

We used to have a blowout about once a year in the Gulf, he tells me, but the water was shallower and the oil was burned so you had very little pollution. This is the first time we've had anything like this anywhere in the world. And in such deep water, everything is new.

It won't be till mid-July that one of the undersea experiments actually works. The robots manage to make a clean cut through the main pipe running up from the wellhead. That increases the scale of the leak but also allows them to install a set of valves over the pipe. For a while the oil keeps flowing straight through. That's intentional. But gradually, and with infinite care to avoid a rupture, those valves are slowly turned off, one by one. The video images show the jet of oil shrinking to a trickle then to a wisp. Finally the view is of plain dark ocean. The leak is over.

It's the evening of July 15, about 8.50 pm London time. I know that for sure because I hadn't expected this phase to occur so quickly and I'm not in the right place – neither in Louisiana nor at the BBC in London. Instead, when the newsroom calls, I'm at home. My brother and his family are visiting and I'm carrying a large bowl of pasta to the table. I rush to my study to file a report. The pasta's cold by the time I'm done.

With the flow stopped, it's time to take stock of the impacts. Some are obvious – the shrimp fishermen have lost a season, maybe two, and have had their livelihoods disrupted. But many have also been employed by BP to help lay boom or skim for oil and all are in line for compensation. The resorts were emptied at the sight of a single tar ball and lost the entire summer trade. Even in late October some ninety miles of coastline were still being hit by oil so compensation is being paid to tourist businesses too. More controversial is the fate of the many businesses that suffered indirect effects of the oil – subcontractors and suppliers.

And what about the environmental damage? Because the *Exxon Valdez* disaster had been the most notorious in American waters until now, it is used as the yardstick to judge this one. For example the numbers of birds affected then and now can be compared and the results are quite surprising.

In the Alaskan spill, hundreds of thousands of seabirds were killed, too many to count accurately.

And in the BP accident? The total number of birds found dead with evidence of oiling was far lower, at 2,263. Another 2,079 were found oiled but alive and were collected. Some 1,200 of them were rehabilitated and returned to the wild.

In one sense the comparison is unfair: the *Exxon Valdez* was a tanker which ruptured in a narrow inlet while the BP leak was 50 miles offshore and a long way down. On the other hand, given how readily the word 'disaster' was used in the Gulf of Mexico, it's fair to ask how bad it really was.

The answer, from most researchers, is that it is still too early to tell. The struggling pelicans may be the least of it. The greatest damage, it's feared, might not be so obvious or so immediate. The worry is that the tiniest traces of oil – or the chemical dispersant used to break it up – could be enough to infect the micro-organisms at the bottom of the food chain. And once absorbed into the web of marine life, they could work their way up, like other pollutants in the oceans, and poison generations of creatures. That's why the mission of the *Seward Johnson* and its submarine is seen as so important.

The quarter-dollar clatters onto the table and the ship's press officer picks it up. We're all watching him intently.

It's heads, he announces, holding up the coin. CNN has won. They'll go first, and they're grinning.

I catch Rob's eye and he looks as disappointed as I feel. I turn to producer Rozalia Hristova. She's spent weeks setting up this opportunity and can't hide her sense of defeat either. It doesn't mean we won't get on the submarine but our odds are suddenly a lot worse.

There's nothing we can do except study the weather forecasts, but they aren't promising and the next morning we wake up to the same, heavy swell. CNN's expedition has been set for midday. When the time comes, the conditions are deemed marginal but just about adequate and I watch their correspondent doing what I want to do: climbing into the acrylic dome of the submarine and then being lowered off the stern. The ship is pitching and the submersible swings wildly until it splashes into the water. I pace the deck, wondering how we can put together a report if we don't get underwater.

When CNN surface two hours later, the waves have become slightly rougher and the task of retrieving the submarine is not straightforward. The vessel's crew are clearly anxious about the wisdom of having launched at all. The correspondent says the visibility was poor because of the turbulence but she's elated and her team excitedly play back their video.

I climb to the bridge to ask the captain when the next launch, our turn, will take place. He grimaces and points to the waves. At this rate there won't be another launch, he says. He'll wait till late afternoon and make a decision then. It's exactly the scenario I'd dreaded. I talk it through with Rob and Rozalia but there's nothing any of us can say. I take another seasickness pill and head for my bunk.

Suddenly it's 5 pm and Rob's waking me. We're on. The sky has brightened and the swell has reduced. The crew are now in a hurry to get going. This is my big moment but I'm groggy with sleep. There's just time to swig some coffee before I'm escorted across the deck to the submarine and led to a ladder that runs up to its hatch. I've rehearsed the moves required to get in: sit on the rim of the hatch, lower one foot onto a console below, stretch the other onto the seat, and then wriggle down. It must be similar to entering a spacecraft – cramped, switches everywhere and air conditioning emitting a loud hum. I worry that a stray elbow or knee will knock something vital.

I'm sitting in the right-hand seat, Don Liberatore is already in the left-hand one. We're both facing the clear, curved window of acrylic. It's so close to us that I can't stretch my legs out and if I lean back I get dangerously close to a bunch of wires. It should feel claustrophobic because it's impossible to move. But the dome offers views in all directions so there's a deceptive sense of space. Far worse was a dive on a British rescue submarine, the LR5, some years earlier: a cigar tube of steel so narrow we had to sit with our heads bent and so hot that another correspondent bailed out before the hatch was shut. This one is more like a very elaborate roller-coaster ride.

Don greets me but he's busy on the radio talking to the support team on deck. There isn't a countdown but, as they run through their checks, it feels as if there should be one. Batteries? Confirmed as fully charged. Oxygen? Full. Seals? Tight. Communications? Good.

Then comes Don's safety briefing. The sub has an exemplary record but he turns to me to explain what to do in an emergency. If he's incapacitated, the technician in the submarine's second chamber at the rear will take over. If the technician is also out of action, I'll have to run things.

Flick these three switches, Don says, one after the other, in this order, to blow the ballast tanks. That'll send you straight up to the surface. He points at three switches. But there are dozens, the whole cockpit is a nest of switches. And the three he's pointing to aren't marked in any special way. I don't ask the obvious: how will I remember which ones to

**Long way down:** off the west coast of Florida, Rob Magee films my departure into the abyss. At this point the mini-submarine is swaying just before being lowered into the water. I'm sitting inside the vessel's acrylic bubble fretting over handling two little cameras. *BBC*

flick and in which order? Don goes on: if the switches don't blow the ballast, you can do it manually.

Manually, of course. That's what happens in movies. Switches never work and people always end up having to pull levers. Open this blue valve, Don says. At least this one is marked, it is genuinely a bright blue, I can see that. And then open these two other valves. That'll shoot you up to the surface, no problem, but do them in the right order: blue first, then the others.

Sure, I say. But I'm the sort of person who can't recall where I've put my own pen, let alone conquer absent-mindedness to rescue a stricken sub. I want to write all this down but I feel too hemmed in to reach into my pocket for a notebook. And, anyway, I'm distracted by far greater worries: there's no room for Rob so I'll be doing all the filming.

Not since the Norwegian whaling ship have I had to handle the stress of getting the right shots. I have with me our smallest camera – what we call 'kamikaze-cam' because we've used it for all kinds of suicidal tasks. It survived the Arctic chill when we tied it to the outside of our ski-plane to land on the ice island. And it's been dunked in the flood water of Tuvalu, the mud of Bangladesh and the algal fuel ponds of California. No surprise, it's not in the best of condition and I realise, just as the hatch is closed, that the masking tape that's meant to hold the battery in place is coming unstuck in the heat. A second, larger camera has also decided to play up: for no apparent reason, its screen has gone blank. Everything is clear for launch – except me. Reluctantly, I have to turn to Don and ask him to hold.

A crewman reopens the hatch. The larger camera is passed out, checked and given back. It's now working. And a roll of masking tape is handed in to rebind the little camera's battery. The filming should now be fine. Should be. No wonder I can't concentrate on Don and his valves.

Minutes later, we are lifted off the deck. A crane hoists us into the air and down over the stern of the ship where we swing above the swell. A few sharp lurches follow and then there's a blast of foam as we drop at speed beneath the surface, surf splashing over the canopy. Don releases several streams of air and we descend. It's quiet and we're soon beyond the surge of the waves, slipping into a darkening, tranquil blue towards the coral of the ocean floor.

It's like scuba-diving without any of the hassle of masks and weights and the dry throat one gets from breathing compressed air. Clouds of marine snow stream past us. It's like being in a brilliant, drifting dream. I can look up and sideways and down – I'm immersed in a world of infinite blue light. It's spellbinding. Not since I entered the unearthly cavern of ice in Antarctica have I arrived somewhere so beautiful. We're almost at the bottom and a reef appears out of the gloom, a sudden burst of orange, red and green, its twists and folds teeming with fish.

Apart from the hum of the ventilation, the only sound is a constant clicking. To manoeuvre, Don does not have a steering wheel but instead switches nine little motors on and off. His fingers are a blur over the controls as he steers our bubble along a coral gully and up over a ridge.

We're hovering so serenely – about one mile per hour – that grouper and angelfish idle near us, untroubled, or even approach us. At various points, Don manipulates the sub's mechanical arm to collect samples of corals, sponges and sea fans which he lowers into an array of collection boxes.

Directing the choice of specimens is his wife Shirley, who's in the sub's second chamber at the back. While looking through a porthole and also watching a video feed from the submarine's camera, she provides an expert commentary over our headsets. The headline, which she's delighted with, is that the corals appear healthy with no visible hint of oil or any damage. Passionate about the oceans, she seems to love hearing the excitement in my voice too. Thrown together on this extraordinary journey, Don and I in the front compartment and Shirley and the second crewman in the rear, we find ourselves in a really enjoyable conversation. But it's fragmented. Don and I can chat because we're next to each other and Shirley and I can talk because our headsets are linked. But Don needs to stay in contact with the ship at the surface so he can't talk directly to Shirley. I become their messenger, and it's hilarious.

Tell Don to pick me that coral, the pink one, she asks me.

I relay the request.

Which one does she mean? There are several.

I pass back the question.

The little one, on the right, over there, Shirley says, as if it's obvious. Why can't men ever see anything?

She wants that one, I say, explaining what she's told me while sympathising with the position he's in.

Why didn't she say she wanted that one in the first place? I don't pass that bit back.

Instead, while Don's collecting the sample, Shirley explains what she's looking for. The very worst would be visible signs of oiling, a black coating over the reefs, which she does not think very likely. More realistic are indicators of stress in the corals – the most severe of which would be 'bleaching' when the corals are ailing or dead and turn white. But short of that, and as a precursor to the collapse of a reef, Shirley is hunting for clues in the genes of coral. She believes there are genetic responses to invisible threats such as toxins and that identifying them could provide an early warning of trouble to come. She won't get answers immediately; this is a project that may take years.

After two hours, we have to return. The time has gone in a flash. I run through my list of essential filming to make sure I've got what we need: interviews with Don and Shirley, a piece to camera, a commentary for radio, a longer video description for the website, shots of coral, the sampling, and Don at the controls. I think I have it all but, just in case, I shoot some scenes twice, once on each camera. One thing worse than not getting on the trip would be failing to get decent material.

We rise gently, the sea brightening until we reach the dazzling light of the surface and some tumultuous waves. For a while, we're tossed around like a beach ball caught in a storm. Don confirms our position to the ship and the *Seward Johnson* approaches. A diver leaps into the water pulling a towline which he attaches to the sub. Soon we're hoisted into the air and swing dramatically. At the ship's stern there's a welcome party. The hatch opens and warm Gulf air surges in. The samples are rushed to the lab.

The question in my mind, as dusk falls on the deck of the *Seward Johnson*, is whether the true effects of this leak will be understood before the next one happens – the world needs oil, new deep wells are being drilled, and the technology can never be faultless. This spill was not as catastrophic as it might have been. But the threat isn't over yet, which is often the case with environmental problems. Some are in-your-face and obvious right now, like the plastic landing on Midway. Others are less tangible and more uncertain, as with the long-term effects of the oil and the potential hazards of climate change. Within months, the spill tumbles from the news agenda, BP returns to profit and a diminishing band of researchers tries to remind everyone that the full impact still isn't known.

But as Don checks over the submarine, I'm high on adrenaline as I describe what the undersea voyage was like. I notice that Rob and Rozalia are smiling at me a little nervously and I realise that I'm talking with the crazed speed of a traveller just back from an alien world.

# EPILOGUE

## Hard numbers

A single pearl of rain catches the light as it slides across a waxy tropical leaf and slips off its edge. I watch another drop swell before it too flashes while delicately tumbling to the ground. It's an exquisite sight, the creation of jewels of precious water right in front of me, and I realise I've never properly noticed it before; the birth of moisture.

I'm in the Mau Forest in Kenya and a light shower soon turns into a drenching, deafening downpour. Cameraman Phil Davies and I try to speak but we're being drummed on and can't hear each other. An old Africa hand, Phil has produced a poncho from his backpack and he and his camera are sheltering beneath it. I hunch forward under the hood of my anorak and there's little to do except enjoy a contemplative state as the drops cascade over me, merge into rivulets on my trousers and then form a stream around my boots that will eventually join one of the twelve rivers which originate here. I'm witnessing why the forest matters.

Getting caught in a storm of this scale would usually be a nightmare on an assignment because heavy rain splatters the lens, turns day into dull twilight and wrecks any chance of a view. But this time it's exactly what we need because our story is about the forest's importance as a supplier of water. As I found in the Amazon, rainforests generate rain, lots of it, the moisture released by the trees rising on warm currents to form clouds and later falling either over the forest or on drier lands nearby. But forests have another role as well: they trap much of the rainfall, with the leaves, undergrowth and soil acting as a giant sponge. While a bare hillside will allow the water to run off unchecked in a wasteful flood, a forest will release its moisture steadily, maintaining a flow downstream at all times of the year, even when it's driest. No wonder Kenya's forests are known as 'water towers'.

But that isn't enough to save them. The trees are being cleared as the demands for timber and firewood combine with a fast-growing population's need for farmland. The result is that the Mau Forest is nearly half the size it was just fifty years ago – and that means its potential as a natural reservoir is being diminished. Short-term needs are damaging long-term value – that's been obvious for years – but, as happens so often, the case for conservation has withered in the face of economic development. In fact, given the scale of deforestation globally, the decades of campaigning must be judged a failure and one reason for this must be the vagueness of the conservation argument. The calls to save the trees have not been convincing, perhaps because the case has lacked the more readily understood language of money, the kind of financial values that might persuade people that a forest is worth more than the cash fetched for its timber.

That is now starting to change. Calculations have put a price tag on the Mau Forest and the 'service' it provides in generating the raindrops beating on my jacket. Sponsored by the UN Environment Programme, it's the first study of its kind, assessing how much the forest's function as a water tower is really worth, not in a spiritual or social sense but as a hard number. And the result is surprising: $1.3 billion a year.

Just beyond the trees stand plantations of tea, one of Kenya's biggest exports. Amid the waist-high bushes, the pickers bend forward to reach for the youngest, palest leaves which they throw over their shoulders into baskets on their backs. The tea plants need a lot of water and the research estimates that the forest's rain and rivers are worth $136 million a year to the plantations in this region alone.

We hear a similar story at a hydroelectric plant, recently opened with Japanese support. Its generators depend on the Sondu River whose flow begins somewhere close to where I'd sheltered in the trees. Half of Kenya's electricity comes from hydroelectric power and the director at this plant, Alfried Abiero, knows he is ultimately reliant on the Mau Forest upstream.

I ask him what would happen if the forest were cleared.

God forbid, he says.

The estimated value of the forest's water to electricity generation: $131 million a year.

Our final stop is Lake Nakuru, famous for its dazzling flocks of pink flamingos. Its waters are fed from the Mau Forest. We rise in the dark so that we can be in position to film the lake at dawn, the sky turning from black to silver to gold, the colour of the birds emerging as the sun rises. A few minibuses arrive with tourists, their faces awed, like mine. Wildlife is a huge attraction and the tourism industry is one of Kenya's largest. I notice movement a short distance away: a line of zebra fording one of the streams that feed the lake. A dozen cameras click as the animals trot by.

Back in the car, we're set to leave when Phil whispers a single, priceless word: lion. Their coats are pale bronze in the early light and they're approaching. I hold my breath as they pad noiselessly past the cars, heading to the lake to drink water that began life in the forest upstream.

The estimated value to tourism of the Mau's gift of water is $65 million a year.

I find that a typical reaction on hearing these numbers is a lack of comprehension. What do you mean, the forest's water is worth so many millions? It's just free, surely?

But then I explain how the natural world provides 'eco-system services' which are free – but which would be hugely expensive to replace if they weren't available. The penny drops. The tea companies, the hydroelectric man and the tourism authorities have understood that they depend on the survival of the forest which is why they support the Kenyan Government's plans to preserve the trees. For them, this particular green agenda not only makes sense as a do-good act to satisfy the requirements of corporate social responsibility. It also makes business sense. The suits have become tree huggers.

The problem is that this new kind of environmental economics bumps into an awkward reality: the Mau Forest is not empty of people. Tens of thousands live inside it and they're mostly extremely poor, like Margaret Kwamboka and her husband Kennedy. I meet them while they're planting pea seeds in a plot of land hacked out of the jungle. Such is their rush to cultivate crops – to raise money to pay for their children's schooling – that they have not even bothered to clear the remains of the trees which have been felled; the old stumps dot the little field like boulders, interrupting the neat rows carved in the soil. The peas are planted around them, this land transformed in a hurry.

I ask Margaret if we can talk. She speaks good English but hasn't needed it for a while.

I wonder if she understands the value of the trees that used to grow here.

Yes, she says.

Next comes a trickier question: one Kenyan Government scheme involves moving everyone out as the only sure way to preserve the forest.

So, could you afford to leave?

No, there's nothing we can do, Margaret replies. I am afraid because I don't have anything. How will I feed my children?

Margaret and her family represent all that's hardest about life on a crowded planet. Kenya as a whole will obviously do better if the forest continues to stand and to deliver water, in other words if the environment is put first for the benefit of wider society. But imagine the upheaval for her of being shipped somewhere else, the disruption and uncertainty, not to mention the moral ambiguity of putting trees before people. Pricing the natural world is a new and powerful tool for conservation. It doesn't provide a ready answer about what to do – at what point a sustainable future should take priority over day-to-day need – but it does make the choices clearer.

I'm standing, glass in hand, chatting to the chairman of a very large supermarket chain and he's ditched the small talk to steer the conversation to climate change, to what his company could or should do about it. He seems open to ideas, even hungry for them, but sincerity is hard to judge. His chain has started projects in all the obvious areas: adding carbon footprint labels, encouraging carrier bag recycling, switching to fridges and freezers that are fitted with doors to stop the waste of energy used for chilling.

My first thought is that none of this will amount to much, that I've heard it all before. This is the easy, cheap stuff that any company can do. Maybe the accusation of greenwash – from the most ardent campaigners – has a ring of truth. But then I pause to reflect on the sort of attitudes that were typical when I started in this job in 2003. Back then, did I ever imagine finding myself talking climate to a business leader? Would he or she (or me) have bothered to discuss carbon audits or plastic waste? How many of us had even heard of this stuff? In a few short years, something fundamental has changed: thinking about sustainability has entered the mainstream and green initiatives are now so commonplace that it's hard to get anyone excited about them.

Someone with us raises a question for the chairman which I hadn't thought of before. Would you, he asks, ever consider editing your product list?

It takes me a moment to work out what 'editing' means in this context. To me, it involves assembling and writing a video report. To the supermarket boss it means deliberately dropping certain items from the shelves because of the environmental damage they cause – editing out the airborne mangetout from Peru or the budget biscuits rich in palm oil bought from uncertain sources. It's a highly sensitive topic. Trying to shape consumer behaviour by limiting choice carries a grave commercial risk: that of losing customers to rival stores. But stocking everything and merely following public opinion could be seen as a denial of responsibility – we don't like this stuff but people seem to want it, so what can we do? This is a tough call because it raises one of the hardest questions. In the absence of an international treaty, governments and businesses must decide individually what they will or won't do. And how far will they go?

We wait for the chairman's answer.

He's clear: we don't believe in editing, he says. We believe in choice but if customers turn away from something, we'll be lumbered with unsold stock and soon learn not to buy any more. In other words – he's saying – we won't lead opinion, we'll follow it.

I'm struck by the thought that the supermarkets have chosen to edit out products before. Public nervousness about genetically modified food, whipped up by campaigners and a few newspapers, led to a rapid and general refusal to stock GM. Maybe that happened because food is so much more personal and tangible than concepts like climate change or sustainability. I leave the conversation thinking that everyone is waiting for someone else to take the lead, and no one's sure if anyone will.

So what has changed since my original accounts of the assignments described in this book? Has the world become more environmentally aware – and has it acted, in earnest, on any of the stories we reporters have brought to the public?

From Greenland, which I visited so innocently in 2004, there's mixed news. The farmer I met, Ferdinand Egede, has become famous for his harvests of potatoes. And the melting of the ice has picked up speed. A major NASA study of two decades of data reported in 2011 that the thaw is raising the sea level more than ever before. But British research has thrown up a countervailing idea about the fate of the ice sheet. When I stayed with Koni Steffen at Swiss Camp, the belief was that the ice sheet's gentle slide towards the sea was accelerated when summer meltwater flowed to the base of the ice and acted as a lubricant. This new study instead suggests that the water gouges out new tunnels inside the ice and leaves the main body of it unmoved. The warming of Greenland is still a threat but the collapse of its ice sheet may not be quite as rapid as originally feared.

Bjorn Andersen and his whaling ship the *Reinebuen* are still in action in the Arctic, and Norway has increased its quota for minke whales. For each of the two years after I was on board, the government allowed 1,052 whales to be killed. As for the *Reinebuen* itself, I heard that it had been returned to the shipyard to be rebuilt. I asked why. The vessel, I was told, apparently had a tendency to roll uncomfortably in the swell. Clearly we were not the only ones to suffer. I was offered a chance to board her again but found it easy to decline.

The Aral Sea has continued to dry up and shrink. It is now only one-tenth of its original size. Satellite pictures show what looks like a small puddle in one corner. My eldest son Jack visited the former port of Muynak in the summer of 2010 to see the fishing boats stranded on the sand. They're still there and the wind-blasted, dusty little town was 'the most derelict, the most desperate' place he saw on his travels through some of the poorest corners of Central Asia. On what used to be Muynak's seafront, he proved braver than me: he bought a local ice cream.

The hole in the ozone layer is not healing, as some suggest. But it's not getting any bigger. It may take decades to be restored and to provide its usual protection against ultraviolet radiation.

The clearance of the Amazon rainforest is slowing from a peak of rapacity ten years ago. Trees are still being felled in vast numbers but new controls are having an effect. However, the spectre of drought has returned. When the rains stopped so alarmingly in 2005, many assumed it was a one-off. But another, more severe drought struck in 2010. Again, the rivers turned to mud, the fish died and new questions loomed: do two droughts within five years start to make a trend? Might the rainforest become savannah as the climate models forecast?

Near the summit of Mauna Loa in Hawaii, scientists still maintain the world's most detailed record of carbon dioxide. When they started in 1958, the level was 315 parts per million. In 2010 it reached 389 ppm. That's 2 ppm higher than when the first edition of this book was published last year. And it's still going up.

The scourge of plastic waste in the oceans is attracting more attention. The Royal Geographical Society devoted an evening to the issue and asked me to chair it. Hundreds attended. I showed a clip of our video report from Midway, and Rob Magee's shots of an albatross chick, which had a plastic hook lodged in its beak, drew gasps. The campaigner David de Rothschild described sailing across the Pacific in a boat made of plastic bottles. And a representative of the plastics industry got a hard time. The most depressing observation came from a professor of oceanography: that there's no point investigating technologies for removing the plastic from the sea because none of them can or will work. We must learn to live with it, he said, and try to stop adding any more.

There were rumours that the metals processing factory in Copsa Mica in Romania had closed. I checked. It is still working but with a reduced workforce.

The Northwest Passage continues to become passable for a few weeks every summer. A Northeast Passage, along the shores of Russia, has started opening, too. Most surprising is the speculation about a third new sea route, directly over the North Pole. At a conference, a man from Shell unveiled a design for a strengthened gas tanker that could sail through broken ice right over the roof of the world. And polar records keep tumbling. The four greatest summer melts have occurred in the last four years. The winter of 2010 saw the lowest extent of Arctic ice for at least thirty years. And in December that year, when the sea is normally frozen, Greenland experienced the novelty of winter rain.

The people of Tuvalu still hope the outside world will help them. Enele Sopoaga, the official who'd told us that the islands had only fifty years left, made an appeal ahead of the UN climate conference at Cancun. We need quick-acting medicine, he said. We do not have a moment to lose. But the sea is still rising, the clock ticking.

The villagers of Gabura Island in Bangladesh have managed to repair their sea wall. For nearly two years they endured the twice-daily flooding of their homes and fields.

But how effectively will their bank of mud resist the next storm?

The giant solar power station near Seville is apparently working well, its mirrors still dazzling the local countryside. But there are many uncertainties about the future of renewable energy. In Spain, Germany and the UK, the recession has meant that subsidies for alternative power are either under strain or being cut. That may only spell temporary trouble. Or it could hobble an infant industry, as some fear. Meanwhile, a key source of low-carbon energy – nuclear power – was also dealt a blow when Japan suffered an earthquake and tsunami in March 2011. The tremors triggered the automatic shutdown of the reactors at the Fukushima Daiichi nuclear power station – as was designed to happen – but a giant wave then overwhelmed the back-up generators so that all emergency cooling was lost. Explosions and fires followed. The nuclear fuel inside three of the reactors began a partial meltdown, two tanks storing old fuel lost their cooling water, and radioactive contamination was released into the wind and sea. It was not another Chernobyl but the crisis forced the evacuation of everyone living within 20km of the plant and rekindled fears of atomic power. China and Germany were among countries to put their nuclear plans on hold. Renewable energy may get a boost as a result, though the easier, cheaper option is to invest in more fossil fuels.

Research published in the journal *Nature* tackled one of the great questions about climate change: can a single weather event ever be blamed on global warming? Until now the answer has been 'No', and I've been very cautious about sticking to that. It's far too glib to link every flood or forest fire to global warming. But a study of the storms in England in 2000 compared the real weather data of that time with computer models in which all man-made greenhouse gases were removed. The conclusion: that the presence of those gases made it twice as likely that the rain would fall as intensively as it did. Here for the first time was a possible connection between climate change and an actual weather event. The sceptic critics erupted. One blogger, who'd watched my report on the news, described how his wife had exclaimed disappointedly that she thought 'this kind of thing had all gone away'. Sorry dear, he'd said. He's right. Like it or not, climate science has not gone away.

And what of that lonely feature near the North Pole that briefly hosted a human presence, the island of 3,000-year-old ice that was our home for a day, the iceberg as big as Manhattan? Within months of our expedition in 2007, the giant structure had split into two chunks and each had drifted several hundred miles south. By the summer of 2010, they too had broken apart into countless, smaller fragments which then also shrank and cracked as the waves, winds and sunshine eroded them. One of those pieces had carried the dents of Duncan's tripod, the grooves cut by our plane's skis and the footprints from my pacing back and forth during a live broadcast on the satellite phone. I often think of how all traces of our visit have now melted into the vastness of the Arctic Ocean, and of how a major geographical feature, the Ayles Ice Shelf, had broken off to become an ice island only for that, too, to vanish from the face of the earth. Its last remains were seen bobbing in the waters off the remote Inuit settlement of Resolute. That's where we began our journey through the Northwest Passage, and where the ice island's journey will come to an end.

## AUTHOR'S NOTE

# Chronology of reports

Although the arrangement of chapters is broadly chrono-logical, I have visited several locations more than once so, for simplicity, I have grouped some episodes by theme. The trips described in the book are dated below:

## Preface

Sermilik Glacier, near Narsarsuaq, Greenland, July 18–22, 2004.

## Chapter 1

Whaling off North Cape of Norway, April 24–29, 2005; Aral Sea, Uzbekistan, June 9–14, 2004; ozone hole, Punta Arenas, Chile, November 18–24, 2004.

## Chapter 2

Amazon rainforest, Brazil, October 3–12, 2003 and July 9–21, 2006, visiting Manaus and Santarem on both trips, also Alter do Chao on the first and Jau National Park on the second. Other rainforest assignments included Borneo, December 6–11, 2007 and Ghana, 2–8 July, 2009.

## Chapter 3

Mauna Loa, Hawaii, March 21–27 2005. The same trip included filming at NOAA's Global Monitoring Division at Boulder, Colorado, which I visited from March 7–10, 2006.

## Chapter 4

Rothera, Antarctica, January 12–25, 2006. Another trip, on a Chilean Navy/NASA/CECS ice-mapping flight, took place on November 21, 2004 over Pine Island Glacier in West Antarctica but without landing.

## Chapter 5

Swiss Camp, near Ilulissat, Greenland, May 8–17, 2005; Yakutsk and Cherskii, Russian Federation, September 5–16, 2006.

## Chapter 6

Kalahari Desert, South Africa, November 20–26 2005; drought in Kenya, November 12–17, 2006; Michael Crichton lunch, London, September 19, 2005.

## Chapter 7

Plastic pollution, Midway Atoll, March 19–30, 2008.

## Chapter 8 .

Copsa Mica, Romania, January 8–11, 2008.

## Chapter 9

Ice Island, Canadian Arctic, May 14–25, 2007; IPCC report launch, Paris, February 2, 2007; Live Earth, Wembley, July 7, 2007; Northwest Passage, October 3–17, 2007. Other Canadian Arctic trips included Baffin Island and Churchill, Manitoba from November 6–14, 2005 and the Catlin Arctic Survey, May 10–16, 2009.

## Chapter 10

Funafuti, Tuvalu, January 15–27, 2008; Gabura Island and Dhaka, Bangladesh, August 31– September 7, 2009.

## Chapter 11

Solar power, Sanlucar La Mayor, Spain, April 16–18, 2007; UN climate talks, Bali, December 12–17, 2007; Kodiak Island and Barrow, Alaska, September 2–12, 2008; Kingsnorth power station, Kent, September 23, 2009; Charleston, West Virginia, November 30–December 5, 2008; Belchatow and Poznan, Poland, December 8–13, 2008; oil drilling near Houston, Texas and algae fuel in Imperial Valley and San Diego, California, October 18–24, 2009; Orkney, November 10–12, 2009; Bolivia, November 15–21, 2009.

## Chapter 12

UN climate conference, Copenhagen, December 6–20, 2009; Sweetwater, Texas, November 20–24, 2010.

## Chapter 13

Venice, Grand Isle and Houma, Louisiana, June 1–8, 2010; BP Crisis Centre, Houston, June 20–23, 2010; Grand Isle and Port Fourchon, Louisiana and St Petersburg, Florida, July 18–26, 2010.

## Epilogue

Mau Forest, Kenya, October 4–8, 2010.


As many viewers have pointed out – some very robustly – these travels on the environmental beat have entailed a high environmental price. They're right, no argument. I'll never forget, once, flying to the Canadian Arctic and watching, mesmerised and appalled, as the sunset turned the jet's exhaust plumes a dirty orange, the lurid streaks scarring the darkening sky for mile after mile. But I'm also told that audience feedback from the coverage has generally been very positive. So my answer to the carbon critics is to express a hope: that the value of the reporting may be seen to outweigh the cost of the footprint.

Beyond that, I've done what any environmentally aware traveller might do: buy carbon offsets for the flights, at my own expense. Offsetting is not an exact science and has attracted plenty of criticism, some of it justified, especially in the early days before any kind of regulation. But there are now schemes which are under proper scrutiny and if they support projects that are worthwhile in their own right – for example, enabling people to have access to cheap, clean power – then they're probably better than doing nothing.

# Acknowledgements

Working in outlandish places on the tightest of deadlines in heat or cold, dust or mud, filing copiously for television, radio and the web, can test any team, however well bonded. When the immutable hour of a live broadcast approaches, it's guaranteed that cables will freeze or laptops overheat. The Internet connection will crash or normally accessible satellites will slip beyond our reach. The producer won't be able to contact London and the cameraman-editor will curse the ailing software preventing the final assembly of a video report. In this crescendo of tension, when long hours have passed since the last meal and a tangle of time zones leaves us desperately short of sleep, there's an inevitable moment when it falls to me to multiply the stress. I'll realise that I have to add to everyone's workload and risk further delay by suggesting something that could not be less helpful: that I need to make a slight change to my script. It's the cue for the one brief flash of sharpness that characterises most assignments. That there aren't more of these is a tribute to the extraordinary skill and decency of the people who make up our small bands on the road. The regulars have featured in these pages repeatedly – Tony Fallshaw, Mark Georgiou, Rob Magee and Duncan Stone – and I'm hugely grateful to them for their talent, energy and friendship.

Broadcasting is only possible in teams and many colleagues deserve thanks for their expertise and comradeship in the distant or difficult locations described here: Steve Adrain, Kevin Bishop, John Boon, Maxine Collins, Nora Dennehy, Tony Dolce, Paul Francis, Roger Harrabin, Tim Hirsch, Dominic Hurst, Tony Jolliffe, Matt McGrath, Glenn Middleton, Alex Milner, Natalie Morton, Joe Phua, Mark Rabbage, Martin Roberts, Malcolm Senior, Ron Skeans, Paul Simpson and Tony Smith.

On trips, it's up to the cameramen, producers and correspondents to make things work but back at base are the editors who take the risk of commissioning the stories. For suggesting or supporting one or more of the assignments in this book or helping make any of this work possible over the past six years, I'd like to thank Jonathan Baker, Kevin Bakhurst, Mark Barlex, Mark Damazer, Malcolm Downing, Amanda Farnsworth, Rome Hartman, Mary Hockaday, Peter Horrocks, Jay Hunt, Craig Oliver, Jonathan Paterson, Mark Popescu, Gary Smith, Simon Smith, James Stephenson, Fran Unsworth, Frances Weil, Sarah Whitehead and Jon Williams. Thanks to Vin Ray for offering me the job in the first place and to my colleagues in the Environment and Science Unit: Jonathan Amos, Judith Burns, Melanie Fanstone, Pallab Ghosh, Mark Kinver, Su Maskell, Becky Morelle, Sarah Mukherjee, Paul Rincon, Christella Robertson, Emily Selvadurai and Kate Stephens. Dave Bristow and Wendy Austin do a great job getting us out and back, Emma Robertson provides the snow boots and mosquito nets and Paul Vary keeps us afloat.

I owe particular thanks to Tony Grant, editor of *From Our Own Correspondent*. For years he has encouraged a personal style for contributions to his programme and unwittingly prepared me for this task. Many of the episodes featured here were first aired under his guidance.

None of the filming could have happened without the help of a great many people and organisations. Most are named in the narrative and, to them, huge thanks. Thanks also to Maria Becket of Religion, Science and Environment; the British Antarctic Survey; the US National Oceanic and Atmospheric Administration; the US Fish and Wildlife Service; NASA; the US Coast Guard; Kenn Borek Air; the captain and crew of the Canadian Coast Guard's *Amundsen*; Sam Barratt of Oxfam; Ian Curtis of Oxford University's Environmental Change Institute; John Hay and Carrie Assheuer of the UNFCCC; the European Marine Energy Centre.

The idea for this book came from Duncan Clark and Mark Ellingham of Profile Books. I'm incredibly grateful to them for making the approach, for convincing me to give it a go and for remaining good-humoured and supportive as the project developed. Julian Alexander provided invaluable guidance. My father, Harry Shukman, kindly read the manuscript. Any mistakes are of course mine.

The flip side of having the privilege of travelling to the furthest corners of the globe is that it means repeatedly being away from home. A big apology is due to my children, Jack, Harry and Kitty, along with a heartfelt thank you for unfailingly finding ways of bringing me back to earth. I owe most though, to my wife, Jessica Pryce-Jones. She has not only put up with my long absences but also found time to offer an unparalleled sign of love and encouragement: reading and commenting on my drafts in the midst of writing a book of her own.

# Index